Palgrave Critical Studies of Antisemitism and Racism

Series Editor

David Feldman
Birkbeck College – University of London
London, United Kingdom

Aims of the Series
Palgrave Critical Studies of Antisemitism and Racism considers antisemitism from the ancient world to the present day. The series explores topical and theoretical questions and brings historical and multidisciplinary perspectives to bear on contemporary concerns and phenomena.

Grounded in history, the series also reaches across disciplinary boundaries to promote a contextualised and comparative understanding of antisemitism. A contextualised understanding will seek to uncover the content, meanings, functions and dynamics of antisemitism as it occurred in the past and recurs in the present. A comparative approach will consider antisemitism over time and place. Importantly, it will also explore the connections between antisemitism and other exclusionary visions of society. The series will explore the relationship between antisemitism and other racisms as well as between antisemitism and forms of discrimination and prejudice articulated in terms of gender and sexuality.

More information about this series at
http://www.springer.com/series/15437

Anne Summers

Christian and Jewish Women in Britain, 1880–1940

Living with Difference

palgrave
macmillan

Anne Summers
London, United Kingdom

Palgrave Critical Studies of Antisemitism and Racism
ISBN 978-3-319-42149-0   ISBN 978-3-319-42150-6 (eBook)
DOI 10.1007/978-3-319-42150-6

Library of Congress Control Number: 2016958215

© The Editor(s) (if applicable) and The Author(s) 2017
This work is subject to copyright. All rights are solely and exclusively licensed by the Publisher, whether the whole or part of the material is concerned, specifically the rights of translation, reprinting, reuse of illustrations, recitation, broadcasting, reproduction on microfilms or in any other physical way, and transmission or information storage and retrieval, electronic adaptation, computer software, or by similar or dissimilar methodology now known or hereafter developed.
The use of general descriptive names, registered names, trademarks, service marks, etc. in this publication does not imply, even in the absence of a specific statement, that such names are exempt from the relevant protective laws and regulations and therefore free for general use.
The publisher, the authors and the editors are safe to assume that the advice and information in this book are believed to be true and accurate at the date of publication. Neither the publisher nor the authors or the editors give a warranty, express or implied, with respect to the material contained herein or for any errors or omissions that may have been made.

Cover image © The Women's Library collection at LSE, 2SJA/K/35/12, Religious leagues for women's suffrage, c. 1913
Cover design by Fatima Jamadar

Printed on acid-free paper

This Palgrave Macmillan imprint is published by Springer Nature
The registered company is Springer International Publishing AG
The registered company address is: Gewerbestrasse 11, 6330 Cham, Switzerland

Acknowledgements

When I began the research embodied in this book, with the generous support of a British Academy travel grant, I knew that I might be looking for the occasional needle in a great many haystacks. The solidarity and expertise of a correspondingly large number of historians and archivists was needed and was, happily, forthcoming to bring the project to fruition.

I am deeply grateful to fellow scholars Ruth Abrams, Sally Alexander, Clyde Binfield, Elizabeth Crawford, David Feldman, Abigail Green, Jenifer Glyn, Naomi Hetherington, Janet Howarth, Jean Holder, Louise Jackson, the late Elaine Kaye, Jill Liddington, Carmen Mangion, Meri-Jane Rochelson, and Gill Sutherland for their many gifts of time, effort, expertise and information.

Within the wonderful freemasonry which guards and interprets the archival record I particularly thank Professor Chris Woolgar and Karen Robson of the Hartley Library at the University of Southampton; Gail Cameron and Teresa Doherty, formerly at The Women's Library at London Metropolitan University, and Liz Chapman, Anna Towlson and Gillian Murphy of The Women's Library at the London School of Economics and Political Science; Jill Butterworth and Clara Li-Dunne at the Armitt Gallery, Ambleside; Alex Grime at the Manchester Jewish Museum and Mark Cunningham of the Manchester Jewish Federation; Annette Mevis at the former IIAV, now Atria, Amsterdam; Rochelle Rubinstein at the Central Zionist Archives, Jerusalem; Alison Behr Turner at the Montagu Centre, London; Stefan Dickers at the Bishopsgate Institute, London; and Giles Mandelbrote at Lambeth Palace Library, London.

Warm thanks are also due to staff at the Bodleian Library, Oxford, the City Library and County Record Office in Manchester, the Marks & Spencer Company Archives at the University of Leeds, London Metropolitan Archives, the Friends' House Library, London, The National Archives, the Tower Hamlets Archives, the Rothschild Archives, London, the Jewish Museum, London and last, but never least, my alma mater the British Library.

My research has benefited from responses both positive and astringent to papers presented at the Institute of Historical Research, University of London, in the Women's History Seminar, the Modern British History Seminar, and the Jewish History Seminar respectively; in the European Jewish History Seminar at the University of Oxford, and at the Parkes Institute Seminar at the University of Southampton. I am grateful to all their convenors for these opportunities. For permission to republish portions of earlier articles, I thank the editors and publishers of *Women's History Review*, *Archives*, and Cambridge University Press and the *Journal of Ecclesiastical History*. Particular thanks are due to the anonymous readers of those articles for their helpful editorial recommendations.

Illustrations are reproduced with the kind permission of the British Library; the Franklin family; Manchester Libraries, Information and Archives, Manchester City Council; the Marks & Spencer Company Archive; the Musée d'art et d'histoire du Judaisme, Paris; The Women's Library at the London School of Economics and Political Science; and the Jewish Museum, London.

Professor David Feldman has encouraged this project from its very earliest stages, and is responsible for propelling me out of my historiographical comfort zone in more ways than one. As series editor he, together with Emily Russell and Rowan Milligan at Palgrave Macmillan, have shown great patience and care in the production of this work, and I am also very grateful to the anonymous external reader whose comments on the entire text were both challenging and constructive. Those faults remaining in the book are, as pavement artists used to say, all my own work.

I wish to record a particular debt of gratitude to Dr Phyllis Lassner, whose interest and encouragement were vital to developing and completing this study of 'Living with Difference'.

To David Lawrence, thanks beyond words.

Contents

1 Introduction   1

Part I   Group Encounters, 1870s–1918   21

2 Women and Men in a Religious Landscape: Britain in the Late Nineteenth Century   23

3 Joint Enterprises: 'The Co-operation of Ladies Who Are Not Christians'   33

4 'Dear Madame Dreyfus'   49

5 'Votes for Women!'   63

Part II   Friendship in Private and Public, 1890s–1930   85

6 'A Dear Good "God-Mother" to Her': Margaret MacDonald and Lily Montagu   87

7 'We Fell in Love with Each Other at First Sight':
   Charlotte Mason and Netta Franklin   113

Part III Continuity and Change, 1920s–1940s   135

8 False Start or Brave Beginning? Lily Montagu
   and Interfaith Initiatives   141

9 Separatism Without Separation: Rebecca Sieff,
   Englishwomen and Zionism   155

10 Refuge and Asylum   175

11 Conclusions   199

12 Coda: Rachel Bernstein goes to Surrey Lane   205

Bibliography   209

Index   229

Abbreviations

BCL	British Commonwealth League
BL	British Library
BUF	British Union of Fascists
CCJ	Council of Christians and Jews
COPEC	Conference on Politics, Economics and Citizenship
FWZ	Federation of Women Zionists
GEC	Germany Emergency Committee
ICW	International Council of Women
ILP	Independent Labour Party
JAPGW	Jewish Association for the Protection of Girls and Women
JAPGWC	Jewish Association for the Protection of Girls, Women and Children
JC	*Jewish Chronicle*
JLVA	Jewish Ladies' Visiting Association
JLWS	Jewish League for Woman Suffrage
JPS	Jewish Peace Society
JRU	Jewish Religious Union
JTS	Jews' Temporary Shelter
LMA	London Metropolitan Archives
LSE	London School of Economics and Political Science
MP	Member of Parliament
MSSA	Manchester and Salford Sanitary Association
NCW	National Council of Women
NUWSS	National Union of Women's Suffrage Societies
NUWW	National Union of Women Workers

ODNB	*Oxford Dictionary of National Biography*
PEP	Political and Economic Planning
PNEU	Parents' National Education Union
RCM	Refugee Children's Movement (Kindertransport)
TAS	Travellers' Aid Society
TNA	The National Archives
TWL	The Women's Library
UJW	Union of Jewish Women
USL	University of Southampton Library
WIC	Women's Industrial Council
WIZO	Women's International Zionist Organisation
WLL	Women's Labour League
WPPA	Women's Publicity Planning Association
WSPU	Women's Social and Political Union
YWCA	Young Women's Christian Association

LIST OF FIGURES

Fig. 4.1	Portrait of Mrs Gamble (Courtesy of Manchester City Libraries)	54
Fig. 4.2	'A letter of sympathy and another of congratulation to Madame A. Dreyfus signed by 1176 women of Manchester, England, September 1899' (Courtesy of Musée d'art et d'histoire du Judaisme, Paris)	58
Fig. 6.1	Portrait of Margaret MacDonald, 1895 (Courtesy of the British Library Board)	89
Fig. 6.2	Portrait of Lily Montagu, 1895–1900 (Courtesy of the Jewish Museum, London)	90
Fig. 7.1	Portrait of Netta Franklin, c. 1895 (By kind permission of the Franklin family)	114
Fig. 9.1	Portrait of Rebecca Sieff 1915 (Courtesy of The Marks & Spencer Company Archive)	158

CHAPTER 1

Introduction

This book began with a letter, dated 1898, which I read in a Swiss archive. 'I have written to Madame Dreyfus' it began, 'on behalf of a number of English women and myself'.[1] The writer was Josephine Butler, a Victorian reformer who united an ardent Christianity with an equally passionate political liberalism. I had studied British women's history, and Butler's campaigns, over many years, but this letter sparked off a series of questions which I had never previously thought to ask. Did Butler have other correspondents or friends—in particular, women friends—within the Jewish community in her own country? The Frenchwoman Lucie Dreyfus, who embodied the international outcry over the trumped-up charge of treason against her husband Captain Dreyfus, was the international liberal celebrity of the hour. What about more ordinary Jewish women nearer home? Josephine Butler's husband, the Reverend George Butler, was a Hebraist; the couple were acquainted with the Chief Rabbi and other Jewish male notables of the day; but they seem not to have been acquainted with these men's spouses. Were Josephine's Jewish counterparts debarred by domestic or religious custom from these relationships? If so, this might have been on account of the sensitive character, considered scandalous by many, of her campaigns on behalf of prostitute women and against the 'state regulation of vice'.[2] What, then, about other Christian women, in less exposed positions? What were the everyday interactions, if any, between Christian and Jewish women in Britain in the decades preceding and following World War I?

These questions matter because they help us to explore the first chapter in the narrative of a multicultural Britain. Between roughly 1880 and 1914, at a time when different sects within the Church, and even within Protestantism, could not always find common ground, around 150,000 people who were not Christians, who prayed in synagogues and in Hebrew, and who read and wrote in a non-European script, settled in this island. Most came from Eastern Europe, were extremely poor and lacked any secular education, my grandparents among them. Britain had seen many waves of immigrants over the previous centuries, all initially arousing varying degrees of hostility among their hosts, but this cohort was without a doubt more 'foreign' than any who had come before. On the eve of World War I, the community had grown to nearly 300,000. The earliest Jewish migrants had been of predominantly Sephardic (Spanish and Portugese) origin; their ranks were augmented by members of Ashkenazi (German) communities. Many had prospered greatly, producing a 'Cousinhood' of notables who established successful financial institutions, entered public life, and with more or less success took responsibility for the needs of their poorest coreligionists.[3] Without obscuring the fact of religious difference, individuals from these prominent families could establish social relationships with their hosts based on affinities of wealth and occupation. The contention that they did not, at least not for long, challenge native Britons' sense of identity may be illustrated by legislation in 1858 (strengthened by the Oaths Act of 1866), allowing (male) Jews to become Members of Parliament without professing Christianity, and by the relaxation of the Anglican clerical qualification in 1871 which allowed (male) Jews to become Fellows of Oxford colleges.

The new wave, however, transformed both the nature of Anglo-Jewry, and Britain's relationship with the Jews. A very few, very rich families could be absorbed relatively easily; but this large body of people, conspicuously alien in so many senses of the word, could not. There was the potential for social unrest in the deprived urban neighbourhoods where they settled *en masse*. The Jewish notables wished to avoid the rise of an antisemitism which could harm them as well as the hugely increased numbers of their dependent brethren, and their fears had substance: a political fringe movement was able to exploit a sense of 'native' grievance to the point where the Conservative government passed the Aliens Act of 1905, the first to institute official controls over entry into the country in peacetime. This situation galvanised those Jewish women and men who felt relatively secure in their citizenship to anglicise the newcomers, and to expand communal welfare provision in order to prevent their poverty becoming a resented burden on the public funds. It was also a spur to building stronger bridges between the minority and host communities. All these initiatives had to take place in the arena we currently call 'civil society', within religious congregations, voluntary associations and a range of charitable activities. This was the one sphere in which women could enjoy something like equality of opportunity with men. Long denied political participation and professional education, women in Britain had for decades taken philanthropic and religious routes into public life and social action. These activities provided the opportunity for some Jewish and Christian women to meet on almost equal terms.

An abundant literature has chronicled the stages by which Christian Britain enacted the legal emancipation of its Jews, and Anglo-Jewry in turn assimilated into and contributed to the host society.[4] Only a small proportion of this literature refers to women, and even less to their relationship to a gentile world.[5] Yet the experience of migration and minority status is not the same for women as for men.[6] In the period under review, social life was often segregated by gender for all classes, and the primary responsibility for childcare and domestic labour (or, for the wealthier classes, the arrangements made for them) devolved on women. Like other working-class women, Jewish women earned family income by taking in 'home work', or setting up shops and market stalls;[7] but their continuing ascription to the domestic sphere made it unlikely that they would be resented as major competitors in business or the labour market. Jewish women were often in closer contact with their gentile neighbours than were husbands working in all-Jewish banks or workshops; encounters with schoolfriends and schoolteachers, social workers, medical officers and Christian evangelists were experienced differently by women than by their male peers.[8] The strong bias towards male leadership in Jewish religious institutions also meant that religion played a different role in women's negotiation of an Anglo-Jewish identity than was the case for the men in the community.

Women were not lawmakers for much of this period; but it must be acknowledged that emancipation, assimilation, citizenship and equality are not values which can simply be legislated into existence. They must always be enacted day-to-day in civil society, on the streets and within a variety of institutions. Middle- and upper-class women's work in the voluntary associational life of the country in the nineteenth and twentieth centuries was based on a strong sense of neighbourliness and social obligation. It helped to shape the development of modern health and welfare services, the provision of education, training, employment and public housing, as well as women's own entry into the political arena. The continuity between pre- and post-World War I developments is important here. The debates on citizenship which women launched with the suffrage campaign took on material form after enfranchisement, through the work of their many national and local organisations. Before as after 1914, these were sites of coexistence and cooperation, where religious and communal difference had to be accommodated as women organised for social improvements or humanitarian relief. To study this aspect of women's history is to see the development of modern Britain in a new light: one which, it is hoped, can bring us to a more rounded understanding of the phenomenon of religious diversity within a relatively stable and democratic society.

This book comprises case histories of individuals and organisations; it does not aspire to be encyclopaedic. The choice of topics has been to some extent dictated by the availability of sources, notoriously more meagre for women's history than for men's. It is partly for this reason that the focus is on middle- and upper-class women, who are the most likely to bequeath a legacy of correspondence and diaries enabling them to be quoted in their own words. Within the Anglo-Jewish community, this class of women was the second, third and even fourth generation of immigrant families, who had developed conscious strategies of acculturation while also preserving a minority social identity. In all communities this class comprised women who had the leisure and means to be active in the voluntary societies which have in turn generated substantial bodies of records. Such organisations were of continuing importance in the decades between the two world wars. Despite the granting of equal suffrage and the passing of formal legislation against sex discrimination in employment, much professional training remained effectively closed to women, and many occupations operated a marriage bar against those women who had succeeded in obtaining relevant qualifications and experience.[9] The historical context is sometimes ignored by those adopting the 'social control' model, which suggests that for Anglo-Jewish women in particular voluntary work offered the means to exert power over social 'inferiors' denied them elsewhere within their own community.[10] The exponents of this paradigm may not, perhaps, have experienced the ennui of acting as Treasurer or Minutes Secretary of a voluntary organisation for years or even decades on end simply because no one else will volunteer for the job. The individuals studied here made willing sacrifices of time and energy, and brought talent and training into the voluntary sector; they were neither egocentrics nor political unsophisticates; their loss of career opportunity can indeed be seen as the country's gain.

Within this group of women I have selected a further subset. Women, whether Christian or Jewish, for whom religion or communal identity was of primary importance, offer better exemplars of the challenges of 'living with difference' than secular gentiles or assimilated Jews. Moreover, an earlier historiography of modernisation, which considered religion largely irrelevant in British society after the late Victorian period, is now increasingly subject to reconsideration: the driving force behind many movements in recognisably modern national and international politics is understood to have been religiously inspired.[11] Nor was religion static or fossilised between the two world wars. Changing currents in both Christianity and Judaism, and in the relations between them, are an important aspect of this country's history, and one in which women played a part which deserves to be better known. It might be argued that the salience of religion in the lives of these particular women owed much to their relative exclusion from secular political and professional spheres before the 1950s; however, current scholarship, and the increasingly active role of women in British churches and synagogues in the new century, which offers them many other opportunities, would suggest otherwise. This analysis shifts racism and political antisemitism from the central place which they occupy in much writing on Jewish–non-Jewish relations in the modern period; I am, nevertheless, aware that different selection criteria could tell a different story about Christian and Jewish women than the one I offer here. Many other books could be written on this subject, and I hope they will be.

Recent literature on Anglo-Jewry between the two world wars stresses the salience of antisemitism and the failings of Western liberalism, but it can be argued that 'The Strange Death of Liberal England' has been greatly exaggerated.[12] It was not the Liberal Party which legislated restrictions on immigration in 1905, or pushed hard for their extension in 1919. Both before and after World War I, mass dissatisfaction with Liberal governments was expressed far more in the rise of the Labour party than in the sprouting of right-wing populist movements. Significant elements of the Protestant 'nonconformist conscience', which had characterised support for the nineteenth-century Liberal party, survived and found their way into the labour movement and even into the Conservative party.[13] Important studies by, in particular, David Cesarani and Louise London, highlighting antisemitism within governing circles, posit continuities between post-1917 anti-alienist, anti-Bolshevist and anti-Zionist rhetoric and a chilling indifference to urgent Jewish concerns as Hitler rose to power. This view of ruling elites has been challenged,[14] and it is contended here that a focus on personal and organisational relationships within civil society produces a different balance sheet of tolerance and 'othering'. Despite official strategic preoccupations, a widespread and continuing complacency that theirs was an empire on which the sun would never set enabled many in Britain to continue to accept the presence of minority populations without undue anxiety. The alacrity with which the settled Jewish families, in conjunction with local authorities, educated their 'poor relations' in the laws and customs of their new homeland provided additional reassurance. (The suggestion that this education was in itself a form of repressive tolerance may be balanced against the positive memories of some of those at the receiving end,[15] and contrasted with the often horrendous experiences of their parents' generation in the Talmud Torahs of Eastern Europe.)[16]

Within these debates, the 'literary turn' has played a substantial role, addressing the overall social and imperial context, and issues of gender which were lacking in previous historical studies in this area.[17] While this newer scholarship has been of great value, its methodology has not been adopted in the present work. It is possible to privilege literary text over material action to the point of being positively misleading. To give just two examples: the bad Jew/good Jewess trope of some conversionist literature [18] did not ever surface in the popular British agitation in support of Captain Dreyfus and his wife, discussed in Chap. 4; and the trope that Jewish women 'did not become potential marriage partners unless they converted'[19] is not borne out by the respective real-life marriages of Hannah, Constance and Annie Rothschild to Archibald Primrose (Lord Rosebery), Cyril Flower (later Lord Battersea) and the Hon. Eliot Yorke. The present study cites some literary texts of the period, but in the context of recorded actions; as far as possible it marries texts with the actions and choices of their authors.

'Deeds, not words' may be a hoary exhortation, but in making moral judgements (and many have been made, or strongly implied) it is vital to record what people actually do. Is it more important, for example, that a voluntary worker meeting German-Jewish refugees off the boat train wrote disobliging remarks about them in a report, or that she stuck it out until 2.00 a.m. on Victoria Station to ensure that they came to no harm?

There is also the problem of generalisation from one section or institution of society to the whole: were the limits that the British government placed on immigration from Nazi Germany and Austria more 'truly' representative of British culture and attitudes to the Jews than the protests against these limits? Do punch-ups in the East End tell us a truth about gentile British society that is more significant than the extraordinary efforts made by members of the National Council of Women, the Women's Citizens' Associations, and many other women's organisations, to provide accommodation for refugees? It is impossible to eliminate elements of subjectivity in an assessment of a culture and a society, but one is on slightly safer ground in the world of deeds; and the under-recording of women's deeds leaves the historical record with an inbalance which requires to be redressed.

There is, nevertheless, a caveat to be entered: it is axiomatic that 'the world of deeds' appears differently to different observers: but the picture also varies with the same observer according to the point in time at which it is viewed. One notable feature of many of the biographies and autobiographies consulted for this book is that, whether or not by conscious design, they omit all mention of involvement in some of the most important political movements of the day, or ignore or downplay the contribution of colleagues on whom they were dependent for years on end. This gap between experience and recollection is of course grist to the historian's mill, and one can only speculate, as I have, as to its significance for the individuals concerned. It is also the reason why, despite my respect for the work of oral historians, and the benefit I have derived from, for example, the interviews with former suffragists conducted by Professor Sir Brian Harrison, I have been content not to seek out interview material for research purposes. The texts which have to be married to life stories are, first and foremost, archival: correspondence between friends and colleagues, minutes of meetings, annual reports: the practical minutiae of practical women, day-to-day details which were easily forgotten subsequently, but which helped to construct the social fabric of the times.

* * * * *

Women who stepped outside the domestic and familial sphere, even where they followed routes acceptable to their male kin, could very soon find themselves in unknown territory. The 'Lady Bountiful' might become a social anomaly when her visits to the poor led her to demand votes for women, or concern herself closely with the plight of prostitutes. To anyone pushing the boundaries of what might be considered 'normal', peer friendships were vital for endurance, success and indeed sanity. Among the women and in the period under review here, therefore, female friendship had particular importance. While there may be no essential difference between male and female friendship (even if women are still widely assumed to have greater aptitude in this area) cultural and historical circumstances endowed these women's relationships with certain features specific to time and place.

To a very considerable degree, these friendships were freely chosen. Even though an individual might accept and hold posts within charitable societies out of a weary sense of obligation, it would always be easier to resign a voluntary post, or form a breakaway organisation—and suffrage history attests to the power of the Pankhurst family to provoke such splitting—than it would be for a male breadwinner to abandon employment in order to escape an obnoxious colleague. Male-dominated political parties and governments experienced their fair share of personal vendettas, but few politicians would give up Cabinet office, or risk driving their party out of power, on the basis of such antipathies alone. Women's organisations were not, by contrast, power players in the conventional sense. The stakes were never so high, and rivalries were rarely as destructive as in the male sphere. In their associative life, women experienced a different balance between choice and obligation, freedom and necessity, and operated within a different moral and emotional economy.

There is now an extensive literature on the erotic aspect of female friendships. Since the 'second wave' of feminism in the 1970s, women historians have done much to explore women's sexuality and to reinstate the importance and staying power of lesbian relationships.[20] Many of the women in this study were spinsters or in arranged marriages, and found, indeed, their greatest emotional fulfilment in each other's company. But many will not have been lesbian. Edith Picton-Turbervill, a Christian social worker who became a Labour MP in 1929, stoutly declared that 'a great deal of nonsense is talked about women's friendships, as though, because they are intimate and dear, they are necessarily silly and unwholesome'. Her autobiography portrays a lively and witty 'little colony of friends', and female collaborations overriding party political ties, which undoubtedly sustained a long career in public service.[21] The close relationships of interwar feminists and professional and charitable pioneers, whether or not sexually inflected, were necessities of life. As will be seen in Chap. 7, Charlotte Mason and Netta Franklin clearly idolised each other; however, it was also essential for Charlotte, if her project directed at mothers as home tutors was to succeed, to have energetic and proselytising women supporters, as well as devoted female staff.

Creative and productive partnerships were often based on sisterhood in the literal sense: the educationists and social workers Rachel and Margaret McMillan, the suffragettes Sylvia, Christabel and Adela Pankhurst, and Netta Franklin and Lily Montagu are well-known examples. Lily freely acknowledged that her career was sustained by the loving care of Marian, the sister with whom she shared her home.[22] Other prominent figures created their own female families and households: the independent MP Eleanor Rathbone established a lifelong partnership with Elizabeth Macadam;[23] Margaret Bondfield, Labour Cabinet minister and the first female member of the Privy Council, shared much of her life with Maud Ward, writing that 'she dug out facts from blue books, etc., and was housekeeper for both when in lodgings, and later when she bought a house at Hampstead which she was good enough to share with me'.[24] The author Vera Brittain wrote in her memoirs *Testament of Friendship* and *Testament of Experience* of the household she shared with Winifred Holtby (as well as with Vera's husband George Catlin).[25] There will have been many others; the known instances of destruction of personal correspondence, by authors fearing the post-Freudian gaze, suggest that no definitive coverage of the topic is achievable.[26]

It cannot be denied that self-interest, ambivalence, insensitivity and prejudice also played some part in these relationships. Voluntary organisations always needed an income. While a woman did not have to be Jewish to be wealthy, there was clearly an advantage in securing a female representative of the Rothschild, Goldsmid or Montagu clans as a member, officer or patron. This did not necessarily cancel out the possibility of genuine cross-denominational friendship. Admittedly, one cannot prove a negative, and it goes without saying that correspondence between the Jewish and Christian women in this study would have been free of overt expressions of antisemitism. The only hint I have found is very much at thirdhand. Lady Anne Burrell was the daughter of Lady Gertrude Denman, head of the Women's Institute. When interviewed in 1977, she referred to the WI Treasurer Helena Auerbach as a 'fat Jewess': a clearly antisemitic statement, as it is difficult to believe that the rest of the WI membership, as famous for their culinary as for their campaigning activities, were slim as wands. She also emphasised that Auerbach and her mother enjoyed merely a 'business partnership', not friendship as such, although she added that

Lady Denman 'listened … a lot' to Eva Hubback, an educationist who was Jewish by birth but not by subsequent identification. It is noteworthy, however, that Lady Burrell was unembarrassedly explicit concerning Lady Denman's prejudice against Catholics, quoting her as saying that 'you couldn't rely on them' because of the influence of their priesthood.[27]

That said, even persons of real goodwill, then as now, could be unconscious of almost comically racist assumptions. Barbara Bodichon, the founder of Girton College, Cambridge, supported the efforts of Phoebe Sarah Marks (later the engineer known as Hertha Ayrton) to obtain a university education and support herself by taking governess posts. While praising her for being 'pure breed', unlike English 'mongrels', she anticipated that her looks might not appeal to a potential employer, and recommended that her protégée wear a hairnet.[28] Millicent Fawcett recalled that her tutor in girlhood was Louisa Browning, aunt of the poet. Alluding to rumours that Robert Browning had Jewish ancestry, she 'sometimes reflected, especially since I have had the opportunity of seeing Palestine, Algeria, Egypt, etc., that possibly Miss Browning's love of bright-coloured clothing may indicate an Eastern strain in her ancestry'.[29] The exoticising and eroticising of Jewish female beauty may perhaps be described as a mainly male interest.[30] Non-Jewish women might allude to the 'black sparkling eyes' of a fellow worker, and imagine Madame Dreyfus with 'hair dark as the night';[31] darkness was indeed difference, and was remarked upon, but in the main without either desire or repugnance.

The Anglo-Boer War of 1899–1902 unleashed much antisemitic rhetoric, some of it coded, amongst supposedly progressive circles. 'International financiers', 'aliens and blackguards in the market-place', persons who were 'patriotic in broken English', and 'the very incarnation of the money idea' were phrases bandied about by non-Jewish suffragists and colleagues at this time;[32] this ambivalence is alluded to in the chapters on the campaigns in support of Captain Dreyfus and the female suffrage respectively. In many instances, these stereotypes were uttered without consideration of the offence they might cause, and without the intention of offence, by people who could honestly say that some of their dearest friends were Jews. Some may have had difficulty in accepting that the individuals they loved and admired belonged to a religious and ethnic community as well as to the milieux and the causes they shared. It might have seemed politest to consider Jews as individuals, rather than as members of a distinct community. Many may well have considered themselves philosemitic, without employing the term. Ambivalence pervades most relationships; obtuseness is not malice; a lapse of tact is not necessarily equivalent to hostility or disdain. Friendships such as those of Lily Montagu with Margaret MacDonald, and Lily's sister Netta with Charlotte Mason, opened up a world of activism in the host society for Jewish women. The expressions of affection and sympathy that I have found in the course of researching this book were underpinned by years of close collaborative working, of lengthy stays in each other's homes and of shared joys and condolence in life's losses.[33] They deserve to be taken at face value.

There is nothing extraordinary about the fact that East European Jewish newcomers were not warmly welcomed by their English and Irish neighbours—or, indeed, that these same East European Jews did not always feel a surge of affection for the German Jewish refugees who reached Britain some thirty years after them.[34] The unfamiliar is, conventionally, unlikeable: anyone singing that 'A Stranger's Just a Friend You Do Not Know' is almost certainly doomed to disillusion and disappointment.[35] By the same token, unjust and ungracious as it may seem, the bright-eyed welcome extended to Jews by certain good-hearted Christians has been treated, both at the time and in subsequent histories, with considerable reserve. Above all this is due to the fact that, unlike Judaism, Christianity is essentially a proselytising religion. In many instances philosemitism has also involved the projection onto actually existing Jewish communities of inappropriate biblical nostalgia and myriad millenarian hopes: the second coming of Christ has often been seen as dependent variously on the conversion of the Jews to Christianity, the completion of their dispersions and their restoration to the Holy Land. The offer of friendship was of course not always attended by a self-interested agenda involving Jewish religious extinction; but suspicions, inevitably, lingered.[36]

Outside explicitly missionary enterprises the issue of conversion existed as an undercurrent in many individual and collective relationships. Jan Marsh has recorded the poet Christina Rossetti's persistence in offering the gospel to her friends the Heimanns: 'how could I love you and yours as I do, ... without longing and praying for faith to be added to your works? Dear old friend, do not be offended with me'.[37] Josephine Butler's readiness to invite Jewish members into her campaigning organisations, and her sympathy with Madame Dreyfus, coexisted with her hope that Captain Dreyfus's sufferings would lead him to Christ.[38] It is also possible that female social workers in areas of Jewish settlement were more involved with missions to the Jews than the official record might suggest. That Annie Macpherson, whose sphere of work was in Spitalfields, was a supporter of the conversionist project is mentioned only in the biography of John Wilkinson, 'the Jewish missionary'.[39] This aspect of her career features neither in the *Oxford Dictionary of National Biography* nor in the life of Macpherson published in 1882 by Clara Lowe:[40] a strange silence, given that it was said of Clara Lowe herself that 'the Mission to the Jews held a very warm place in her heart. It was at her suggestion, and through her influence, that the Bible was translated into Yiddish by Mr. Bergmann'.[41]

Just how fiercely the existential threat could be resented is, somewhat surprisingly, well illustrated in a letter of Lily Montagu. As will be seen, her founding role in the creation of Liberal Judaism exposed her to claims from the orthodox Jewish fold that by anglicising worship and practice she was encouraging total assimilation. However, notwithstanding her indifference to much traditional observance, and her affection and respect for her many Christian colleagues, she was distressed by marriages out of the faith, and even more so by attempts at conversion, writing in 1920: 'I think we have squashed our missionary school. Miss Lazarus and Miss Court have worked hard & stood outside the school & pounced on the children & literally dragged them back to Judaism'.[42] The difficulty of establishing relations of equality, and of steering a course between Jewish Orthodoxy and Christian conversionism, was subsequently to be brought home to her more forcefully when she established the first national interfaith organisation in England.[43]

* * * * *

Every country is, in a sense, exceptional, and the British religious landscape comprised features which were not replicated elsewhere in the West. The predominant distinguishing feature was an established Protestant church whose head was also the secular head of state. Opposition to the established church did not take the form of anti-clericalism—aggressive secularism played a minimal role in nineteenth- and early twentieth-century Britain—but of dissenting strands of 'non-conformist' Protestantism. In Catholic countries, liberal opposition to the dominant national church took a secular and anti-clerical turn; in Britain, the 'nonconformist conscience' accommodated both liberalism and religious belief. This had important consequences for British women. While they were denied formal access to the political sphere, religious cultures were available to them which permitted and even encouraged comment and activism on important issues.[44] Moreover, in the absence of an extensive network of female religious orders, religious and social energies were not diverted into or confined by conventual life.[45] In Britain, therefore, Christian women's example showed Jewish women the possibility of combining social action with religious affiliation. In Italy and France, by contrast, Jewish women were more likely to espouse civil society causes in a secular, republican spirit.[46] The peculiarly British link between religion and citizenship is exemplified by the fact that, in the annals of the international suffrage movement, Britain was alone in producing a Jewish League for Woman Suffrage.[47]

The largest English-speaking Jewish community in this period was, of course, that of the USA. This reached nearly 5 million by 1940, while the Anglo-Jewish community numbered some 300,000. The constitutional separation of church and state, the federal structure and the territorial extent of the USA all make for a religious landscape of Judaism and Christianity which is much more variegated than anything in Europe. The character of the USA as a land of mass inward migration also makes transatlantic comparisons problematic. Relative degrees of acculturation and acceptance notwithstanding, American society was the 'melting pot' where, as Melissa Klapper has written of her own female Jewish research subjects, 'Because notions of identity are fluid rather than fixed, it is impossible to differentiate between some kind of public Jewry and private individuals who happen to be Jewish. American Jewish actors of the past, blessed with free will, ... and the possibility of a sort of voluntary Judaism not available elsewhere, very often found their Jewish identities changing over time and in response to circumstances'.[48] This description would be more difficult to apply to women of the Anglo-Jewish community.

What every Western Jewish community seems to have had in common was an exclusionary male ethos, bolstered in particular by the tenets of Orthodoxy. British Jewry, whose United Synagogue of Great Britain and the Empire to some extent modelled itself on the national established church, remained predominantly orthodox. It was able to establish this as the religious norm, even if one sometimes honoured more in the breach than the observance. As in France and Italy, this provided an impetus for Jewish women to seek outlets for activism outside the fold. What a religious concept of citizenship facilitated in Britain was fostered in France and Italy by the ethos of republicanism; but Jewish-identified women in Germany seem to have found themselves restricted, by a politically salient antisemitism on the one hand, and a *Kulturkampf* between Protestantism and Catholicism on the other, in their freedom to act in the name of shared egalitarian principles.[49] It should be noted that in Germany and the USA, 'Reform' Judaism offered women a much more inclusive worshipping and educational environment than Orthodoxy[50] and this may have given female congregants more confidence in striking out and, in many cases, assimilating into the larger civil society. However, in the American as in the British community, the Jewish male consistently excluded the Jewish female from positions of communal responsibility and leadership.[51] The story of Jewish women is, therefore, also the story of Jewish men: of responses to the experiences of migration, discrimination and minority status, of aspirations to a sense of control which were often fulfilled at the expense of women. After decades of communal exclusion and historiographical neglect, however, it is certainly time to place women at the centre of the narrative.

In 1900 an East End clergyman stated that the issue of Jewish-Christian relations was one 'in which everyone is taking a part by his conversation or by his action, inasmuch as everyone has dealings with Jews'.[52] This was wholly inaccurate at the time (not just because it excluded the possibility of female interactions), and it was not true thirty years later. Even at the beginning of this new century, I find that many people who have in fact had many 'dealings with Jews' know remarkably little about the religion of Judaism, about modern Jewry's paths of migration, or about communal institutions which have flourished in this country for at least 150 years. As much of the content of what follows will, therefore, be unfamiliar, I hope the reader will begin at the beginning and thus discern the scaffolding on which the narrative of individual and group relationships is constructed. The recognition that Jewish history is fully a part of British history is long overdue, and a broadly chronological framework is intended to assist progress from the known to the unknown.

Notes

1. Bibliothèque Publique et Universitaire de Neuchâtel, Fonds Felix Bovet Ms 2098/86 1116, Josephine Butler to Felix Bovet 24 Jan. 1898: 'J'ai écrit à Madame Dreyfus pour exprimer de la part d'un groupe de femmes Anglaises et de moi même notre sympathie pour elle et sa famille'.
2. The most recent biographies of Butler are Jane Jordan, *Josephine Butler* (London, John Murray, 2001) and Helen Mathers, *Patron Saint of Prostitutes: Josephine Butler and a Victorian Scandal* (Stroud, The History Press, 2014). See also Anne Summers, *Female Lives, Moral States: Women, Religion and Public Life in Britain, 1800–1930* (Newbury, Threshold, 2000).

3. Todd M. Endelman, *The Jews of Britain 1656–2000* (Berkeley and Los Angeles, University of California Press, 2002), pp. 127, 130; Chaim Bermant, *The Cousinhood: the Anglo-Jewish Gentry* (London, Eyre & Spottiswoode, 1971).
4. Among many publications, see: Bill Williams, *The Making of Manchester Jewry, 1740–1875* (Manchester, Manchester University Press, 1976); Geoffrey Alderman, *The Jewish Community in British Politics* (Oxford, Clarendon Press, 1983); David Cesarani, *The 'Jewish Chronicle' and Anglo-Jewry* (Cambridge, Cambridge University Press, 1994); David Feldman, *Englishmen and Jews: Social Relations and Political Culture, 1840–1914* (New Haven & London, Yale University Press, 1994).
5. However, see Rickie Burman, '"She looketh well to the Ways of her Household"' in Gail Malmgreen, ed., *Religion in the Lives of English Women, 1760–1930* (Beckenham, Croom Helm, 1986); Tony Kushner, 'Sex And Semitism: Jewish Women in Britain in War and Peace' in P. Panayi, ed., *Minorities in Wartime* (Oxford, Berg, 1993); Lara V. Marks, *Model Mothers: Jewish Mothers and Maternity Provision in East London 1870–1939* (Oxford, Clarendon Press, 1994); Burman, 'Middle-class Anglo-Jewish Lady Philanthropists and East European Jewish Women' in Joan Grant, ed., *Women, Migration and Empire* (Stoke-on-Trent, Trentham, 1996); Susan L. Tananbaum, 'Philanthropy and Identity: Gender and Ethnicity in London', *Journal of Social History* 30 (1997), pp. 937–61.
6. American scholars, particularly the late Paula E. Hyman, have been the pioneers in this field. See Charlotte Baum, Paula E. Hyman and Sonya Michel, *The Jewish Woman in America* (New York, Dial Press, 1976); Paula E. Hyman, *Gender and Assimilation in Modern Jewish History: the Roles and Representation of Women* (Seattle, University of Washington Press, 1995). A valuable recent contribution by an American historian of Britain is Susan L. Tananbaum, *Jewish Immigrants in London 1880-1939* (London, Pickering and Chatto, 2014).
7. Burman, 'Jewish Women and the Household Economy in Manchester, c. 1890–1920' in David Cesarani, ed., *The Making of Modern Anglo-Jewry* (Oxford, Blackwell, 1990), pp. 55–75.
8. Tananbaum, *Jewish Immigrants*, p. 87.
9. Deirdre Beddoe, *Back to Home and Duty: Women between the Wars 1918-1939* (London, Pandora, 1989). As late as 1966, a marriage bar existed in local government employment in Scotland: personal information, Esther Croxall Higgins.
10. Nadia Valman, 'Jewish Girls and the Battle of Cable Street' in Tony Kushner and Nadia Valman, eds, *Remembering Cable Street: Fascism and Anti-Fascism in British Society* (London, Vallentine Mitchell, 2000), pp. 186–9, summarises much of the literature on this topic.

11. See, e.g., Philip Williamson, 'The Doctrinal Politics of Stanley Baldwin' in Michael Bentley, ed., *Public and Private Doctrine: Essays in British History Presented to Maurice Cowling* (Cambridge, Cambridge University Press, 1993); the same, 'Christian Conservatives and Totalitarian Challenge 1933-40', *English Historical Review* 115:462 (2000); 'National Days of Prayer: the Churches, the State and Public Worship in Britain 1899–1957', *English Historical Review*, 128.531 (2013).
12. George Dangerfield, *The Strange Death of Liberal England* (London, Constable, 1936). On the weaknesses and ambiguities of British liberalism see, for example, Bryan Cheyette and Nadia Valman's introduction to their edited volume *The Image of the Jew in European Liberal Culture 1789–1914* (London, Vallentine Mitchell, 2004), and Phyllis Lassner and Lara Trubowitz, eds, *Antisemitism and Philosemitism in the Twentieth and Twenty-first Centuries* (Newark, University of Delaware Press, 2008).
13. Philip Williamson, 'The Doctrinal Politics of Stanley Baldwin'.
14. David Cesarani, *The 'Jewish Chronicle' and Anglo-Jewry*; Louise London, *Whitehall and the Jews, 1933–1948: British Immigration policy, Jewish Refugees, and the Holocaust* (New York, Cambridge University Press, 1999). For an opposing view, see W.D. Rubinstein, *A History of the Jews in the English-Speaking World: Great Britain* (Basingstoke, Macmillan, 1996), especially Chs. 4 and 5. It is worth remarking that anti-Zionism and anti-Bolshevism would not have had uniform electoral traction in this period. Harry Defries, *Conservative Party Attitudes to Jews 1900–1950* (London, Frank Cass, 2001), pp. 84–5, states that even anti-alienism did not emerge as a specific local issue during the election campaign of December 1918.
15. The classic statement is Bill Williams, 'The Anti-Semitism of Tolerance: Middle-Class Manchester and the Jews 1870–1900' in Alan J. Kidd and K.W. Roberts, eds, *City, Class and Culture: Studies of Social Policy and Cultural Production in Victorian Manchester* (Manchester, Manchester University Press, 1985). For a personal experience which begs to differ, see below, 'Coda'.
16. Israel Joshua Singer, *Of a World That Is No More* (London, Faber, 1970).
17. Nadia Valman, *The Jewess in Nineteenth-Century British Literary Culture* (Cambridge, Cambridge University Press, 2007); Naomi Hetherington and Nadia Valman, eds, *Amy Levy: Critical Essays* (Athens, Ohio University Press, 2010).
18. See Valman, *Jewess*.
19. Paula E. Hyman, 'Does Gender Matter? Locating Women in European Jewish History' in J. Cohen and M. Rosman, eds., *Rethinking European Jewish History* (Portman, Littman Library, 2009), p. 64.
20. See, e.g. Lillian Faderman, *Surpassing the Love of Men: Romantic Friendship and Love between Women from the Renaissance to the Present* (New York,

Morrow, 1981); Lucy Bland, *Banishing the Beast: English Feminism and Sexual Morality, 1885–1914* (London, Penguin, 1995); Martha Vicinus, ed., *Lesbian Subjects: a Feminist Studies Reader* (Bloomington, Indiana University Press, 1996) and *Intimate Friends: Women who loved Women, 1778–1928* (Chicago, University of Chicago Press, 2004).
21. Edith Picton-Turbervill, *Life is Good* (London, Frederick Muller, 1939), pp. 93–4, 150–1, 158, 183.
22. Lilian H. Montagu, *My Club and I* (London, Neville Spearman Ltd & Herbert Joseph Ltd, 1954), p. 9, referring to 'my "better half"', ... Our lives are entirely intertwined, she supplementing me in some of my many deficiencies'.
23. Susan Pedersen, *Eleanor Rathbone and the Politics of Conscience* (London, New Haven, Yale University Press, 2004), pp. 77–82, 163–75. Pedersen also points out, pp. 155–6, the importance to Rathbone of a substantial legacy from her half-sister Elsie.
24. Margaret Bondfield, *A Life's Work* (London, Hutchinson, 1948) p. 76. Bondfield maintained, p. 36, that her concentration on the labour and trades union movement was 'undisturbed by love affairs'.
25. First published in 1940 and 1971 respectively.
26. This topic is further touched on in Chap. 7.
27. The Women's Library (henceforth TWL) 8SUF/B/173, interview with Lady Burrell, Tape 67. On the Women's Institute, see Simon Goodenough, *Jam and Jerusalem* (Glasgow, Collins, 1977), and Val Horsler, *Women's Century: an Illustrated History of the Women's Institute* (London, Third Millennium Publishing, 2015); on Hubback see Brian Harrison, *Prudent Revolutionaries: Portraits of British Feminists between the Wars* (Oxford, Clarendon Press, 1987), Ch. 10.
28. Evelyn Sharp, *Hertha Ayrton 1854–1923* (London, Edward Arnold, 1926) pp. 38–52. Beatrice Potter, afterwards Webb, in 1883 wrote scathingly of Eleanor Marx's unorthodox appearance, particularly her 'curly black hair, flying about in all directions': Yvonne Kapp, *Eleanor Marx* (London, Virago, 1979), Vol I, p. 284; Kapp counters this with reference to 'innumerable testimonies to her [Marx's] neat if not modish attire'.
29. Millicent Fawcett, *What I Remember* (London, T. Fisher Unwin, 1924), pp. 38–9. Browning's maternal grandfather is thought to have been the German-Jewish George William Weidemann according to www.scotlandspeople.gov.uk/.
30. Carol Ockman, *Ingres's Eroticized Bodies: Retracing the Serpentine Line* (London, New Haven, Yale University Press, 1995); Norman Kleeblatt, ed., *John Singer Sargent: Portraits of the Wertheimer Family* (Exhibition catalogue, Jewish Museum, New York, 1999), p. 32, n. 21.

31. Sylvia Pankhurst, *The Home Front* (London, Hutchinson, 1932), p. 431, describing Minnie Lansbury; 'The Noblest Woman in the World; the Story of Madame Dreyfus', *Woman's Life* 16.203 (28.10.1899), pp. 281–2.
32. E. Pethick-Lawrence, *My Part in a Changing World* (London, Victor Gollancz, 1938), pp. 122, 124; J. Ramsay MacDonald, *Margaret Ethel MacDonald* (London, Hodder & Stoughton, 1912), p. 232; Claire Hirshfield, 'The Anglo-Boer War and the issue of Jewish Culpability', *Journal of Contemporary History* 15.4, (1980), p. 623.
33. See in particular the correspondence between Millicent Fawcett and Helena Auerbach in the Atria archives; and that between Charlotte Mason and Netta Franklin in Chap. 7.
34. See, e.g. Karen Gershon, ed. Phyllis Lassner and Peter Lawson, *A Tempered Wind* (Evanston, Northwestern University Press, 2009).
35. 'A Stranger's Just a Friend'. Recorded by Jim Reeves. Written by Gilbert Gibson.
36. On British philosemitism, see W.D. Rubinstein and H.D. Rubinstein, *Philosemitism: Admiration and Support for Jews in the English-speaking World 1840–1939* (1999); Donald M. Lewis, *The Origins of Christian Zionism: Lord Shaftesbury and Evangelical Support for a Jewish Homeland* (Cambridge, Cambridge University Press, 2010); A. Sutcliffe and J. Karp, eds, *Philosemitism in History* (Cambridge, Cambridge University Press, 2011).
37. Jan Marsh, *Christina Rossetti* (London, Viking, 1995), p. 215.
38. See Chap. 4.
39. *The Life of John Wilkinson, the Jewish Missionary, by His Youngest Son Samuel Hinds Wilkinson* (London, Morgan & Scott, 1908), pp. 205–6, 282.
40. Clara M.S. Lowe, *God's Answers: a Record of Miss Annie Macpherson's Work at the Home of Industry, Spitalfields, London, and in Canada* (London, J. Nisbet, 1882).
41. Mary H. Steer, *Opals from Sand: a Story of Early Days at the Bridge of Hope* (London, Morgan & Scott, 1912), pp 54, 57.
42. London Metropolitan Archive (henceforth LMA) ACC/3529/03/001, Lily Montagu to Rabbi Mattuck, 21 April 1920.
43. See Chap. 8.
44. See, for example, Clare Midgley, *Women against Slavery: the British Campaigns 1780–1870* (London, Routledge, 1992); Summers, *Female Lives*.
45. This is not to denigrate the contribution of Catholic sisterhoods to social and public service. Sioban Nelson, in *Say Little, Do Much: Nursing, Nuns and Hospitals in the Nineteenth Century* (Philadelphia, University of Pennsylvania Press, 2001), sets out the literally pioneering roles of nursing orders in Australia and the USA. She also shows how the twentieth century

brought increasing restrictions on these nuns' mobility and leadership functions.
46. Luisa Levi D'Ancona, '"Notabili e Dame": nella Filantropia Ebraica Ottocentescas: casi di studio in Francia, Italia e Inghilterra', *Quaderni Storici* n.s. 114 (2003); and 'Jewish Women in non-Jewish philanthropy in Italy 1870–1938', *Nashim* 20 (2010).
47. See Chap 5.
48. Melissa R. Klapper, *Ballots, Babies and Banners of Peace: American Jewish Women's Activism 1890–1940* (New York, New York University Press, 2013), p. 14.
49. Peter G.J. Pulzer, *The Rise of Political Anti-Semitism in Germany and Austria* (New York, John Wiley, 1964); Christopher Clark, 'The Jews and the German State in the Wilhelmine Era' in M. Brenner, R. Liedtke and D. Rechter, eds, *Two Nations: British and German Jews in Comparative Perspective* (Tübingen, M. Siebeck, 1999), pp. 181–2; Marion A. Kaplan, *The Jewish Feminist Movement in Germany: the Campaigns of the Jüdische Frauenbund 1904–1938* (Westport and London, Greenwood, 1979), pp. 68, 82–3.
50. Melissa R. Klapper, *Jewish Girls Coming of Age in America, 1860–1920* (New York, New York University Press, 2005), pp. 32–3, 178–9.
51. Mary McCune, *"The Whole Wide World, Without Limits": International Relief, Gender Politics, and American Jewish Women, 1893–1930* (Detroit, Wayne State University Press, 2005), p. 65.
52. Canon Samuel Barnett, Introduction, in Charles Russell and Harry Samuel Lewis, eds, *The Jew in London* (London, T. Fisher Unwin, 1900), p. xxiii.

PART I

Group Encounters, 1870s–1918

CHAPTER 2

Women and Men in a Religious Landscape: Britain in the Late Nineteenth Century

Before the last three decades of the nineteenth century, few British cities and towns had substantial Jewish communities. This very new, very large and very visible body of immigrants from Eastern Europe entered into a modernising society—'the workshop of the world' and the centre of a vast empire—and also into a religious landscape. The established religion was one specific form of Protestantism—Anglicanism, or the Church of England, whose head, the reigning monarch, was also the secular head of state. The myriad other forms of Protestantism came under the heading of Dissent, or nonconformity. No longer outlawed or subject to major civic restrictions as under the Tudor and Stuart monarchs, these had retained their distinctive congregational characters. All, whether Anglicans, Methodists, Baptists, Congregationalists or Quakers participated to a greater or lesser extent in a distrust of Roman Catholicism. This was reinforced by prejudice against that other great immigrant wave of the century, which preceded the Jewish influx: the rural and predominantly Catholic Irish fleeing poverty and actual famine in hopes of a better life in English and Scottish cities.

The religious institutions of Anglo-Jewry, despite strenuous attempts at unification, were almost as fissiparous as those of the host community. From 1870 the United Synagogue linked a large number of orthodox Ashkenazi (East European) congregations within Britain and, eventually, its empire, under the authority of the Chief Rabbi. However, many

© The Author(s) 2017
A. Summers, *Christian and Jewish Women in Britain, 1880–1940*,
Palgrave Critical Studies of Antisemitism and Racism,
DOI 10.1007/978-3-319-42150-6_2

orthodox synagogues remained outside this body, some combining in the Federation of Synagogues. Their congregations often comprised very recent immigrants who considered the ministers, rituals and liturgy of the United Synagogue to be tainted by association with Protestant forms and English manners. Meanwhile the Sephardi (Spanish, Portuguese) congregations, whose members' settlement in Britain predated that of the Ashkenazim, maintained their autonomous organisation under their own leader, the Haham. A small number of Reform congregations, often associated with immigrants from Germany, existed in London and the provinces; and the Jewish Religious Union (JRU), inaugurated in 1902 to discuss ways of reviving intellectual discussion and congregational participation, gave birth in 1911 to the Liberal Synagogue which endorsed radical departures from orthodox liturgy and practice.

It should be remembered that for the whole of the nineteenth century, and while the Jewish presence in Britain was numerically still negligible, many of the most important initiatives to improve the lives of the disadvantaged—whether through the abolition of slavery, the reform of prisons, the education of children or opposition to state regulation of prostitution—had been driven by a powerful urge to 're-Christianise' society at large, in which women such as Elizabeth Fry, Mary Carpenter and Josephine Butler played a crucial part. Campaigns and missions were launched to rescue and regenerate Britain from the effects of intellectual cynicism, from the dangers of revolutionary politics or from simple demographic drift as old urban parish boundaries failed to cope with and care for the rapid movement of families from the surrounding countryside in search of employment. For decades the densely populated East End of London had been one of the most favoured locations for these initiatives to relieve poverty and reclaim souls. But from the 1870s, the arrival of thousands of people who—unlike their Irish predecessors—had never been Christians in the first place, actually put such projects into reverse.

A few examples may suffice for many. The published memoirs of Mary Steer, from 1879 head of the Bridge of Hope mission on the Ratcliff Highway, indicate at best a very ambivalent attitude to the influx of Jews into the district. Early in her career she associated with women whose mission was to convert the Jews, but her own principal vocation was to re-Christianise the native poor. She admitted with something like sadness that social standards in the area had improved over her lifetime, saying that 'the Jews who have invaded us, notwithstanding their many insanitary habits, are at least temperate.'[1] (Although most foreigners were 'dirty foreigners' to the British at this time, the Medical Officers of Health for the East End in fact considered that Jewish mothers brought up cleaner and healthier children than did any of their neighbours.[2]) In the second edition of her memoir, Steer wrote that it had broken her heart to sell her premises to Jewish philanthropists: so much of the drunkenness and prostitution which had disfigured the neighbourhood having disappeared, her work there was no longer needed.[3]

In 1880 Octavia Hill, now celebrated for her work on housing schemes and the National Trust, accused Canon Samuel Barnett and his wife Henrietta Barnett (now equally celebrated for bringing beautiful music and paintings into the East End, and for the model housing experiment of Hampstead Garden Suburb), of failing to win enough souls to Christ in Whitechapel through 'want of real affection for the Church' and avoidance of 'critising [sic] or making, or dwelling on, differences between yourself & any single human soul'. She did, however, concede that 'I do not think that many people know the special difficulty you have in St. Judes, partly because of the Jews & Catholics'.[4] And in the late 1890s a Thrift Society, started in connection with the Barnetts' former parish, ended up in the hands of the Chief Rabbi's wife. As the *Jewish Chronicle* reported, 'since most of those coming to it were Jewish Mrs Adler was asked to become Joint Treasurer; eventually Mr Bartholomew, the co-Treasurer, proposed to stand down and leave it to become a wholly Jewish charity'.[5] How the parish felt about this change is not recorded.

What may have been a cause of resentment and even despair to some Christians was seen as an opportunity by others. Perhaps the one thing on which most Christian denominations could agree was that it was their duty—even if more honoured in the breach than in the observance—to convert the Jews to the Gospel. Clusters of recently arrived and desperately poor Jewish immigrants were particularly exposed to such overtures. Indeed, in a working-class area with a substantial Jewish population like London's East End or Manchester's Red Bank, the Jewish individual leaving the family home might never feel that she was observing the Sabbath on the wrong day of the week, or encounter too many temptations to feed on forbidden pork, eels or oysters; but she would run a gauntlet of missionary agencies offering tea, sympathy, medical facilities and a heavy dose of messianic enthusiasm. Jews, unlike mere Unitarians, or even lapsed Christians, occupied such a significant niche in the messianic imaginary that there would always be parties reluctant to live and let live. One East End recipient of medical aid from the Christian Mission to the Jews in

Bateman Street cheerfully recalled that 'its zealous workers had no more hope of making converts than selling refrigerators to Eskimos but they persevered, with admirable forbearance on both sides'.[6] Not all acts of generosity towards Jews came with a conversionist price tag attached, but all this activity was a matter of grave concern to communal leaders and a goad to them, in turn, to increase and strengthen both their religious institutions and their welfare provision for their own flock.

At this point, both the religious and the more secular institutions of Anglo-Jewry faced contradictory challenges. The longer-established families and their rabbis wished to provide for the needs of their poorer brethren as a matter of religious duty. They were also anxious lest the Jewish poor inflame antisemitism in Britain by becoming a burden on such welfare provision as was supplied by local authorities and funded by ratepayers. They also feared that the welfare provisions of the host community might impair Sabbath and dietary observance. A powerful impulse to educate and transform the new immigrants into good, and inconspicuous, British citizens as quickly as possible was countered by the fear that the process of social assimilation might estrange Jews from their ancestral religion as efficiently as the blandishments of the Christian missionaries. Finding the balance between social acceptance and religious identity required the material, mental and spiritual resources of the entire community. However, Anglo-Jewry was not only divided along sectarian lines but restricted, in both secular and religious spheres, to the resources of just one half of the community.

Men were, and in the majority of cases still are, Anglo-Jewry's representatives to the outside world, and the self-appointed guardians of the integrity of the faith. Very deep structures of feeling have underpinned their resistance to women's communal participation on anything like equal terms. It is fair to say that historically most societies have been dominated by men, and therefore that assumptions of domination and leadership have been for centuries a crucial element in the masculine sense of private and public identity. This identity has sometimes been threatened where men are members of a social minority, or have been colonised by another society. The gentile world did not always treat Jewish men as equals, often denigrating them in terms such as 'weak' or 'effeminate', terms which were also used of colonial subjects.[7] Such slights and pejoratives, spoken or implied, may have strengthened the resolve of male Anglo-Jewry to form a bulwark of defence for the community, and to maintain and even increase the dominance of their own sex in synagogue and home.

It is, of course, the case that the most important tenets of Orthodox Judaism—kashrut (the dietary laws) and Sabbath observance—are centred on the home and principally managed by the materfamilias. Apologists for the division of labour in Judaism have emphasised its sanctifying of marriage and the value placed on motherhood, while glossing over the inequity of Jewish divorce law and the absence of any religious role for single women. Mothers were expected to impart initial religious instruction to their own children, but far more strenuous efforts were made for the institutional religious education of boys than of girls. Orthodox girls did not, in this period (and in most cases before the 1970s), receive any of the intensive training which led to the bar-mitzvah ceremony for boys, marking the end of religious childhood. The conduct of all synagogue services was performed by men alone, and while women's bequests to synagogues and charities were willingly accepted, they were rarely allowed any role in synagogue management and financial housekeeping before the 1950s.[8] Communal leaders recruited in their own image, looking in the first instance to a younger generation of men to reinforce and succeed them in, for example, the Jewish Board of Guardians. Modelled on the British local institution known as Poor Law Guardians, which provided (often very harshly) for the needs of the destitute, this was the body through which the settled and prosperous Jewish families attempted to help the more recent arrivals.

While British churches certainly made little attempt to become gender-equal institutions before the late twentieth century, the different strands of Christianity nevertheless afforded their female adherents a number of routes into public life and action. Christian women whose names and campaigns have found their way into mainstream British history found that their religious convictions enabled them to articulate critiques of local and national governance. The religious convictions behind the reforming careers of such women were variants of Protestantism; their sense of mission struck chords with many of their male co-religionists, even where the women were condemning prevailing standards of male conduct. By the 1850s, churches in Britain also offered women more formal institutional roles: Protestant deaconesses and Anglican sisterhoods adapted earlier Roman Catholic practice; and the Anglican parish became almost wholly dependent on women for its system of house-to-house 'district visiting'. It was with the sanction of their parents' religion that many Christian women were inspired to trust their own instincts and competence beyond the confines of home and family.[9]

It would not be reasonable to expect Anglo-Jewish womanhood to have produced national social reformers such as Elizabeth Fry or Josephine Butler within a few decades of settlement. It was difficult enough for them to overcome the opposition of their own male establishment. In 1881, over twenty years from its foundation in 1859, the Jewish Board of Guardians—ceding with visible reluctance to pressure from subscribers—formally constituted a Ladies' Visiting Committee, which presented its first report in 1885.[10] Ironically, these under-regarded women were becoming the community's real experts in welfare work. They had long presided over small welfare organisations for women in their own congregations and neighbourhoods. As will be seen, they took note of their Christian neighbours' activities, and went on to form collaborations with their Christian counterparts in new charitable initiatives. They pioneered new ways to negotiate the assimilation of modern practices and the maintenance of communal identity. By the 1880s they were doing so in the company of Christian women who experienced little contradiction between their personal faith and their public lives, and who could almost always count on the support of their respective denominational hierarchies. As members of the overall religious majority, Christian women could confidently frame committee business with their own prayers, and could set up programmes of action in tandem with local clergy. Jewish women, as the subordinate group within a social and religious minority, inevitably felt very much at a disadvantage.

A number of them had already felt impelled to become interpreters of Judaism through the medium of authorship. In this they would appear to have been following the example of their Christian opposite numbers, whose translations, compositions of hymns and published homilies and tracts were legion. However, given their subordinate status within their own community, Jewish women often had to be cautious in the presentation of similar works. They certainly did not emulate the evangelical writer and educationist Hannah More, who 'took that lively interest in the public secular affairs of her country that Jeremiah and Ezekiel did of old, and on the same plain ground that where the state professes to be modelled and the executive to act on principles of God's instilling ... nothing done by the state can be indifferent to the church or unworthy the anxious watchful regard of Christians'.[11] It was not until the end of the nineteenth century, with their participation in national women's philanthropic gatherings, and the emergence of the religious suffrage leagues, that some Jewish women began to feel that their religious convictions entitled them, as well as their Christian colleagues, to pronounce publicly on matters of state.

When they published prayers of their own composition, Jewish women justified their ventures in pedagogical and domestic terms. Anna Maria Goldsmid's translations of German Reform Judaism texts, published in 1839, were ostensibly to facilitate mothers' home teaching of religion.[12] In 1870 sisters Constance and Annie de Rothschild published a two-volume *History and Literature of the Israelites* for use in schools; in 1876 their aunt Charlotte de Rothschild published *Prayers and Meditations for Daily Use in the Households of Israelites*. Another writer, Annette (Annie) Salaman, published a collection of scripture texts, *Footsteps in the Way of Life*, in 1874, and a children's book, *Aunt Annette's Stories to Ada*, in 1879, the year of her early death. In 1897, Julia Matilda Cohen (Mrs Nathaniel L. Cohen), later the first President of the Union of Jewish Women, published an *Infant Bible Reader*, which she followed up ten years later with a selection and interpretation of the psalms for children, together with 'a prayer book for home use in Jewish families'.[13]

Nevertheless, the target reader of many such publications was often the Christian adult. When in 1890 Constance, now married 'out' to Cyril Flower, published *Mehayil el Hayil*, 'From Strength to Strength', Lessons for Jewish Children, her friend the Liberal MP A.J. Mundella diplomatically divined the lessons intended for adult readers, thanking her for the book, 'and the insight it will give of the teachings and faith of the most gifted of the human race'.[14] Four years later, Rachel Simon née Salaman published her own *Records and Reflections*, citing Charlotte de Rothschild as her exemplar; she might also have cited her late sister Annette Salaman. Wife of Sir John Simon, Liberal MP and Sergeant at Law, Rachel Simon had developed highly ecumenical habits of religious reading and institutional worship but was explicit that her purpose was 'to remove some of the prevailing misconceptions in regard to my ancestral religion'. In her relatively privileged social position she may not have been exposed to crude attempts at conversion, but she felt it necessary to point out that Judaism 'is not a system adapted for the childhood of the human race only as so many good people of other creeds suppose, nor is it an old ruin to be erased and a new edifice built in its place'.[15] Here, of course, she touched on the heart of the matter. Christian doctrine insisted that the 'New' Testament subsumed the 'Old', which had been fulfilled in Christ's ministry and sacrifice on earth. This justified the conversionist project, and consigned Jewish theology and practice to the dustbin of history. Hence the confused but wholly sincere inquiry of one of Constance Flower's correspondents, the Countess of Pembroke: 'Thank you so much for your very interesting letter on the Talmud & Bible—I do not quite understand is our Old Testament yours too? or has that come solely to us—…'.[16]

With the exception of Julia Cohen, whose father was a key figure in the foundation of the United Synagogue, none of these female apologists wrote from the orthodox mainstream of Anglo-Jewry, a fact which further underlined their minority status. All emphasised the ethical teachings of Judaism at the expense of the praxis from which—the rigorous observance of kashrut and Sabbath apart—they were excluded. Many of the discontents felt by Jewish women regarding their unequal religious status surfaced in a more public and political mode in the suffrage movement, where they campaigned alongside Christian suffragists voicing similar sentiments.[17] The culmination of these discontents may be seen in the career of Lilian (Lily) Montagu. She was born into a strictly orthodox home, which was nevertheless involved to a high degree in secular national politics: her father, the financier Samuel Montagu, later Baron Montagu of Swaythling, was the founding President of the orthodox Federation of Synagogues, and also Liberal MP for Whitechapel.[18] She inaugurated in 1899 the movement for religious renewal within the community which twelve years later, to his dismay, produced the first Liberal Jewish congregation in Britain. Throughout her life she attempted to make a more accessible, and more gender-equal, version of Judaism available to her coreligionists, and at the same time to make her religion more intelligible and acceptable to the outside world.[19] That a woman should have been a prime mover in this radical religious movement should not, in the circumstances, evoke surprise.

Notes

1. Mary H. Steer, *Opals from Sand: a Story of Early Days at the Bridge of Hope* (London, Morgan & Scott, 1912), p. 91.
2. See Lara V. Marks, *Model Mothers: Jewish Mothers and Maternity Provision in East London 1870–1939* (Oxford, Clarendon Press, 1994); also Vanessa Heggie, 'Jewish Medical Charity in Manchester: Reforming Alien Bodies', *Bulletin of the John Rylands University Library of Manchester* 87.1 (2005), p. 131, reference 106.
3. Mary H. Steer, *The Bridge of Hope Mission: a Jubilee Thanksgiving* (London, Gillett Bros, 1929), pp. 125–6.

4. London School of Economics (henceforth LSE) Coll Misc 0512, Letters of Octavia Hill to Henrietta and Samuel Barnett; Hill to Samuel Barnett, 6 August 1880.
5. *Jewish Chronicle* (henceforth *JC*), 28 February 1902, p. 9.
6. Stanley Jackson, *A Short Walk from the Temple* (London, Michael Joseph, 1970), p. 28.
7. Within a large literature on colonialism and masculinity, see: Mrinalini Sinha, *Colonial Masculinity: the Effeminate Bengali and the Manly Englishman in the Late Nineteenth Century* (Manchester, Manchester University Press, 1995); Martin Summers, 'Diasporic Brotherhood: Freemasonry and the Transnational Production of Black Middle-Class Masculinity', *Gender and History* 15.3 (2003), pp. 550–74; Janaki Nair, '"Imperial Reason": National Honour and New Patriarchal Compacts in Early Twentieth-century India', *History Workshop Journal* 66 (2008), pp. 208–26.
8. It is not the case that by the 1920s Jewish women in Britain had the right 'to participate fully in the running of many synagogues and community institutions', as stated in Helen Jones, 'National, Community and Personal Priorities: British Women's Responses to Refugees From the Nazis, From the mid-1930s to Early 1940s', *Women's History Review* 21.1 (2012), p. 134; this in turn is quoted from Clare Midgley, 'Ethnicity, "Race" and Empire' in June Purvis, ed., *Women's History: Britain 1850–1945: an Introduction* (London, UCL Press, 1995), p. 252.
9. See, for example, F. K. Prochaska, *Women and Philanthropy in Nineteenth-century England* (Oxford, Clarendon Press, 1980); Jessica Gerard, 'Ladies Bountiful: Women of the Landed Classes and Rural Philanthropy', *Victorian Studies* 30.2 (1987); Anne Summers, *Female Lives, Moral States: Women, Religion and Public Life in Britain 1800–1930* (Newbury, Threshold Press, 2000); Kathryn Gleadle, *The Early Feminists: Radical Unitarians and the Emergence of the Women Rights Movements, 1831–1851* (London, Macmillan, 1995); Sandra Holton, *Quaker Women: Personal Life, Memory and Radicalism in the Lives of Women Friends, 1780–1930* (London, Routledge, 2007); Sue Morgan and Jacqueline de Vries, eds,, *Women, Gender and Religious Cultures in Britain, 1800–1940* (London, Routledge, 2010).
10. University of Southampton Library (henceforth USL) MS 173/1/12/4 , Jewish Board of Guardians 22nd Annual Report, p. 46; the same, 26th Annual Report, p. 73.
11. *Personal Recollections By Charlotte Elizabeth* [Charlotte Elizabeth Phelan, afterwards Tonna (1790–1846)] (London, R.B. Seeley & W. Burnside, 1841), p. 211; for the latest scholarship on More (1745–1833), see *Oxford Dictionary of National Biography* (henceforth *ODNB*).

12. Michael Galchinsky, *The Origin of the Modern Jewish Woman Writer: Romance and Reform in Victorian England* (Detroit, Wayne State University Press, 1996), pp. 194–5.
13. Mrs Nathaniel L. Cohen's *The Infant Bible Reader* was advertised in the *JC* of 8 October 1897; it is not in the British Library catalogue, which lists only her *The Children's Psalm-Book ... together with a Prayer-Book for Home Use in Jewish families* (1907). Julia Cohen's father, Jacob Waley, was thought to be only the second Jew to be called to the English bar. He became Professor of Political Economy at University College London and President of the Anglo-Jewish Association.
14. British Library (henceforth BL) Add MS 47911 ff. 95–96, A. J. Mundella to Mrs Flower, 25 April 1890.
15. *Records and Reflections selected from her Writings during half a century ... by Lady Simon* (London, Wertheimer & Lea, 1894), pp. 38–9.
16. BL Add MS 47911 ff. 89–90, Lady Pembroke to 'My beloved Constance', n.d. c. 1888.
17. See Chap. 5.
18. For an account of Samuel Montagu's career, see Chaim Bermant, *The Cousinhood: the Anglo-Jewish Gentry* (London, Eyre & Spottiswoode, 1971).
19. Ellen M. Umansky, *Lily Montagu and the Advancement of Liberal Judaism* (New York, E. Mellen Press, 1983).

CHAPTER 3

Joint Enterprises: 'The Co-operation of Ladies Who Are Not Christians'

Before the years of large-scale Jewish immigration, individual Jewish women from a small number of socially prominent and extremely wealthy families had collaborated with Christian women and men in a variety of voluntary initiatives.[1] From the 1860s Louisa Lady Goldsmid, whose husband was the Liberal MP for Reading, was a key supporter of movements to improve women's educational and employment opportunities. She was often treasurer of any committee she joined: as Emily Davis, founder of Girton, the first college for women at Cambridge University, candidly admitted to a colleague, the Goldsmid wealth was a guarantee against deficit.[2] Similar considerations may have played their part elsewhere, and at later times; for example, in Helena Auerbach's service as Treasurer of the National Union of Women's Suffrage Societies and, post-1918, of the Women's Institute; and in Henrietta Franklin's long service as Secretary of the Parents' National Education Union.[3]

It was inevitable that the immensely wealthy wives and daughters of the Rothschild dynasty would be drawn into charitable collaborations, though theirs were of a less radical character. In 1864 Baroness Mayer (Juliana) de Rothschild, together with Lord Shaftesbury, launched what became known as the 'penny dinner' movement, when their Destitute Children's Dinners Society was set up in London in connection with a Ragged School in Westminster.[4] In the same period Juliana's sister Lucy Cohen served on the Working Committee of the Princess of Wales's Branch of the National Aid Society (later to become the British Red Cross),[5] while her sister-in-law Charlotte de Rothschild patronised, surprisingly perhaps, the fundraising efforts of her friend the Catholic convert Lady Georgiana Fullerton.[6] But it should be noted that Charlotte de Rothschild's long-term commitments in this period were to Jewish charities, such as the Jewish Ladies' Loan and Benevolent Society, the Norwood orphanage or the Jews' Free School, and over the years these involved significant investments of time, often on a regular weekly basis.[7] The more demanding aspects of philanthropic work were conducted on parallel lines which did not often meet.

By the mid-1880s, such Jewish women were occupying a social space which had been transformed. Thanks to mass immigration, their religious community was expanding exponentially; and where they had previously found acceptance as individuals and as a slightly exotic source of charitable funding, they were now the public, English-speaking face of a large body of resident destitute foreigners. The influx threw up new challenges to established charitable practice. At the same time, changes were taking place in the landscape of Christian women's philanthropy, as different denominations sought to pool knowledge, and reduce the duplication of effort, in a range of similar and overlapping projects. Charitable workers on all sides were seeking each other's help for reasons other than (or at least supplementary to) the perennial issue of finance. Possibly because she had married into a non-Jewish family but had retained, through the prestige of her Rothschild origins, a role in Jewish charitable life, Constance Flower was to become an important bridge between Jewish and Christian women's organisations.[8] A pivotal event in this narrative is the formation in 1885 of the Jewish Association for the Protection of Girls and Women (JAPGW), originally 'the Jewish Ladies' Society for preventive and rescue work', of which she was the convener.

JAPGW is said to have come into being when two prostitute women taking shelter in a Christian mission in London refused to eat non-kosher food or to listen to Christian sermons, and were referred by the organisers to Mrs Flower.[9] Her first step had been to assemble a group of Jewish ladies to whom Mrs Herbert, wife of the London minister who had initially encountered these two women, 'gave a stirring address' on rescue work in March 1885, which immediately produced a resolution to form a committee.[10] In contrast to their Christian counterparts, Jewish women in the early 1880s had no experience whatever in 'prevention and rescue work' among prostitute women: it came as a tremendous shock to the community to learn that cases of the 'social evil' existed in their midst.[11] Indeed, it could be said that the shock generated was somewhat disproportionate to the numbers of 'fallen' women involved. Mary (later Lady) Jeune, the writer and philanthropist, who had for some years managed a home for girls who were first-time offenders, said that out of around 3000 cases 'about fifteen only have been Jewesses'. Early inquiries made to workhouses and penitentiaries revealed almost no Jewish inmates, and those attempting street rescue work reported that a 'visit to Poplar had been a fruitless one, also Mrs Emanuel & Mrs Oppenheim's visit to the Strand, no Jewish girl having been seen either night'.[12]

As the committee proceeded to set up their refuge for 'fallen' or endangered girls and women, they referred constantly to Christian colleagues for advice and practical help, visiting Christian institutions, placing Jewish staff there for training and themselves appointing Christian staff where none could be found within the Jewish community. The Jewish committee, as time went on, felt their limitations deeply; the number of girls to be rescued might be relatively few, but some had 'fallen' so far that they were found altogether too difficult to deal with, and were referred to Christian homes or to the workhouse. They also sought the help of and cooperation with the National Vigilance Association (NVA), which monitored instances of sexual abuse and immorality and attempted to protect its victims, particularly where legal advice was needed to prosecute cases.[13]

However, the Jewish Ladies, even if they initially felt out of their depth, were responsible for one innovation of the greatest interest and service to the host community. This was the appointment of a male agent who would go to the London docks to meet any (but mainly East European) Jewish girls arriving by ship from Rotterdam, Antwerp and Hamburg, as well as to Liverpool Street Station, where passengers arrived from Harwich.[14] They arranged this in November 1885, at almost exactly the moment that several Protestant societies, notably the Young Women's Christian Association (YWCA), sent representatives to a meeting in London to establish yet another 'protective' organisation, the Travellers' Aid Society (TAS). This aimed to group together organisations already working to help girls and women leaving home in search of work to find suitable lodgings and employment, and to escape the clutches of sexual predators.[15] By February 1886 the Jewish and Christian groups were in discussions as to how to work together, with Constance Flower acting as go-between.

The TAS committee had heard that 'there was great need of visiting the German boats arriving at St. Catherine's docks', and considered this a task for which the immigrant community possessed the necessary linguistic skills.[16] A Mrs Nathaniel Cohen[17] was asked to be the Jewish Ladies' representative, and when she attended her first TAS meeting, accompanied by the (male) dock agent, she demonstrated the symmetry of communal needs by pointing out that he was actually encountering more Central and East European Christian than Jewish girls at the docks. In his words, 'for every two Jewish girls there were twenty Christians'. Not only did he need directions as to where they should be referred, but there was a case to be made for the two organisations' paying an equal share of his salary and expenses.[18] This happy symmetry did not last, however, as by November 1887 the TAS considered the agent to be doing 'far more work' for the Jewish Society than for their own, so that they should therefore be paying only one quarter of his salary.[19] Five years later the TAS was grumbling that 'Christian girls [were] conducted by Sternheim [the agent] to places of which nothing was known'.[20]

Despite this and other areas of disagreement, a relationship based on mutual need persisted. The 1892 Annual Report thanked the JAPGW for 'allowing non-Jewish young foreigners to lodge at one of their Homes in cases where … ignorance of English renders it impossible for them to make themselves understood in any ordinary Home'; and that for 1895 reaffirmed that 'We should often be in great perplexity if we could not commit our Russian and Polish girls to their kind care'.[21] This may be an example of the emollient tone of published Annual Reports in comparison with the scratchier sound of minutes of day-to-day transactions: Annual Reports invite new subscriptions, and spin is not a modern invention. Nevertheless, it is clear that by 1896 the Jewish Ladies were well embedded in the practice of intercommunal cooperation. Their growing confidence in their activism and their independent initiative was demonstrated when they accepted an invitation to the second conference of the National Union of Women Workers (NUWW). This was a convention of like-minded philanthropists and reformers—not, as its name might suggest, a trade-unionist organisation—which later became known as the National Council of Women. Once again, Constance Flower (now Lady Battersea) acted as bridge, having already become one of the National Union's Vice Presidents.

As we can see, such societies came together for solidly practical reasons, and not for the specific purpose of interfaith or interdenominational communication, however much they may have congratulated themselves on this unintended consequence of their actions. It is, for example, interesting to note that it was only in July 1891, more than five years after the TAS's invitation to a Jewish representative, that it decided to ask Cardinal Manning to recommend a lady representative of the Roman Catholic community; and none had been appointed by the end of 1892.[22] Moreover, if there were occasional misunderstandings between representatives of the Jewish and the host community, there were also dissensions within the latter. The distance between Catholic and Protestant communities was manifest, but there were also sharp degrees of difference between Protestants: these concerned particularly the YWCA's tendency to present itself in its printed literature as the principal, if not indeed sole, sponsor of the Society.[23]

However, while the Protestant groups concerned may have bickered among themselves, they were certainly agreed upon one thing: that they had formed a society 'having a distinctly religious and Christian basis'.[24] And they had been fully aware of this when issuing their original invitation to Rebecca Cohen in 1886. With some delicacy, they had minuted 'It was decided to tell Mrs. Cohen that the Travellers' Aid will be willing to co:operate [sic] as far as possible, &[sic] that if she felt she could work with the Young Women's Christian Association, the "Travellers' Aid" would be very glad to welcome her on their General Committee'.[25] Some of the connotations of that phrase 'if she felt' became apparent in October 1890, when the President, Lady Frances Balfour, composed a prayer for TAS meetings. Either through accident or tactful design, it referred to 'Almighty God' and 'our Heavenly Father', but not to Jesus Christ. However, some months later this prayer was rejected by the general committee in favour of 'the Collect "Prevent us O Lord" and the Lord's Prayer'. The Jewish representative attending the meeting, a Mrs Nathan Joseph, 'expressed on the part of the Jewish Ladies' Association, her perfect readiness to accept any form of Prayer agreed upon'.[26]

The issue of public prayer in 'non-denominational' meetings resurfaced some years later on a national platform, at a conference of the National Union of Women Workers. The earlier incarnation of the NUWW was the 'Central Conference Council', which had from 1891 to 1894 published a journal, *The Threefold Cord*. The first issue proclaimed: 'Our standard is the Christian standard; our hope is the Gospel of the Incarnation; our aim the realization of our union with each other ... Can we not unite in making our Magazine a true organ of the Christian womanhood of our country'.[27] This was an only slightly coded call to cross-denominational Protestant union, subsequently somewhat muted in the stated constitutional purpose of the NUWW 'to advance the social, moral and religious welfare of women'.[28] Non- or cross-denominationalism was not, however, un-denominationalism; and its practice was variously interpreted by the Anglican and nonconformist membership.

Mary Clifford, for example, an Anglican who was President from 1904 to 1906, wrote in 1890 of an early gathering: 'We met in the Friends' Meeting House ... Notwithstanding this, the tone was on the whole, one felt, rather Churchy, and I think it's very sweet of the Non. Cons. [*sic*] to endure with entire meekness the unconscious attitude of superiority that Church people take. At the same time, it seemed to be a proof that they recognised the value of our ways and our stand'.[29] After the 1897 conference, when Mrs Alfred Booth (sister-in-law of Charles Booth of the famous London survey) stepped into the rotating presidency, *The Woman's Signal*, an important journal of women temperance reformers and suffragists, spoke with considerably less meekness: 'It is an advantage that Mrs. Booth is a Nonconformist, she being a member of the Presbyterian Church ... There has been hitherto a feeling amongst many dissenting ladies that the "Union of Women Workers" was too exclusively managed by prominent Churchwomen; but it is, of course, meant to be quite unsectarian ...'.[30]

That year's annual conference had seen a never-to-be-repeated intervention on the subject of public prayer. It appears that from 1891, if not earlier, every conference day had begun with prayer (initially in an 'adjoining room'), and within a short time every meeting of the Executive Committee did likewise. It is a token of the continuing eclecticism of the NUWW that in 1897 its members included Louise Creighton, wife of the Bishop of London, and her friend of many years, the Fabian socialist Beatrice Webb. But eclecticism could only stretch so far. On 28 October 1897 Webb proposed that the NUWW should omit prayers from its formal agenda, 'in view of the fact that the Union invites the co-operation of ladies who are not Christians'. She claimed to represent 'the Comtists or Agnostics' and added grandly: 'It is very easy for me to say that I am not a conforming Christian, because I am independent of public approval'. This was not, she argued, the situation of those attending the conference, such as teachers or nurses, whose livelihoods might be at stake, and who wished to be neither hypocritical, nor discourteous, nor conspicuous by their absence. 'I understand', she continued, with what she may have considered a correct coinage, 'that members of the Jewish Church do not object to be present at Christian prayers, but they are not free to take part in them'. She thought that Roman Catholics felt a stronger objection to being present. The proposal was seen off with scant regard for such scruples. It was replaced with an amendment that objectors might remain absent and ask the Secretary to keep their places for them. The amendment was framed by Mary Clifford and seconded by Constance Flower.[31]

Presumably the election of a nonconformist President in 1897 took non-denominationalism as far as it would go for the time being. The incident provoked Webb to write in her diary: 'So ended my official connection with the bishops' wives.' She continued: 'It is difficult to know when and where it is wise to make a stand and insist on equality of treatment as a matter of principle', and wondered why 'only the narrow-minded and uneducated' [should be] 'allowed to have strong convictions'.[32] NUWW members were far from being 'uneducated', but it is certainly true that they considered strong convictions something of a Christian, and indeed Protestant, not to say Anglican monopoly. Religious minorities could not claim equal standing. Even a Rothschild, whose social standing might have led her to think herself, like Webb, 'independent of public approval', made no such claim; when Constance, Lady Battersea, became President between 1902 and 1904, she left undisturbed existing arrangements for prayers and services at conferences or Executive meetings. So did her coreligionist Henrietta (Netta) Franklin in her time as President of what was now the National Council of Women from 1925 to 1927, although increasing numbers of Jewish women were attending national conferences in the interwar period.

It is touching but indicative to read in the memoirs of Eva Isaacs, Marchioness of Reading, that on becoming President of the National Council of Women in 1957, she thought she was the first Jewess to do so. She recalled that the Annual General Meeting, as always, began with a service in the local (Anglican) church, where the President read the lesson: 'The vicar agreed to my selecting my own passage' and she generally chose Isaiah.[33] In 1945 an official history of the NCW had spoken of the importance of the religious orientation of the founders as a thing of the past, adding: 'to-day an occasional heartfelt sentence, the saying of the Lord's Prayer before each Executive meeting, and the inclusion of a church service in the meetings of the Conference, are all that represent the religious fervour of the early gatherings'.[34] In the face of such serene unselfconsciousness, that Eva Isaacs should have had so little sense of precedent or entitlement is unsurprising.

* * * * *

In May 1902, five years after the NUWW's prayer debate, a conference was held in London to inaugurate the Union of Jewish Women (UJW). The UJW has no founding myth, and so far relatively little documentation concerning its origins has come to light. The communal press supported the initiative, but there is no evidence that male leaders of the community were pushing for a new organisation. One of the UJW's objects was to bring together from London and the provinces those Jewish women who were already involved in the kinds of organisations and activities represented in the NUWW, and to recruit more educated women, particularly from the younger generation, into their ranks.[35] The initiative was the suggestion of Mrs Anna Simmons, widow of the Reverend Laurence Simmons, of the Manchester Reform Congregation. She proposed it to a drawing-room meeting held in 1900 at the home of Louise de Rothschild, mother of Constance Flower. Together with Mrs Gertrude Spielmann, Anna Simmons became one of the two organising secretaries of the conference which, they announced in the *Jewish Chronicle* of 27 September 1901, would 'discuss matters concerning the social, moral and spiritual welfare of our community'.[36]

Anna Simmons's experience of working in Jewish communal and Christian interdenominational charities in Manchester was immense[37] and none of the organisers of the new Union could be said to have lacked occupation. Why did they feel the need to set up yet another organisation? One small hint as to the organisers' motives may lie in a fictional sketch by Constance Flower, published in the *Jewish Chronicle* on the eve of the conference, where one young voluntary worker enthuses: 'I rejoice to think that instead of losing our identity in one of the big Conferences, we Jewish "working" women, are actually going to have one of our own'.[38] A stronger hint was given by Julia Cohen in her introductory speech: 'one often hears people say, "I don't care to work if it is only to benefit Jews. I like undenominational charity". But in this country, charity work is very largely organised on denominational lines, and we Jews, a small minority, must inevitably fall in with the general lines of the majority'.[39]

Cohen immediately qualified her statement, perhaps mindful that the guest of honour was Millicent Fawcett, head of the non-denominational and law-abiding suffrage movement to which many present were sympathetic. She pointed to the cross-denominational links of the TAS and JAPGW, as well as to the involvement of Jewish women in 'philanthropic work of national benefit, even if it be carried on through other denominational channels'. As she was well aware, many in her audience had years of experience in such voluntary work. Most recently, they had moved into patriotic organisations active for the duration of the Anglo-Boer War, such as the Victoria League and the Soldiers' and Sailors' Families Association. These seasoned workers urged their younger listeners to learn the ropes by participating in rent-collecting under the aegis of Octavia Hill, by reading the works of the social reformer Helen Bosanquet, and by contacting and training under their local branch of the Charity Organisation Society, the Metropolitan Association for Befriending Young Servants, or the Working Girls' Clubs movement.[40]

All the above would suggest that by 1902 it was unproblematic for social activists to move between the Jewish and non-Jewish worlds. Constance Flower told the conference how pleased she would be to announce that the UJW wanted to affiliate to the NUWW. Prominent speakers—her sister Annie Yorke, the Chief Rabbi's daughter Henrietta 'Nettie' Adler, Lily Montagu and her sister Netta Franklin, as well as several JAPGW representatives—were later that year to be found participating in the national conference of the NUWW, under Flower's presidency. The known practice of Christian public prayer appeared to be no obstacle to participation, and there seems to have been no overt expression of a sense of exclusion from any part of national organisational life. But Constance Flower's short story hinted at a paradox at the heart of Jewish women's participation in the wider associational world. If the desire to reinforce a communal sense of confidence played its part in the birth of the UJW, this suggests quite strongly that the very process of going out into the gentile world produced a felt need for Jewish women to strengthen their collective institutions and identity.

For in truth, the context in which Jewish women undertook the care of 'their' poor could not be a simple parallel with comparable activities in the host community; and mingling with Christian social peers represented only the tip of a larger iceberg of political and welfare issues. The massive involvement of the well-to-do among the Jewish community in relieving the poverty of their coreligionists was driven by anxiety as well as generosity. The year 1902 marked the end of the Anglo-Boer War, during which, Jewish patriotic charitable endeavours notwithstanding, Jewish financiers had been portrayed as instigators of, and profiteers from British military involvement.[41] It was also the year in which the Royal Commission on Alien Immigration was set up, which resulted in the Aliens Act of 1905, the first of several such restrictive measures. And Jewish philanthropy was still driven by the fear that if Jews left a welfare vacuum among their own people, Christian conversionists would hasten to fill it. As Julia Cohen had reminded the inaugural conference of the UJW, poor Jews might be lost to the community if they sought help 'from essentially Christian charity, whatever the conditions attached to it, may be'.[42]

Christianity could, of course, operate against Jewish identity in ways less direct than missionary conversion. Conditions of employment could often penalise Jewish religious observance. UJW leaders were keenly aware that fidelity to religion could entail material hardship as well as social disadvantage to their less privileged sisters. The religious sectarianism of British philanthropy to which Cohen had alluded was brought home to the UJW, for example, as it set itself the task of helping middle- and lower-middle class women to obtain professional training. Organisers were particularly keen to increase the number of Jewish nurses. However, aspiring Jewish probationers were mainly restricted to the London Hospital in the East End, which accommodated the religious observances of Jewish patients. The UJW minutes for February 1903 include a terse note that 'Miss S. Joseph was unable to enter King's College Hospital, as all nurses must attend chapel'. (It is relevant that in this period, only one London hospital, St George's, accepted practising Catholics for nursing training.)[43] By May 1903, the UJW had declared as its principal object 'To help in finding employment for educated Jewesses struggling against difficulties and disabilities arising from adherence to the tenets of our faith'.[44] There is no record of the UJW's challenging such exclusions, much less discussing them in a 'mixed' public domain. Their response was to assume the obligation, as prominent and prosperous community representatives, to compensate those who suffered from them.

If Jewish women occupied any particular role within the philanthropic community, as within the nation as a whole, it was one defined largely by absences and negatives. They were, while cooperating with the host community's labours, to take care of their own people, and to ensure that they caused, in the classic Jewish phrase, 'no trouble'. It was thus hardly to be expected that, in a gentile context, Jewish women's organisations would have asserted their communal rights, or made a general stand against religious discrimination. If their religious sensitivities were taken into account from time to time, this was an issue of privilege only. The religious culture of British public life in this period did not invite them, in Beatrice Webb's words, 'to make a stand and insist on equality of treatment as a matter of principle'.[45] Moreover, the broad spectrum of the nineteenth-century women's movement was not uniformly hospitable to the concept of rights. For many women, and not just 'the Bishops' wives', the concept of moral and social obligation had a stronger purchase in justifying their actions in the public sphere than claims based on a sense of equality and entitlement. The springboard for social action was often the conviction of the right of every soul to seek salvation through Christ. As a language of universal rights, this had distinct limitations for a religious minority.[46]

However, it might also be argued that, problematic as this Christian female environment could be, it employed a language of religion and obligation which was utterly familiar to Jewish women, and which enabled them to make the transition from domestic and communal to local and national engagements. While these activities might have been discussed with parents and spouses, they do not seem to have raised issues of contention. As secularisation was not demanded as the price of public action, communal identity could be maintained through organising along parallel lines which were allowed to meet, or at least coexist. On an individual level, as we shall see, devoutly held but differing religious beliefs were no barrier to affectionate and long-standing working friendships. The formal surface of organisational life was sometimes stirred by outside events to reveal a genuine depth of fellow feeling.

One such event was General Allenby's entry into Jerusalem in December 1917, or as it was very widely described in Christian Britain, Jerusalem's 'deliverance from the Turks'. In that month the proudly Anglican Mary Clifford, who was nearing the end of her life, wrote to her NUWW colleague Constance Flower:

> Dearest Lady Battersea,
> I cannot help writing you a line of rejoicing [her emphasis] at the good news which has just reached us here today about Jerusalem. ... isn't it splendid to think that at last the worst sorrows and trials of your Nation are over and that to us has been given the honour of redressing these wrongs![47]

And Millicent Fawcett, head of the National Union of Women's Suffrage Societies, wrote to the treasurer, Helena Auerbach,

> We are rejoicing greatly, as I know you both must be over the delivrance [*sic*] of Jerusalem. How wonderful & intensely romantic it all is: all the more so because it coincides with the anniversary of the victory of the Maccabees. ... I shall try to be at the Te Deum in St Paul's this afternoon.[48]

These loving letters demonstrate the acknowledgement of difference and its acceptance. Their religious discourse was very different from the racialised language of the anti-immigrant movement or the anti-Jewish propaganda of some opponents of the Anglo-Boer War. In the discourse of Christian philanthropy, particularly its conversionist tendency, there was relatively little scope for the language of revulsion and expulsion; in principle, conversionists operated a strategy of inclusion, and offered the Other an (often unwanted) embrace. Thus the salience of Christianity—even in its conversionist forms—within British women activists' lives and organisations before 1914 may, in a final paradox, have protected women of the Jewish community from the overt expressions of racialised hostility which were current elsewhere. In this respect, the religious organisations of civil society may have treated Jewish women with greater civility than a more secular civil society treated their male peers.

Notes

1. On comparable developments in the world of male philanthropy, see Abigail Green, 'Rethinking Sir Moses Montefiore: Religion, Nationhood, and International Philanthropy in the Nineteenth Century', *American Historical Review* 110.3 (June 2005), p. 650.
2. Letter of Emily Davies to Helen Taylor, 5 June 1866, cited in Elizabeth Crawford, *The Women's Suffrage Movement: a Reference Guide 1866–1928* (London, UCL Press, 1999), p. 247.
3. See Chap. 7.
4. Angela Burdett Coutts, *Woman's Mission* (London, S. Low, Marston & Co., 1893), pp. 18–19.
5. Anne Summers, *Angels and Citizens: British Women as Military Nurses 1854–1914* (Newbury, Threshold Press, 2nd ed, 2000), p. 124.
6. Letters of Charlotte de Rothschild to her son Leopold, 15 March 1864; 16 May 1865; 17 and 20 July 1866, concerning her friendship with and support for the Catholic charities of Lady Georgiana Fullerton: Rothschild Archive 000/84; online transcriptions at http://www.rothschildarchive.org/RESEARCH/?DOC=/RESEARCH/ARTICLES/clderltrs.
7. Gerry Black, *J.F.S.: the History of the Jews' Free School, London since 1732* (London, Tymsder Publishing, 1998), pp. 59–62.
8. On the life of Constance de Rothschild, see the entry in *Oxford Dictionary of National Biography* (henceforth *ODNB*); and Lady Battersea (Constance Flower), *Reminiscences* (London, Macmillan, 1922).
9. Battersea, *Reminiscences*, p. 418.

10. University of Southampton Library (henceforth USL) MS 173/2/1/1, JAPGW Minutes for 23 March 1885; see also Paul Knepper, '"Jewish Trafficking" and London Jews in the Age of Migration', *Journal Of Modern Jewish Studies* 6.3 (2007).
11. See Edward J. Bristow, *Prostitution and Prejudice: the Jewish Fight against White Slavery 1870–1939* (Oxford, Clarendon Press, 1982).
12. USL MS 173/2/1/1, JAPGW Minutes, 8 and 15 May, and 3 July 1885.
13. See JAPGW Minutes, *passim*; see also Louise A. Jackson, *Child Sexual Abuse in Victorian England* (London, Routledge, 2000), Ch. 7. I am particularly grateful to Dr Jackson for her generous help with this section of my research. The NVA was set up in the wake of the Criminal Law Amendment Act of 1885 which, amongst other measures, raised the age of (hetero)sexual consent to sixteen, and intensified the formal criminalisation of homosexuality. It also lobbied for increasing censorship of publications and performances. After 1899 it was closely linked to the International Bureau for the Suppression of the White Slave Traffic, of which the Chief Rabbi Dr Hermann Adler became a Committee member.
14. USL MS 173/2/1/1, JAPGW Minutes, 24 April 1885, 6 and 27 November 1885; The Women's Library (henceforth TWL) 4 TAS/A/1/1 p. 31, General Committee Minutes, 30 June 1886.
15. TWL 4TAS/A/1/1, pp. 1–2, 12. Societies included: Metropolitan Association for Befriending Young Servants; Girls' Friendly Society; National Vigilance Association; Girls' Helpful Society; Young Women's Help Society; Reformatory and Refuge Union; Amies de la Jeune Fille; British Institute in Brussels. YWCA representatives dominated the Executive Committee. Lady Frances Balfour was president.
16. TWL 4TAS/A/1/1, General Committee Minutes p. 26, 26 February 1886.
17. This was not Julia, but Rebecca Cohen, whose death was lamented in the TAS's Annual Report for 1890, p. 17.
18. TWL 4TAS/A/2/1, Executive Committee Minutes f. 12, 25 May 1886; see also 4TAS/A/1/1, General Committee Minutes p. 31, 30 June 1886.
19. TWL 4TAS/A/1/1, General Committee Minutes p. 44, 14 November 1887.
20. TWL 4TAS/A/2/1, Executive Committee Minutes f. 160, 18 November 1892.
21. TWL 4TAS/B/1, *Report for the year 1892*, p. 17; *Report ... 1895*, p. 26.
22. TWL 4TAS A/1/1, pp. 124–5, General Committee Minutes, 17 July 1891; 4TAS A/2/1, f. 166, Executive Minutes 16 December 1892.
23. TWL 4TAS A/1/1, p. 105, General Committee Minutes, 24 November 1890.
24. Ibid.

25. TWL 4TAS/A/1/1, pp. 28–9, General Committee Minutes, 26 February 1886.
26. TWL 4TAS/A/2/1, ff. 88–9, prayer following Executive Minutes of 18 July 1890; TWL 4TAS/A/1/1, pp. 101–2, General Committee Minutes, 14 November 1890. The collect ends with the words 'through Jesus Christ our Lord'. Lizzie Joseph née Samuel was the second wife of the architect Nathan Solomon Joseph.
27. *The Threefold Cord* I, October 1891, editorial introduction.
28. London Metropolitan Archive (henceforth LMA) X76/2, n. p., 2nd annual report of the Central Conference Council, 1894; Maria Ogilvie Gordon, *Historical Sketch of the National Council of Women of Great Britain* (M.O. Gordon, 1937), p. 7.
29. G.M. Williams, *Mary Clifford* (Bristol, J.W. Arrowsmith, 1921), pp. 181–2, letter (to unknown), 16 November 1890, referring to a conference in Birmingham.
30. *The Woman's Signal*, 4 November 1897, p. 297; the editor was Lady Henry Somerset. Her sister was Adeline Duchess of Bedford, noted for her interest in prison conditions for women, and for her links to Constance Flower.
31. National Union of Women Workers (henceforth NUWW), *Women Workers* (conference report) (1897–8), pp. 178–81.
32. Norman and Jeanne Mackenzie, eds, *The Diary of Beatrice Webb* Vol. 2 (London, Virago, 1983), pp. 124–5.
33. *For the Record: the Memoirs of Eva, Marchioness of Reading* (London, Hutchinson, 1972), pp. 192–3.
34. H. Pearl Adam, ed., *Women in Council* (London, Oxford University Press, 1945), p. 11. Gertrude Horton noted the differences between the Townswomen's Guilds and the rural Women's Institutes in the interwar period: the latter used to begin each meeting with a hymn. The former did not, because it would 'keep people out ... [The WI] expected people who were not holding their beliefs just to shut their ears'; interview, TWL 8SUF/B/139. Recently, secularists in Britain have drawn attention to the continuing custom in many local authorities of commencing formal council proceedings with Christian prayer.
35. *Jewish Chronicle* (henceforth *JC*), 12 July 1901, p. 17
36. *JC*, 27 September 1901, p. 8.
37. Amongst other activities, she established close working relationships with the Bishop of Manchester and other clergy in the relief of local poverty, and was a member of both the Manchester Jewish Ladies Visiting Association and the Manchester and Salford Sanitary Association on which it was modelled (see following chapter): *JC*, 6 June 1902, p. 19; Rickie Burman, 'Middle-Class Anglo-Jewish Lady Philanthropists and Eastern

European Jewish Women', in Joan Grant, ed., *Women, Migration and Empire* (Stoke-on-Trent, Trentham, 1996), pp. 127–8.
38. 'Round the Tea Table': Constance Flower (Lady Battersea), *Waifs and Strays* (London, A.L. Humphreys, 1921), p. 261. (Sketch first published in *JC*, 9 May 1902, p. 20.)
39. *JC*, 16 May 1902, pp. 10–11.
40. Ibid.
41. See, e.g. Claire Hirshfield, 'The Anglo-Boer War and the Issue of Jewish Culpability', *Contemporary Review* 15.4 (1980), pp. 619–31.
42. *Report of the Conference of Jewish Women ... 13th and 14th May, 1902* (*JC* 1902), p. 74.
43. USL MS 129 AJ 26/B/1 p. 16, UJW Executive Minutes, 11 February 1903. Information on Catholic nurses from Dr Carmen Mangion, Birkbeck College.
44. USL MS 129 AJ 26/ D/1, News Cuttings: *Jewish World*, 5 June 1903, account of UJW General Committee meeting, 27 May 1903.
45. Norman and Jeanne Mackenzie, eds, *The Diary of Beatrice Webb* Vol. 2 (London, Virago, 1983), pp. 124–5
46. Christianity rather than socialism demanded identification with the poor: Katherine St John Conway's response to the plight of striking women cotton workers was: 'They stand between me and Christ'; Stephen Yeo, 'A New Life: the Religion of Socialism in Britain 1883–1896', *History Workshop Journal* 4 (1977) pp. 11–12.
47. Battersea, *Waifs and Strays*, p. 194.
48. Atria (formerly Aletta, formerly IIAV), Amsterdam, Fawcett-Auerbach Letters Folder 10, Fawcett to Auerbach 11 December 1917. Ironically, Auerbach was affiliated to that wing of the Zionist movement which sought to establish a haven for Jews in East Africa rather than Palestine. See Meri-Jane Rochelson, *A Jew in the Public Arena: the Career of Israel Zangwill* (Detroit, Wayne State University Press, 2008).

CHAPTER 4

'Dear Madame Dreyfus'

In June 1899, the conviction for treason which had been passed on the French army officer Captain Alfred Dreyfus four and a half years previously was referred for retrial in Rennes, Brittany. Dreyfus was brought back to France from his exile and imprisonment on Devil's Island; liberal opinion in France, and indeed worldwide, saw this as a triumph of the campaign to prove his innocence, and felt confident that the new hearing would produce an acquittal. However, in September 1899 Dreyfus was instead condemned to a shortened sentence of ten years' imprisonment on account of 'mitigating circumstances'. A disgusted Dreyfus renounced his right of appeal, but on 19 September accepted President Emile Loubet's offer of a pardon, on the condition that he could continue his efforts to prove his innocence.[1]

The news of Dreyfus's non-acquittal provoked outrage, and nowhere more widely or more vehemently than in Britain. On 11 September the editors of the *Daily Chronicle* described it as 'an emotion to which we recall no parallel in our experience of modern political affairs'. Some expression of this feeling was called for, and it was proposed to send 'a national address of sympathy to Captain Dreyfus, which, without containing any expression of a wounding character to the French nation or army as a whole, would satisfy the sentiment of deep pity and indignation which animates the entire country without distinction of class or party'.[2]

© The Author(s) 2017
A. Summers, *Christian and Jewish Women in Britain, 1880–1940*,
Palgrave Critical Studies of Antisemitism and Racism,
DOI 10.1007/978-3-319-42150-6_4

On the following day the *Daily Chronicle* published a letter from the journalist and novelist Charlotte O'Connor Eccles, suggesting that it would 'be a graceful act if the women of the British Islands gave practical expression to their sympathy with Madame Dreyfus by organising a testimonial to her'. The original proposal was promptly modified, and the decision taken to send the address to Madame Dreyfus and her family: a demonstration would be held at Hyde Park on 17 September, where sheets would be handed round for last-minute signatures, and in the meantime readers outside London could post theirs to the newspaper. At least 112,000 signatures were received within ten days[3] and, as the archives of the Dreyfus family reveal, many individuals wrote to Lucie Dreyfus directly.[4] The names of the signatories of the address, and of the men and women who wrote independently, certainly bear out the *Daily Chronicle*'s initial claim on 11 September to represent 'the sentiment ... which animates the entire country without distinction of class or party'.

They included the mayors of 165 towns; members of the London Stock Exchange; employees of schools and local authorities, of the staffs of Barclays and Co., of the publishers Eyre and Spottiswood, and the Alhambra theatre; hundreds of working men, including those employed at the Victoria Works, Brentwood (and 190 at High Wycombe); soldiers of the Durham Light Infantry; members of many different churches and Bible classes. The political classes supplied male names such as Lord Rosebery (widower of Hannah Rothschild), Keir Hardie and several members of the Gladstone family. Other prominent male signatories included Charles Darwin's son, the botanist Francis Darwin, the music-hall star Dan Leno, the author George Meredith, the journalist and campaigner Percy Bunting and even the arch-opponent of Jewish immigration into Britain, Arnold White, who offered £20 towards expenses.

Women easily made up half, if not more, of the signatories and correspondents. They included well-known philanthropists and social and political campaigners, such as Catherine Marsh, Josephine Butler, Jane Cobden Unwin, Laura Ormiston Chant, Florence and Rosamond Davenport-Hill, Margaret Lonsdale, Florence Balgarnie, Lady Henry Somerset and Baroness Angela Burdett-Coutts; educationists and authors such as Dr Sophie Bryant, Helena Swanwick, and Marie Corelli; thespians such as Elsie Fogerty, Lily Langtry, Ellen Terry, Lena Ashwell; and titled ladies such as Muriel Countess Delawarr, Lady Selina Scott, Mabel Countess Russell and Margaret Brooke (the Maharanee of Sarawak). Collective responses included those from the Theatrical Ladies' Guild, the Guild of

Women Bookbinders, local branches of the Women's Liberal Association and the Women's Christian Temperance Union, and from working schoolteachers, clerks, washerwomen, sempstresses and nurses.

They also wrote directly to Madame Dreyfus in their hundreds, as woman to woman, addressing their 'Sister in Distress', writing as 'a wife and mother', declaring that 'Every English Wife's heart aches with you', and that 'Every Woman's heart in England bleeds for you & we pray for you & your dear little children, & husband'; 'no pang of agony you had suffered but found its way into the heart of all Englishwomen at home and abroad. . . . accept this halting and imperfect offering of sympathy both personally and from every woman in my household' (this last from Baroness Burdett-Coutts, presumably on behalf of herself and her domestic staff).[5] But—particularly in the light of O'Connor Eccles's acclamation of their heroine as 'The Mater Dolorosa of modern politics'[6]—the question arises: how, if at all, did they perceive and approach Lucie Dreyfus's identity as a Jewess?

Certainly Lucie's identity as a woman was conceived in a traditional manner, one conceived to be non-problematical at a time of fierce debate over the suffrage and the 'New Woman'. At the Hyde Park demonstration on Sunday 17 September, Mrs Ormiston Chant felt confident in declaring: 'there was not a man or woman but would feel hearty admiration for her who had so nobly met and conquered every obstacle in her struggle to get the infamous verdict reversed. (Cheers). ... The courage shown by Mme Dreyfus was an object-lesson for the women of the world'.[7] These sentiments were echoed in the female periodical press. But if Lucie Dreyfus was described, rightly, as dauntless, she was also portrayed and admired for being self-effacing. She had addressed herself to kings and statesmen and mastered the extraordinarily complex brief for the defence, but this was solely for the sake of her family. She was an exemplary wife and mother, not a modern, independent feminist heroine. As for her French nationality and her Jewish family origin, these were very frequently ignored: the latter may have been seen as something of an embarrassment, comparable to a disability to which it would be impolite to refer.

The description in *Woman's Life* of 'that beautiful woman with the majestic figure, tall and graceful, with clear complexion, and hair dark as the night' might perhaps have been a coded attempt to indicate that Madame Dreyfus looked Jewish, but not in a bad way. The article stated that the proof of her husband's innocence 'was her mission. That proof was her religion', which perhaps permitted any little doctrinal awkwardnesses to be conveniently ignored.[8] A year earlier, *The Woman's Signal* had drawn attention to Mme Dreyfus's campaign in France and internationally to secure a retrial; this article was more explicit, referred to an 'anti-Jewish conspiracy', and attributed the words 'Jehovah will, ere long, crush his enemies' to Lucie. It did not describe her as tall or majestic. Instead, Madame Dreyfus was referred to as 'the plucky little wife ... the little wife still waits'.[9] Indeed, post-Biblical Jewish men and women were not generally considered by their host societies to be physically imposing. One example among many of the conventional use of this diminishing adjective is in the published memoirs of the social worker Mary Steer, whose missions in the East End of London have been referred to above. Each individual Christian who ever helped her is acknowledged by name; but in recounting an episode where she received help from generous Jews, Steer refers to them merely as 'a little Hebrew lady and her brother'.[10]

Do the letters written directly to Mme Dreyfus tell us more? A great many of the writers say they are praying for her, and it is noteworthy that they do not mention the name of Christ. Tactfully, they invoke 'the Divine Pity and Compassion' and 'our God, who hears the sorrowful sighing of the poor prisoner'. Burdett-Coutts writes most gracefully: 'May the Almighty support you throughout. "His days are but grass" but though the path in the wilderness is long and heavy the Promised Land is reached at last'. And some go closer to the matter, following the *Woman's Signal* in invoking 'The God of Justice, JEHOVAH' and 'The God of the Jews Jehovah'. Charlotte Roberts, of Northumberland, expressed a particular Christian and, indeed, philosemitic rationale for sympathy with the Jewish prisoner:

> We have seen a good deal in our papers about 'his being a Jew' and therefore being condemned, surely that should to all Christians have been an extra reason for Captain Dreyfus being extra well treated as according to our beliefs
> 'It was a Jew who shed his blood
> Our pardon to procure
> It is a Jew who sits above
> Our pardon to ensure'
> and for that reason alone if necessary all honor [*sic*] should be paid to all innocent descendents [*sic*] of Abraham.

For many gentile women, the drama of this noble soldier and his dauntless wife was easily assimilable to the value system of their own religious (and mainly Protestant) formation. It could without discomfort be accommodated within familiar biblical teachings. While some correspondents may, like Josephine Butler, have nurtured the paradoxical hope that Captain Dreyfus's intense sufferings could lead him to identify with and acknowledge the stricken Christ,[11] none was so tactless as to say so to Madame Dreyfus herself. And, in contrast to the tropes of much Victorian fiction (particularly that of a conversionist persuasion), there was, self-evidently, no bad Jew/good Jewess dichotomy at work here.[12] Nor was it thought odd of God to choose these particular Jews. If there was a religious villain in the story, it was the Roman Catholic Church, hand in glove with another old enemy, the French army. In the face of this evil dyad, the martyred Dreyfus family appeared as honorary, or virtual, Protestants.

* * * *

Much of the furore over the Dreyfus affair involved Francophobia, anti-Catholicism and the self-congratulation of British liberals, male and female, rather than any informed understanding of the position of the Jewish minority in Europe, or ordinary acquaintance with Jewish lives in Britain. However, there was one letter to Mme Dreyfus which clearly represented something more. This was a Manchester initiative, a message of sympathy signed in September 1899 by 1776 women of every creed and class. Taken together with information from other sources, it demonstrates a web of local connections formed by charitable collaborations between Jewish and Christian women over the previous two decades. These relationships were based on practical action in pursuit of realistic goals, and would appear to have been free of the element of romanticisation which characterised some of Mme Dreyfus's other female admirers (Fig. 4.1).

On 14 September 1899, the *Manchester Guardian* printed the following letter from S.A. Gamble:

> Amongst the many expressions of sympathy with Captain Dreyfus, I have looked in vain in your paper for the suggestion of a letter from women in Manchester to his noble wife. Knowing how strong the feeling for her is, and that it only needs expressing, I submit the following, which, in conjunction with some friends, I hope to send, and shall be glad to hear from any others willing to sign.
>
> 'Dear Madame Dreyfus, We have no desire to intrude upon you in this hour of sore trial, but we do wish to express the deep sympathy we feel, and the respect and admiration you have won from us. We have followed with close attention your noble efforts and those of other members of your family to free your beloved husband from injustice and imprisonment and to prove

Fig. 4.1 Portrait of Mrs Gamble (Courtesy of Manchester City Libraries)

to the world his innocence. Our hearts have been wrung by his suffering and our heads bowed in shame over the insult and injustice heaped upon him by the unrighteous verdict and sentence of Saturday last. We join with thousands throughout the world in praying that ere long truth may triumph, that this verdict may be annulled, and that you and he may be speedily reunited in a life of happiness and usefulness.'[13]

Sarah Anne Gamble—who either did not know of the *Daily Chronicle* initiative, or who was perhaps moved to emulate it—succeeded in appending 1776 female (and some male) signatures to her letter, which had been dated 13 September, and signed by her, by the Lady Mayor of Manchester, Mrs W.H. (Eleanor) Vaudrey, and by a Helen B. Thomson. Mrs Gamble (1844–1926) was prominent in many social and charitable Manchester spheres. She was a founder member of the Women's Christian Temperance Association and a pillar of the Band of Hope; she was active in the Church of England mission to women and girls brought before the police courts. She was also a committee member of the Ladies' Branch of the Manchester and Salford Sanitary Association (MSSA).[14] It was through this latter organisation—known under a slightly bewildering number of names in the nineteenth century[15]—that she is most likely to have established links with similar women in Manchester's Jewish community.

The MSSA itself was formed in 1852, 'to promote attention to Temperance, Personal and Domestic Cleanliness and to the Laws of Health generally'. Ten years later the Manchester and Salford Ladies' Health Society (also known as the Ladies' Sanitary Reform Association) was formed. This modelled itself on the Ladies' Sanitary Association, formed in London in 1858, one of many initiatives proceeding from the National Association for the Promotion of Social Science, possibly the most gender-equal of all Victorian voluntary organisations.[16] These societies tried to educate the poor and their charitable visitors through lectures and tracts; but they went further, investigating the bad housing, water supplies and drainage which were beyond the capacity of individual families to remedy, publicising their findings and referring them to the municipal authorities. They took the established practice of house-to-house parish district visiting and extended it from a system of pastoral care and ad hoc charitable provision to a systematic attempt to improve the health and living conditions of the poor. District visiting had long been a female domain,[17] and the MSSA would appear to have handed over this aspect of its work to the Manchester and Salford ladies in the 1860s. Food, medicines, household soap and nursing assistance were given by both volunteer and paid visitors, and a children's holiday scheme devised. In 1878 the ladies formally affiliated to the MSSA, and became its Ladies' Branch.[18]

The Ladies' Branch had many Jewish subscribers, and in 1882, when its Committee was considering work in the districts densely populated by recent Jewish immigrants from Eastern Europe, it would have been able to consult with such women (or, rather, 'ladies') as Anna Simmons, wife of the minister of the Reform synagogue. She was constantly active in cross-communal welfare undertakings. She came to know, for example, the Bishop of Manchester both in his capacity as President of the Ladies' Branch, and as President of the Manchester Relief Fund for Russian Jews. It was said that she and her husband helped their Gentile brethren so often that the clergy of the Church of England and the Romish Church in their turn were quite willing to associate themselves in work for poor Jews. There was, apparently, some muttering within Manchester Jewry when she arranged a Christmas tree and seasonal woolly gifts for poor children in Ancoats;[19] and it is true that at this stage the Reform congregation had closer links to the wider community than their orthodox coreligionists. Anna Simmons may have recruited others to the Ladies' Branch, such as Mrs Salis Simons, who in 1902 recalled having become conscious of 'how wide a gulf had grown between our pleasant villa suburbs ... and those narrow, wretched courts and alleys'; she began reading MSSA literature in the 1870s, and became a member in the 1880s.[20]

Other links between Jewish and Christian women may have originated in less formal ways. The Ladies' Branch reports indicate that neighbourhood acquaintances facilitated the recruitment of members and collection of subscriptions. In 1886, for example, a Mrs Salomons paid 5 shillings via the Misses Wright and Hamilton; the Salomons family lived in Victoria Park, as did the health lecturer Anne Romley Wright. A Mrs Henriques paid 10 shillings via Mrs Hardie; Mrs E.M. Henriques and Mrs James Hardie, wife of the workhouse Medical Officer and Manchester Royal Infirmary surgeon, both lived in Higher Broughton. And Mrs Edward Behrens was living in Fallowfield (where Mrs Gamble and Anna Simmons also resided) when she paid 2 guineas via a Mrs Renshaw.[21] However, whether these transactions were the beginning of relations between Jewish and Christian neighbours, or built on pre-existing connections in suburban districts such as Rusholme and Higher Broughton, is unclear. What is certain is that the Ladies' Branch had a marked influence on a number of its Jewish subscribers, and that the conversations which began around 1882 led to the creation of a major new Jewish voluntary institution. In 1884, the Jewish Sanitary Association—soon renamed the Ladies' Association for Visiting the Jewish Poor and Attending to their Sanitary Condition, and ultimately the more manageable Jewish Ladies' Visiting Association (JLVA)—was formed. Its first President was Abigail (Mrs Edward) Behrens, its Vice President Emily (Mrs E.M.) Henriques, its first Honorary Secretary was Anna Simmons, and Hedwig Dreyfus, wife of a distant relative of Captain Alfred Dreyfus, was its first Treasurer.[22]

The JLVA's programme was initially to undertake all home visits personally: members were to visit at least five houses at least once a fortnight. Personal visiting remained a commitment, but the Association very soon appointed a paid district visitor, employing a second in 1893, and between 1899 and 1903 supervising a third visitor paid by the city council to visit both Jewish and Irish immigrants' homes. By the early 1900s, the visitors were sending daily reports to the city's Medical Officer of Health. Work was at first focused at the domestic level; needy cases were to receive money and material help. The latter included free bars of carbolic soap, and some at reduced prices; tickets entitling them to meat and milk; and help from Jewish medical charities. Advice and assistance in infant care were offered. Over time, other functions developed: the Association supported social and educational gatherings after school hours for women and girls, introducing special Sabbath services in 1893; and it commissioned sewing work and started a children's holiday scheme. It also maintained a fund for rescue work, and established links with the Church of England temperance mission at the police courts, where Sarah Gamble would have been one of their Christian colleagues.[23]

Rescue concerns, the Police Court Mission, and the links which continued to be maintained with the Ladies' Branch of the MSSA, kept like-minded Jewish and Christian women in touch with each other and part of the same civic community. Eleanor Vaudrey, herself a subscriber to the MSSA Ladies' Branch, sealed this connection in April 1899 when she and the Lord Mayor presided over the Annual General Meeting of the JLVA, held at the Town Hall.[24] It is, therefore, unsurprising to find JLVA members featuring prominently among the Jewish signatories to the letter to Mme Dreyfus which had been organised largely by their colleagues from the Ladies' Branch. Committee members and many subscribers can be identified, as well as many other unmistakeably Jewish surnames, on the 36 pages of this document which have been preserved. Addresses as well as signatures were given, and it is possible to see that Jewish and non-Jewish women across the residential spectrum—in the city centre, Red Bank and Cheetham, Bury New Road, Higher Broughton, Moss Side, Fallowfield and Rusholme, to name only a few districts—were sharing, and would have known themselves to be sharing, in an act of collective compassion and a declaration of faith in the ultimate triumph of justice (Fig. 4.2).

The story of the Manchester letter has a mysterious twist in its tail. Unlike the letters and signatures sent in response to the *Daily Chronicle* appeal, it was, in fact, never despatched to France. Shortly before Christmas

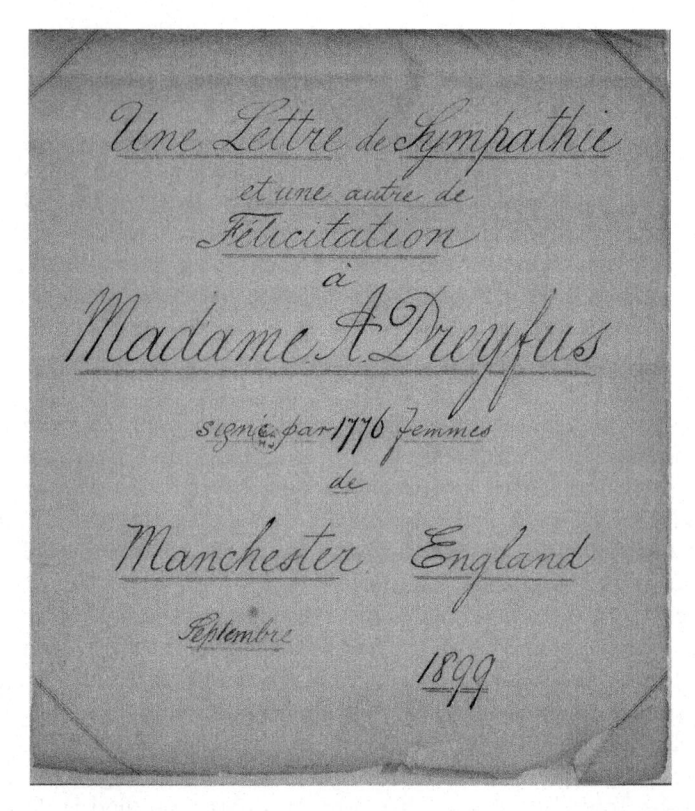

Fig. 4.2 'A letter of sympathy and another of congratulation to Madame A. Dreyfus signed by 1776 women of Manchester, England, September 1899' (Courtesy of Musée d'art et d'histoire du Judaisme, Paris)

1934 Oliver Harvey, an official at the British embassy in Paris, wrote to the now Lieutenant-Colonel Alfred Dreyfus, Knight of the Legion d'Honneur, enclosing the Manchester document. It had been sent to the embassy by a Mrs Small, of Church Cottages, Ashendon, near Aylesbury in Buckinghamshire. How she obtained it, and why it had remained in Britain, is unknown. The failure to send the document in 1899 was certainly not due to the then Captain Dreyfus's decision to accept the French President's offer of a pardon on 19 September. On the contrary, on 21 September a letter of congratulation had been appended to the original letter of sympathy, expressing 'the supreme joy' of the writers on learning that 'your beloved husband has been given back to you and your family', and their hope that he would be restored to health and his innocence, 'in which we all believe', finally established.

What can have happened? Such manifestly well-organised women could not simply have forgotten to put their precious document in the post. While it is true that a political crisis was looming in September 1899 which was to eclipse the Dreyfus Affair in the public imagination, there is no evidence that the signatories were particularly exercised by the impending war between Britain and the Boer settlers in South Africa. However, Manchester Liberals and socialists, supported by the *Manchester Guardian*, formed a powerful centre of opposition to the war. Political partisanship on either side might have proved a distraction. More unhappily, the anti-war movement lent itself to expressions of antisemitism, when it denounced Jewish businessmen and mine-owners in South Africa as warmongers, rather than focussing on their gentile colleagues, or adventurers and politicians such as Cecil Rhodes, Leander Starr Jameson and Joseph Chamberlain. Keir Hardie, who addressed his sympathy to Lucie Dreyfus in September but fully endorsed the attribution of collective guilt to the Jews of South Africa (and had no quarrel with his party's statement, in the *Independent Labour Party News* of October 1899, that the Jew was 'the very incarnation of the money idea'), was not an isolated case.[25] He may have been unaware of his German comrades' maxim that antisemitism was 'the socialism of fools'. While the initiators of the Manchester letter do not appear to have been socialists of any description, it is impossible to rule out similarly ambivalent and paradoxical sentiments among the signatories.

That speculation aside, what can be definitely learned from these 1176 Manchester names and addresses? Exploring the origins and composition of the Manchester letter, however limited the biographical information available to us, certainly demonstrates that Christian and Jewish women, or at least 'ladies', knew each other as colleagues and were unembarrassed at sharing information about the social problems of their respective communities. Their experience of charitable collaboration was solid enough to provide a platform for new and spontaneous forms of social action. It enabled them to progress from the local to the national, and even to international levels of intervention. As elsewhere in Britain, relationships built up in the conventional female sphere of philanthropy could begin to take a more political turn. Sympathising with Lucie Dreyfus was not, of course, the most controversial stand one could take in Britain in 1899. As the *Manchester Evening News* had put it, in a rather double-edged comment, 'If they never find another topic upon which they may agree, Jews and Gentiles throughout the length and breadth of England are unanimous in their opinion about the Dreyfus affair'.[26] A different matter, and a much greater challenge, was involved in demanding the parliamentary suffrage, in campaigns which intensified with the new century.

Some connections can be traced between the Manchester letter and the links later forged between Jewish and Christian women in the campaign for equality and for the suffrage which is discussed in chapter 5.[27] Estelle (Stella) Isaacs, whose mother was Annie Isaacs, a founder member of the JLVA and signatory of the address, became an active supporter of the Women's Social and Political Union, launched by the Manchester Pankhurst family in 1903.[28] In 1907, the children of Abigail and Edward Behrens actively encouraged and assisted the purchase of their family home, 'The Oaks', Fallowfield, by the university when it wished to extend residential accommodation for women students. Edward Behrens Wing was later said to be haunted by 'a kindly ghost, Abigail, the wife of Edward Behrens'.[29] Other Jewish Mancunian girls of the younger generation, such as Rebecca and Elaine Marks, may have been more influenced by their suffragist teachers than by the charitable interventions of their mothers.[30] The themes which are revealed in the Dreyfus episode—the evolution of philanthropic into political action; the cooperation of women of different creeds and formations, irrespective of ambivalent social sentiments, in pursuit of a common goal—emerge yet more strongly from the suffrage narrative, to be sustained not for the duration of a brief cause célèbre, but for more than a decade's worth of struggle.

Notes

1. Within a very large literature, see: Eric Cahm, *The Dreyfus Affair in French Society and Politics* (London, Longman, 1996); Pierre Birnbaum, *The Anti-Semitic Moment: a Tour of France in 1898* (New York, Hill and Wang, 1998); Martyn Cornick, 'The Dreyfus Affair—Another Year, Another Centenary. British Opinion and the Rennes Verdict, September 1899', *Modern and Contemporary France* 7.4 (1999); Ruth Harris, 'Letters to Lucie: Spirituality, Friendship and Politics During the Dreyfus Affair' in Ruth Harris and Lyndal Roper, eds, *The Art of Survival: Gender and History in Europe, 1450–2000* (Oxford, Oxford University Press, 2006).
2. *Daily Chronicle*, 11 September 1899, p. 4.

3. Ibid., 12 September 1899, p. 4; 16 September 1899, p. 5; 21 September 1899, p. 4.
4. These records have been consulted online, at the website of the Musee d'art et d'histoire du Judaisme, Paris: http://dreyfus.mahj.org/consultation/index.php; henceforth MAHJ.
5. MAHJ. All quotations from letters are from this source, unless otherwise stated.
6. *Daily Chronicle*, 12 September 1899, p. 4.
7. Ibid., 18 September 1899, p. 6.
8. *Woman's Life*, 28 October 1899, p. 281.
9. *The Woman's Signal*, 24 November 1898, p. 326.
10. Mary H. Steer, *Opals from Sand: a Story of Early Days at the Bridge of Hope* (London, Morgan & Scott, 1912), p. 160.
11. Bibliothèque Publique et Universitaire de Neuchâtel, Fonds Felix Bovet Ms 2098/86 1116, 1 September 1899, Josephine Butler to Mme Bovet: 'If dear Alfred Dreyfus were to read attentively now the Gospel history, surely he would find in it everything to answer to the mystery of his own martyrdom, & would be attracted to the Divine Victim of human injustice, the Incarnation of Divine Justice & Love'.
12. See Nadia Valman, *The Jewess in Nineteenth-century British Literary Culture* (Cambridge, Cambridge University Press, 2007).
13. *Manchester Guardian*, 14 September 1899, p. 6; *Manchester Evening Mail*, 14 September 1899, pp. 4, 5.
14. Obituary, *Manchester City News*, 27 November 1926; Annual Report of the MSSA for 1886.
15. In addition to the names in the text above: Manchester and Salford Ladies' Public Health Society; Manchester and Salford Ladies' Sanitary Association; Ladies Health Society; Ladies' Sanitary Reform Association.
16. Lawrence Goldman, *Science, Reform and Politics in Victorian Britain: the Social Science Association, 1857–1886* (New York, Cambridge University Press, 2002).
17. Anne Summers, 'A Home from Home—Women's Philanthropic Work in the Nineteenth Century' in Sandra Burman, ed., *Fit Work for Women* (London, Croom Helm, 1979); F.K. Prochaska, *Women and Philanthropy* (Oxford, Clarendon Press, 1980), Ch. 4.
18. Information from website of John Rylands Library, Manchester University.
19. *Jewish Chronicle* (henceforth *JC*), 6 June 1902, p. 19. Anna Simmons née Herzfeld died in January 1912.
20. *JC*, 23 May 1902, p. 21; *Report of the Conference of Jewish Women ... 13th and 14th May, 1902* (*JC* 1902), pp. 27–8.
21. Information from the Annual Report for 1886 of the MSSA, *Slater's Directory of Manchester*, (Manchester, Slater, 1888) and census information for 1881, 1891 and 1901.

22. Minutes of the Manchester Jewish Ladies' Visiting Association, Manchester Central Library mf2687; Annual Reports of the JLVA, Manchester County Record Office M 182/5/2.
23. Bill Williams, *Jewish Manchester: an Illustrated History* (Derby, Breedon Books, 2008), pp. 68–72; Rainer Liedtke, *Jewish Welfare in Hamburg and Manchester c. 1850–1914* (Oxford, Clarendon Press, 1998), pp. 174–8.
24. *JC*, 28 April 1899, p. 25.
25. Claire Hirshfield, 'The Anglo-Boer War and the Issue of Jewish Culpability', *Contemporary Review* 15.4 (1980), p. 623.
26. *Manchester Evening News*, 15 September 1899, p. 2.
27. The impact on French feminism of Frenchwomen's participation in the pro-Dreyfus campaign is discussed by Françoise Blum, 'Itinéraires féministes a la lumière de l'Affaire', in Michel Leymarie, ed., *La Posterité de L'affaire Dreyfus* (Villeneuve-d'Ascq, presses universitaires du septentrion, 1998), pp. 94–9.
28. Personal information from Stella Isaacs's grandson David Jacobs.
29. Mabel Tylecote, *The Education of Women at Manchester University 1883 to 1933* (Manchester, Manchester University Press, 1941), pp. 89–90.
30. See Chap. 9.

CHAPTER 5

'Votes for Women!'

If it is understandable that Jewish men in England clutched jealously to themselves their roles as guardians of Judaism, as communal leaders, as representatives of the community to the outside world, and as paterfamilias in their own homes, it is equally understandable that this was a source of discontent to many of their wives, sisters and daughters. A spirit of mutiny was brewing. Ten years after she had helped to set up the Union of Jewish Women—whose rationale had, in part, been to recruit a younger generation into the ranks of Jewish welfare organisations—Gertrude Spielmann expostulated: 'Who has ever heard of a Jewess taking the chair at a mixed Committee, or being offered any communal honour? ... the intelligent, strenuous girl of to-day, who prepared herself by studying Sociology and training at Women's Settlements or C.O.S. Offices will not work on our communal charities'.[1] The Jewish League for Woman Suffrage (henceforth JLWS), of which Spielmann was a founder member, was about to see the light of day. The 'status incongruity' which saw the projects of a cohort of younger women such as Nettie Adler and Lily Montagu receive public recognition among Christian women in the National Union of Women Workers, but only the most grudging acceptance by the Visiting Committee of the Jewish Board of Guardians, could not be contained indefinitely. Indeed, by the time the JLWS came into existence in 1912 Jewish women and, indeed, some Jewish men were already prominent members of a suffrage campaign which over the previous four decades had become a large and many-stranded movement.[2]

To mention a few activists, from the south of England alone: Netta Franklin and many female members of the clan into which she had married were enthusiastic members of the constitutional (non-militant) National Union of Women's Suffrage Societies (NUWSS), of which Helena Auerbach was Treasurer. Israel Zangwill was much in demand as a speaker for the (militant) Women's Social and Political Union (WSPU), until the Pankhurst family's autocratic style of leadership drove him with many others into forming the United Suffragists.[3] Netta's nephew Hugh Franklin remained faithful to the WSPU's brand of direct action, enduring imprisonment and forcible feeding on several occasions.[4] Rose and Nellie Cohen and Millie Gliksten were pillars of Sylvia Pankhurst's equally militant East London Federation of Suffragettes.[5] At the other end of the political spectrum, Louise Samuel was Honorary Secretary of the Conservative and Unionist Woman Franchise Association.[6]

By the turn of the twentieth century, there were just two institutions formally receptive to at least some form of gender equality within Anglo-Jewry. One comprised the many Jewish Literary Societies which flourished in different parts of London and the provincial cities. Like a latter-day version of the National Association for the Promotion of Social Science, these societies provided a forum for Jewish women and men to meet on virtually equal terms. Women sat on the executive committees of their local branches, as well as acting as honorary and administrative secretaries. Several moved seamlessly from such participation into contributing, as writers and translators, to the *Jewish Review*, which the West End Jewish Literary Society founded at the end of 1909. Given its later history, it is interesting to read of the rearguard action mounted at the 'preliminary meeting of gentlemen' which founded that Society in January 1903. One single motion was discussed—and rejected: 'That ladies shall not be eligible for membership of the Society'.[7]

The West End Society's meeting of November 1903 heard a paper on 'Women and their Emancipation' presented by Frederic Franklin; subsequently Nettie Adler, Gertrude Spielmann, Hannah Hyam and Lily Montagu spoke on their different experiences of social work. In April 1912 Gertrude Spielmann spoke on 'Woman's Place in the Synagogue', and the following November, the month in which the JLWS was founded, she spoke on 'Jews and the Woman's Movement'.[8] Early in 1913 the *Jewish Review* gave these demands, if not the League itself, a wider airing by publishing both a translation of Bertha Pappenheim's paper 'The Jewish Woman in Religious Life', given at the Women's Congress in Munich in 1912, and Spielmann's two addresses, amalgamated into a single article.[9] The editor of the *Jewish Review* was the Reverend Joseph Hochmann, minister of the New West End Synagogue.[10] He was a founding activist in the JLWS, as were all the women named above; and the names of several lesser-known female participants mentioned in the Society's minutes are to be found among the authors of letters to the *Jewish Chronicle* in support of women's suffrage.

A notable group active in the Union of Jewish Literary Societies was a Jewish Study Society, with an all-female committee, which was established by 1902 in order to produce simpler study materials for religious education.[11] This committee was connected with a second contemporary organisation supporting gender equality, the Jewish Religious Union (henceforth JRU). The JRU had originated in an initiative of Lily Montagu, who in 1899 contributed a seminal article to the *Jewish Quarterly Review* on 'The Spiritual Possibilities of Judaism To-day'. She went on to persuade the scholar Claude Montefiore to head a group of men and women concerned with the revitalisation of Anglo-Judaism. Initially a broadly based vehicle for reform, the Union experienced its first split on the rock of 'mixed seating'. It was the custom for men and women to sit separately in synagogues, often with a cloth or lattice screen veiling the women from men's eyes. When in 1909 the JRU constituted itself as the first Liberal Jewish congregation in Britain, it made a point of allowing male and female worshippers to sit together.[12]

The female membership of the Liberal Jewish movement[13] appears to have included some of Montagu's associates in the girls' club movement,[14] and her sisters Marian Montagu and Netta Franklin were also staunch champions of religious reform. These intelligent and outward-looking daughters of Baron Montagu of Swaythling—truly, a patriarch's patriarch—each found their own way to depart from the unbending Orthodoxy of their upbringing. They were also to become suffragists, and the link between their commitment to religious reform and to gender equality was anything but coincidental. The first official meeting of the JRU, attended by over seventy men and women, was held at Netta Franklin's home.[15] Many subsequent meetings of the JLWS were held there also.

* * * * * *

Why should Jewish suffragists have felt the need for an additional organisation, given their integration into existing campaigns? The religious leagues for woman suffrage were late but distinct additions to the campaign scene. The Church League (Anglican), the Free Church League, the Catholic Women's Suffrage Society, the Friends' (Quaker) League for Women's Suffrage and the Scottish Churches' League were established between 1909 and 1912; and in November 1912 the Jewish League brought up the rear.[16] It has been suggested that religious women already involved in the suffrage movement wanted to bring their coreligionists on board.[17] This would fit the facts where, for example, an NUWSS activist such as Netta Franklin was concerned, but is not the whole story. Militant suffragettes had forced the question of votes for women into the public domain in such a way that—in contrast to the decades of quiet constitutional campaigning—it had become almost impossible to ignore.

To many religious communities, it seemed increasingly necessary to assert—or re-assert—that politics was too important to be delegated to the secular realm. Church and synagogue were alike intent on recovering lost ground. The new leagues believed that religion could provide the answer to the 'woman question', and much else besides; each denomination wanted to demonstrate pride in its traditions, and to offer its own contribution to social debates. At the Jewish League's first public meeting, Helena Auerbach said that 'Jews should not fail to take their full share in the social progress of the country', and Netta Franklin declared that 'Judaism had taught the world to do justice ... they had no right to be here at all, unless they tried to make the world better'.[18] Moreover, religious suffragists had a further agenda: they were now prepared to make demands in a public arena for greater gender equality within their respective congregations, as well as at the ballot box.

Other founders of the JLWS gave further reasons for their initiative. On 6 November 1912, Ruth Franklin, an active member of the North Kensington Suffrage Society, wrote to Philippa Strachey, Secretary of the London Society for Women's Suffrage (a branch of the constitutional NUWSS) 'about a new Suffrage Society that I have been trying to form ... I think we shall touch a new set of people, who have not been worked as yet, more especially in the East End, & [*sic*] in the provinces'.[19] Hannah Hyam, interviewed in spring 1913, stated: 'what had made her a suffragist was her experience among the working women of the East End. ... Recent legislation directed to remedy women's wrongs had been the result of the arousing voice of women demanding the franchise'. An orthodox Jewess, she had come via years of voluntary work to the conviction that conditions would not improve until women became citizens on equal terms with men.[20] Louise Samuel, of the Conservative and Unionist Women's Suffrage Society, followed a similar trajectory, stating that it was while she was engaged in 'philanthropic work' that she had become a suffragist.[21]

While recent writing on the charitable activity of middle- and upper-class Jewish women has characterised it as a form of 'social control',[22] this is to ignore the increasingly political aspect of their initiatives. Lily Montagu, for example, was tireless in her efforts to improve working conditions by ensuring that girls in Jewish clubs knew and could insist on their legal rights as employees; Nettie Adler was dedicated to checking the abuse of child labour, and opening up training opportunities for the young.[23] They were almost certainly among those targeted in a complaint to the *Jewish Chronicle* that 'the young girls of the Jewish girls' clubs are being influenced by some members of the Committee, helpers and others interested in the suffragette question to the detriment of the welfare and good manners of the members'. As early as 1911, indeed, the members of the West Central Girls' Club had passed a resolution in favour of woman suffrage.[24]

From the start the JLWS provoked contradictory responses within the communal press. The *Jewish Chronicle* stated, as a matter for commendation, that Jews were following the example of other religious denominations. However, this was suspect in some quarters, where following suit indicated assimilation. Opposition was aroused by a statement in the League's first manifesto that it wished to promote a 'more active participation of the synagogue in the social movements of the day'. A correspondent sneered that the suffragists were intent on converting the synagogue into 'a Whitefield's Tabernacle in order to disseminate Feminist rhodomontade more easily', and his antipathy was not entirely uninformed.[25] When Hannah Hyam said of legislation to improve working women's lives, 'She regarded this as Holy work and therefore Jewish work',[26] she spoke in the spirit of the British nonconformist conscience. What would have been a commonplace for many Christians of her generation was, for many Jewish men, deemed too secular, too un-Jewish, and certainly too controversial for a minority community that did not wish to try the tolerance of its hosts or plunge ever further into internecine squabbles.

The statement on 'active participation' was, in fact, very soon withdrawn from League communiqués, but the commitment to combat 'social evils' was not deleted from the League manifesto. JLWS members pointed out that, as Jewish (male) leaders took every opportunity to voice their horror of the 'White Slave Trade' and to support measures to suppress it, communal political engagement was nothing new.[27] However, there was a major difference, in that no one in their senses was likely to make a public stand in favour of the White Slave Trade, and that by denouncing it neither the JLWS, the Chief Rabbi, nor the Jewish male elite were either taking a revolutionary stand, challenging the status quo or even 'making trouble'. Suffragism, however, did all three. And to a large extent, opponents tended to tar all suffragists with the militant brush: in March 1912, *Jewish Chronicle* readers were horrified by reports of a shopkeeper complaining that his window had been broken by 'a dirty little Jewess!'[28] The founding core of the JLWS may well have been dismayed to find their inaugural public meeting reported in the communal press just above the news that Hugh Franklin had been convicted of setting fire to a first-class railway carriage.[29] Nor was the League's goal of advertising Jewish religious virtues to the gentiles seen to be enhanced when, a year later, three young Jewish militants, sisters Phoebe and Esther Rickards and a Miss Russell, disturbed the Day of Atonement services at the New West End Synagogue with cries of "Votes for Women!"[30] Such actions alienated those British Jews who hoped to counter antisemitism by demonstrating that they were law-abiding citizens of their adopted country.

* * * *

For many historians, the topic of suffrage in the East End is completely bound up with the history of the East London Federation of Suffragettes, formed by the militant Sylvia Pankhurst in 1912 as a breakaway movement from that of her equally militant mother Emmeline and sister Christabel.[31] In fact many other suffrage organisations became active in the area: the Church League for Women's Suffrage, for example, had branches in Bow, Hackney, Poplar, Lewisham and East Ham.[32] However, the non-sectarian and non-militant London Society for Women's Suffrage developed possibly the most comprehensive coverage of the area. From the very thorough district surveys and branch reports which the London Society compiled, it is possible to see, or in some cases to speculate, how its policy towards the East End evolved. At the end of 1909, its agent Laura Donnell surveyed the area as a campaigning prospect on the eve of the 1910 general election. Her conclusions, often echoing those of settlement workers and Liberal Party agents, were largely pessimistic. Of Whitechapel she reported: 'I do not think Whitechapel is a constituency to trouble much about. The people take no interest in the Women's Suffrage & [*sic*] a large number of them are foreign Jews, who do not always vote'. Of neighbouring St George's in the East, again: 'I do not think that it is worth spending much time in this constituency. The Woman's Question is not one that would interest the inhabitants—who are mostly non-English speaking Jews'.[33]

Three years later, however, constitutional suffragism was a highly visible presence in these same districts. To some extent this may have been a competitive reaction to the activity of Sylvia Pankhurst and the militant East London Federation. A more immediate prompt was the need to organise for the Whitechapel bye-election of April 1913. A third factor may have been the formation of the East End branch of the JLWS. Here, Laura Donnell's initial assessment of feminist inertia in these constituencies was largely echoed by the Jewish press. The Jewish League's ambition to take its message to the East End was mocked in the *Jewish Chronicle*, and the female vote derided as 'caviare'—a luxury which the poverty-stricken immigrant community did not need and would not want. In the spring of 1913 it was reported with undisguised satisfaction that during the League's first public meeting at the Old Boys' Club, Mile End Road, all the speakers, male and female, were 'frequently interrupted by a section of the audience, several of whom adopted a very hostile attitude' and that the meeting terminated somewhat hurriedly.[34] However, the sceptics on all sides were, it appears, underestimating the East End's appetite for political argument. The London Society was soon able to set up branches in Whitechapel, Bow, Bethnal Green, Mile End and Limehouse; and Jewish and Christian suffragists were to be found taking up overlapping memberships in both the religious and secular wings of the constitutional campaign.

Press reports show that the East End branch of the JLWS confounded communal expectations, distributing literature in both English and Yiddish, organising lectures and debates with other Jewish organisations and, less solemnly, celebrating the secular new year 1914 with a dance, organised together with a local Literary and Social Union.[35] Its most prominent activists were Dora Lazarnick, together with her mother and sister, and the (male) chairman, one J.H. Schneiderman. (Bizarrely, among those attending meetings in October and November 1913 was none other than 'Tribich Lincoln').[36] It has been argued that Jewish women were not involved with the East London Federation because the Pankhursts were antisemitic, but there is almost no evidence supporting this.[37] On the contrary, Sylvia Pankhurst's operations in the East End relied heavily on a number of Jewish associates.[38] The surviving records of her East London Federation do not mention the JLWS as such; however, it is intriguing to find Dora Lazarnick and her sister among the signatories to a testimonial and gift presented to

Sylvia in May 1914.[39] It is undeniable that some members of the militant tendency expressed antisemitic sentiments, as will be illustrated later in this chapter; however, the overwhelming rationale for Jewish non-cooperation with the East London Federation of Suffragettes lay in the fact of its tactics; Jewish suffragists favoured the non-militant tendency.

By spring 1914 Jewish and Christian constitutional suffragists in the East End were, under the aegis of the London Society for Women's Suffrage, collaborating on a regular basis.[40] The committee membership of the London Society's branch in Whitechapel and St George's-in-the-East was impressively eclectic. Those settlement workers who were reported by Laura Donnell to be sympathetic but pessimistic about campaign prospects, and too busy to help, were now caught within the London Society's widely cast net. They included Mrs Dorothy Wise, of Poplar, of the Church League for Woman Suffrage; Helen Steer, of an older generation than most of her colleagues, whose memoirs, as we have seen, reveal her ambivalent, not to say negative attitudes to both new and more established members of Anglo-Jewry; Mary Hughes, the Vice President of the branch, a Protestant settlement worker increasingly drawn to the Quakers, and daughter of the author of *Tom Brown's Schooldays*; and a younger settlement colleague, Rosa Waugh, also drawn to Quakerism.[41] She was the youngest child of the Reverend Benjamin Waugh, founder of the National Society for the Prevention of Cruelty to Children. A very different kind of Christian from Helen Steer, Rosa Waugh's father shunned sectarianism and cooperated with clergy of all denominations, including the Chief Rabbi.[42]

The Jewish Committee members included Alice Franklin, Hannah Hyam, Miriam Moses and Ida Samuel. It is noteworthy that these were all women who maintained their Jewish identity throughout their lives: Alice Franklin's postwar career was in the Townswomen's Guild, and Miriam Moses and Ida Samuel were Liberal local councillors even before 1914. It is a remarkable comment on the political culture of the East End that in 1931 Miriam Moses became not only the first woman mayor of Stepney, but the first Jewish woman mayor anywhere in Britain. This she achieved while retaining (like Nettie Adler, initially a Municipal Reform and later a Progressive councillor) her lifelong Jewish praxis of Shabbat and kashrut.[43] It could be said that the composition and activities of the Committee were paradigms of relations between Jews and Christians in this period. They accommodated a range of different attitudes to the immigrant minority, from the implicit hostility of Helen Steer to the positive approach of the

London Society head office, which considered ordering no fewer than 10,000 Yiddish pamphlets to be printed in the first quarter of 1913.[44] Franklin, Hyam, Moses and Samuel started as they meant to go on: understanding that they might not, initially, be liked or welcomed, but valuing the opportunity to achieve social goals through which they themselves might, in turn, come to be valued.

* * * *

By far the most overt display of Jewish-Christian cooperation emerged, however, not from these different East End committees, but from the parent branches of the religious leagues. It appears that the Jewish League was responsible for the first interfaith initiative: having in July 1913 sent a representative to a protest at Caxton Hall against the notorious 'Cat & Mouse (Temporary Discharge for Ill-Health of Prisoners) Act', the JLWS organised in August a combined protest of all the religious suffrage societies against the forcible feeding of suffragette prisoners.[45] The first interfaith suffrage meeting, where the Bishop of Lincoln, Edward Lee Hicks, introduced the 'Jewish Rabbi', (the Reverend G.G. Green) the only non-Christian speaker, as 'part of the rock from whom we are all hewn', took place on 8 October at Hampstead Town Hall.[46] By this time all the religious societies had signed up to 'A Manifesto and Call to Prayer'. A 'National Week of Prayer' was to be held in November, following another joint meeting at Caxton Hall.[47] The Church League reported the 'fine speech' of Reverend Hochmann on this occasion at some length, and the *Free Church Suffrage Times* described him as 'an example of the Hebrew genius for "the immensities"'. Hochmann had spoken of 'an ethical standard of social service as opposed to social plunder; of the rule of love as opposed to the rule of force'. All participants supported the Church League's proposal to set up a standing joint committee of representatives of religious suffrage societies.[48]

The warmth of the pre-1914 response of the Christian, and particularly the nonconformist, Leagues to their Jewish comrades is very striking. An article on the JLWS in the *Free Church Suffrage Times* asserted: 'the Puritans founded their theocracy on the Old Testament, so affinities exist between Jews and Nonconformists which do not exist between other religious bodies. ... One leaflet of the Jewish League might have been ours ...because "Justice and liberty have been our ideals"; and rejecting the doctrine of physical force is like our "Nonconformist conscience", which asserts that righteousness exalteth a nation'. The Jewish intention '"to serve our country with our spiritual heritage, as well as with our material and intellectual endowments" ... reminds us of our genius for civic righteousness'.[49] The reforming tendencies in Judaism, which could in some sense be understood as a drive to turn Jews into 'honorary Protestants', would seem to have achieved their goal with this accolade. Far from 'making trouble' by entering the political arena, Jews had been recognised as kindred spirits. They had assumed the mantle of the nonconformist conscience, and with it, attained a level of naturalisation that the mere removal of legal disabilities was powerless to bestow.

This spirit of goodwill and collaboration was sustained until the outbreak of war. Four members of each League took part in a 'Poster Parade' at the opening of Parliament in spring 1914, an event which was to be repeated monthly.[50] Joint meetings took place in Cricklewood in March 1914, and in Swiss Cottage the following May.[51] Most interfaith activities took place in London; it is interesting to note that at a Brighton meeting in December 1913, the mother of Marie Stopes represented the Scottish Churches.[52] Thursday 18 June 1914 marked, unbeknownst to participants, the final event in the interfaith campaign. A joint procession led to Hyde Park, where every denomination had its own platform, but subscribed to a joint resolution to the Government.[53] The Leagues met again only in March 1918, when the NUWSS organised a central London celebration of the grant of the female franchise.[54]

Brief as it was, this episode presents a stark contrast to another pre-1914 interfaith grouping, the all-male scholarly club founded in 1904 as the London Society for the Study of Religion. Meeting in members' homes, it was described by a Christian member as 'a private, though not a secret society', to which admission 'was far from easy'. Its prime movers were Claude Montefiore, the Unitarian Joseph Wicksteed, and the Roman Catholic Baron Friedrich von Hügel, said to have '"pledged each other absolutely"' on the strict privacy of the whole affair, promising non-communication to outsiders'.[55] When an attempt was made to renew interfaith activity on a national basis in the 1920s, it was certainly not in this spirit, and the impulse came to a considerable extent from veterans of the prewar women's movement.[56]

Christian and Jewish suffragists necessarily followed separate paths in pursuit of the gender issues which were specific to their own denominations. It is interesting to compare and contrast their relative successes in this area. The JLWS, whose manifesto mildly stated the objective 'to further the improvement of the status of women in the Community and the State', had called for a synagogue's female seatholders (i.e., subscribing members in their own right) to have the vote on matters of synagogue management. By April 1913 it was, indeed, hoping to alter the Act of Parliament governing the United Synagogue 'by the omission of the word "male" from Clause 42, the effect being that women would then be enabled to vote at Synagogue elections'.[57] The Anglican League, similarly, wanted women to be able to vote and serve on equal terms on parish councils and on parochial church councils. This Anglican demand was granted in 1914, with the barrier to membership of higher councils abolished in 1919.[58] By July 1914, the Council of the United Synagogue, representing the majority of British congregations, had got as far as debating—and rejecting— the demand for the female seatholder vote.[59] A few individual synagogues (West London, New West End, Brondesbury) had implemented this reform earlier, and others (Great Synagogue, Borough Synagogue, North London, Hammersmith and Hampstead) had done so in 1914 in response to the League's initiative.[60] However, although the ultra-respectable, non-political Union of Jewish Women formed a sub-committee to campaign for this reform in September 1919,[61] the United Synagogue as a national body did not grant equal seatholder voting until 1954.

In 2012 women became eligible to become chairmen of individual synagogues and trustee officers of the United Synagogue centrally. They were first elected to the executive of the United Synagogue in July 2014.[62] The Federation of Synagogues was reported in May 2010 to be on the verge of giving women voting rights,[63] but at the time of publication has not done so at a national level. It is worth pointing out that these feminist issues relate to governance and administration only; they do not encroach on priesthood, ministry or participation in synagogue ritual. Two different campaigns with contrasting outcomes may be cited: soon after 1918 and the granting of the vote, former Christian suffragists began to raise the issue of women priests for the Church of England, while the Council for the Amelioration of the Legal Position of the Jewess was formed, principally to campaign for a reform of the Jewish law on divorce.[64] The Church of England now ordains women to the priesthood, and in July 2014 its lay and clerical assemblies voted to consecrate women as bishops; orthodox Jewish divorce law remains, notoriously, unchanged.[65] Orthodox synagogues retain, it hardly needs saying, an outright ban on female ministry. Where the Anglo-Jewish community is concerned, the historical case for 'the feminisation of religion' remains, it is fair to say, less than overwhelming.[66]

Was there ever a possibility that it could have been otherwise? The many Jewish men who did support female suffrage—the Reverends Hochmann, Joseph, Green and Mattuck, the secular Israel Zangwill, Hugh Franklin, and Sir Alfred Mond—were either on Judaism's Reform or Liberal wing, or largely detached from its institutional life. They were not part of the religious mainstream of Anglo-Jewry. As we have seen, the JLWS as a whole, despite its prominent Reform and Liberal membership, wished not to split off from the mainstream, but to convert it to the League's viewpoint. They could be forgiven for thinking that the time was ripe. They had succeeded against expectations in the East End; and, far from bringing the predicted storm of shame and discredit onto their coreligionists in the eyes of the host community, they could claim to have actually enhanced gentile esteem for Judaism's spiritual teachings.

Had they, perhaps, done too well? Might they not have achieved a level of naturalisation equivalent to assimilation, to a dissolution of Jewish religious identity? It is hard not to see the campaign for gender equality as part of the westernising trend evident in the movements for Reform and Liberal Judaism, a trend open to the criticism that it apologised for, and was embarrassed by, signs of Jewish distinctiveness. Many Anglo-Jewish women (and men), to the right and to the left of these movements, subscribed to the gentile denigration of traditional Judaism as a species of 'orientalism'.[67] In 1901, for example, the *Jewish Chronicle* had greeted the news of the proposed Union of Jewish Women as demonstrating 'that our conception of woman's relationship to man is rapidly being de-orientalised'. Gertrude Spielmann described the occupants of the synagogue ladies' gallery as 'segregated as in the Harem of the East'.[68]

Jewish feminists were also conscious that some gentile counterparts went so far as to blame Judaism for the oppression of women in Christian Europe. Such sentiments had been publicly expressed by the American feminists Susan B. Anthony and Anna Howard Shaw in the 1880s. Among British feminists, Elizabeth Wolstoneholme Elmy denounced; 'the Mosaic legend of the "Fall"—a myth in which is concentrated or fossilised the ancient Oriental depreciation of woman and the primitive ignorance of the sacredness of maternity ...' and Florence Farr declared that 'the degradation of women in the past originated in the region of the country round Mount Ararat. The lowering of their status occurred when the white races adopted the Assyrian Semitic scriptures'. Farr's was an explicitly racist agenda; in 1910, in *Modern Woman: Her Intentions*, she wrote 'I am told that in nearly every city of ill-fame in the world the profits arising from the procuring of girls are collected by the Chosen Nation ...it remains for white women to fight now'.[69]

This posed a major dilemma for Jewish suffragists who wanted to present themselves as religiously identified, and indeed to claim that they were egalitarian because, and not in spite of, their religion. How could they distance themselves from the 'orientalist' slur, and dissent from existing Jewish practice, without seeming to reject or denigrate their own faith? They attempted to escape the dilemma by asserting the existence of an earlier, more egalitarian Judaism. One 'Justitia' claimed in the *Jewish Chronicle* that women's subordinate position was 'one of the oriental anachronisms of our religion', and not substantiated by the Torah. The WSPU member K.S. Birnstingl argued in similar vein that 'the nation which thousands of years ago produced Miriam as a leader of her people ... and Deborah as judge, prophetess and military commander, should surely in this twentieth century, C.E., stand forth as advocate for the equality of the sexes'.[70] Miriam and Deborah featured in more than one of the speeches at the first public meeting of the JLWS, and at subsequent gatherings.[71] The Liberal Synagogue's Rabbi Mattuck opined that 'In spite of the Oriental origin of Judaism there had been a development in respect to woman away from Eastern ideals ... consequent to the essential teachings of Judaism'.[72]

The distinction between an 'essential' Judaism which could be traced back to biblical antiquity but which was somehow *not* 'oriental', and a rabbinic Judaism which had been elaborated in Europe in more recent times but which *was*, was an affront to both logic and common sense. But it was perhaps the only means by which its proponents could appear to represent their religion while simultaneously intending to change it. While the suffrage campaign lasted, they could act out a Judaism which they desired, but which did not yet exist. The strategy did not survive the granting of suffrage and the coming of peace.

It is clear from the record that many suffragists wished to retain their Jewish identity, and that both religious and secular suffrage organisations made it possible for them to do so. There was no conversion agenda on the part of the Christian leagues. Within the secular organisations those Jewish suffragists such as Henrietta Leslie and Hugh Franklin, who felt almost completely estranged from their religious background, were under no external pressure to distance themselves from the Jewish community.[73] In at least one instance, quite the reverse: among the many invitations to speak with which Israel Zangwill was deluged was, for example, one which Emmeline Pethick Lawrence pressed on him in 1907: 'There is a very large representation of your religious community in Manchester as you know, which would be drawn to the Meeting if you were speaking, as well as the many people who know you through your literary work'.[74]

It is also undeniable that there were individual suffragists whose attitudes to Jews were, like Helen Steer's, ambivalent, negative, or at the very least compartmentalised. Pethick Lawrence, while admiring Zangwill and financially supporting one of Lily Montagu's philanthropic ventures,[75] was among those who blamed 'international financiers'—widely used code for South African Jewish businessmen—for the outbreak of the Anglo-Boer War.[76] Sylvia Pankhurst could not have managed her campaign in the East End without her Jewish helpers, but she denounced Home Secretary Herbert Samuel, two decades later, as a 'Jew-in-Office'.[77] In 1912 Flora Drummond attempted to deny her statement, reported in the *Jewish Chronicle*, that 'the Jews were dominating the country in the persons of Sir Rufus Isaacs and Mr Herbert Samuel, and the women now emphatically protested against these dictators making their laws. If they were English it would not so much matter, but they were not'—but her denial lacked conviction.[78] The religious suffrage campaign would perhaps have needed more years than the outbreak of war allowed to build really solid bridges between Christian and Jewish worshippers. But it is important to take note of these interfaith and intercommunal activities, as well as Millicent Fawcett's demonstration of affection for Helena Auerbach when Jerusalem fell to the Allies, if one is also to recall racist, xenophobic or graceless remarks from others on the suffragist spectrum.

★ ★ ★ ★

Sources on the history of the JLWS are few and far between. All publications and theses on this and related topics rely heavily on coverage in the *Jewish Chronicle* of the day. Other printed primary sources include the Christian suffrage publications, and a small number of printed JLWS leaflets, some of which survive in the British Library and The Woman's Library. In the latter repository, the archive of the London Society for Woman Suffrage holds only a few manuscript references to the League, including some in the minute book of the Whitechapel branch of the London Society. It seems strange that the many distinguished names on the masthead of the League's leaflets and numbered among its members do not appear to have referred to it in their archived correspondence: one might, for example have expected to find the League mentioned in Zangwill's correspondence with Helena Auerbach in the Central Zionist Archive, and with Nina Davis Salaman in Cambridge University Library, or in Netta Franklin's correspondence with Charlotte Mason in the latter's archive at Ambleside, but this is not the case.

It is true that the League's lifespan was short, as it maintained only a titular existence after war was declared in August 1914. Moreover, one of the League's most important activists, the Reverend Joseph Hochmann, largely disappeared off the radar of Anglo-Jewry after 1916.[79] Little trace remains of less celebrated foot soldiers, whose names may of course have changed on marriage, and whose lives may have been changed and constrained by childbearing; we may never know what League membership meant to them in postwar years. However, strangest of all is the silence on the topic in the surviving correspondence and published memoirs of Netta Franklin and Lily Montagu.[80] All these lacunae may prompt a rethinking of Linda Kuzmack's statement that for 'Anglo-Jewish women ... Suffrage became a vital symbol of their social acceptance as Englishwomen as well as of their political, religious and communal emancipation'.[81] This could have been true for the duration of the campaign; but was certainly not so subsequently. It is possible that the history of the struggle for the vote later became so overwhelmingly linked in the popular imagination with militant tactics that the Jewish community, ever desirous of being thought worthy of law-abiding British citizenship, may have wished to suppress all memory of its participation.[82] One might also surmise that the link between voluntary public service and political intervention became weaker between the two world wars. However, this hypothesis does not entirely square with what we know of Netta and Lily's interwar activities, and does not necessarily bring us to a solution of the conundrum.

Notes

1. Winifred Raphael, *Gertrude Emily Spielman [sic] 1864–1949* (Sevenoaks, Caxton and Holmesdale Press, 1950), pp. 75–6. C.O.S., the acronym of the Charity Organisation Society, was sometimes referred to by its clientele as 'Cringe or Starve'.
2. See, among many others: Jill Liddington and Jill Norris, *One Hand Tied Behind Us: the Rise of the Women's Suffrage Movement* (London, Virago, 1978); Susan Kingsley Kent, *Sex and Suffrage in Britain 1860–1914* (Princeton, Princeton University Press, 1987); Sandra Holton, *Suffrage Days: Stories from the Suffrage Movement* (1996); Elizabeth Crawford, *The Women's Suffrage Movement: a Reference Guide 1866–1928* (London, UCL Press); Ian Christopher Fletcher, Laura E. Nym Mayhall and Philippa Levine, eds, *Women's Suffrage in the British Empire: Citizenship, Nation*

and Race (London, Routledge, 2000); Sandra Holton and June Purvis, eds, *Votes for Women* (London, Routledge, 2000); Harold L. Smith, *The British Women's Suffrage Campaign 1866–1928*, 2nd edn revised (Harlow, Longman, 2010).

3. Meri-Jane Rochelson, *A Jew in the Public Arena: the Career of Israel Zangwill* (Detroit, Wayne State University Press, 2008), p. 147.
4. Archival material on Hugh Franklin's exploits, which included taking a horsewhip to Winston Churchill and setting fire to a train, is held at The Women's Library (Fonds 7HFD) and in the Museum of London, Special Collections Group C Vol. 3, pp. 92–3. See also the memoir of his sister, Helen Bentwich, *If I Forget Thee: Some Chapters in Autobiography, 1912–1920* (London, Elek, 1973).
5. Sylvia Pankhurst, *The Suffragette Movement* (London, Virago, 1984) [originally published London, Longmans, 1931], pp. 465, 498; the same, *The Home Front* (London, Hutchinson, 1932), pp. 243, 274.
6. *Jewish Chronicle* (henceforth *JC*), 31 January 1913, p. 20.
7. University of Southampton Library (henceforth USL) MS 122/1/7, West End Jewish Literary Society, Minutes of General Meetings, 11 January 1903.
8. The same, 29 November 1903, 4 February 1906, 12 December 1909, 27 February 1910, 21 April 1912, 3 November 1912.
9. Bertha Pappenheim, 'The Jewish Woman in Religious Life', trans. Margery Bentwich, *The Jewish Review* 3 (1912–1913), pp. 405–14, paper originally read at the Women's Congress, Munich 1912; Gertrude Spielmann, 'Woman's Place in the Synagogue', *The Jewish Review* 4 (1913–1914), pp. 24–35.
10. USL MS 122/1/6, West End Jewish Literary Society, Minutes of Executive Meetings, 4 October 1909; see also Central Zionist Archive (henceforth CZA) A 120/384, correspondence between Hochmann and Israel Zangwill in 1910. Hochmann, also known as Hochman and Hockman, had a picaresque career. He resigned his post in 1915 (his relations with the Chief Rabbi were uniformly bad, and he was alleged to have arrived for Sabbath services on horseback); he 'went into the trenches and after the war he was called to the Bar and became the legal adviser to the King of Siam': Elkan Levy, 'The New West End Synagogue 1879–2004', www.newwestend.org.uk/docs/EDLlecture.pdf:. In later life he renewed his membership of the New West End: Louis Jacobs, *Helping with Inquiries* (London, Vallentine Mitchell, 1989), p. 106 and p. 415, reference 44. Wikipedia, citing Kevin Allen, records that Hochmann refused to divorce his wife Vera, a semi-professional violinist said to have become Elgar's muse. His feminism may have been a short-lived phenomenon.

11. *The Jewish Literary Annual* (London, Union of Jewish Literary Societies, 1903), p. 11.
12. See Ellen M. Umansky, *Lily Montagu and the Advancement of Liberal Judaism* (New York, E. Mellen Press, 1983).
13. Information here is scanty. Lily Montagu, in *The First 50 Years: A Record of Liberal Judaism in England, 1900–1950* (London: The Younger Members Organization and the Alumni Society of the Liberal Jewish Synagogue 1950), p. 5, recalled that a group of men and women formed around Montefiore, but listed only the men by name. Her biographer writes that Montagu sent copies of her *Jewish Quarterly* article to prominent men and women, but 'she failed to record either the names or number of those who responded favourably'; Umansky, *Lily Montagu*, p. 169.
14. *Jewish Religious Union Bulletin* 5 (1914), p. 7; London School of Economics and Political Science (henceforth LSE) MS WIC D2, Clubs' Industrial Association Minutes, 3 July 1901, 8 October 1903.
15. Umansky, *Lily Montagu*, p. 171.
16. Jacqueline de Vries, 'Challenging Traditions: Denominational Feminism in Britain, 1910–1920' in Billie Melman, ed., *Borderlines: Genders and Identities in War and Peace 1870–1930* (London, Routledge, 1998), pp. 265–84; Sophia A. Van Wingerden, *The Women's Suffrage Movement in Britain 1866–1928* (Basingstoke, Macmillan, 1999), pp. 112–13. Reliable secondary sources on the JLWS, as distinct from the religious suffrage movement as a whole, are quite meagre. Linda Kuzmack, *Woman's Cause: the Jewish Woman's Movement in England and the United States, 1881–-1933* (Columbus, Ohio State University Press, 1986), is a pioneering work of broad scope, inevitably simplifying some matters of chronology and detail. My thanks to Dan Lyndon for lending me his University of Westminster MA thesis on Jewish involvement in the suffrage movement in Britain. This text is unfortunately not publicly available. Ruth Abrams, *Jewish Women and the International Woman Suffrage Alliance 1899–1926* (Ph.D., Brandeis University, 1996), contains much invaluable information.
17. Jacqueline de Vries, 'More than Paradoxes to Offer: Feminism, History and Religious Cultures' in Susan Morgan and Jacqueline de Vries, eds, *Women, Gender and Religious Cultures* (London, Routledge, 2010), p. 201.
18. *JC*, 20 December 1912, pp. 18–19.
19. The Women's Library (henceforth TWL) MS 2LSW/E/15/01/14.
20. *JC*, 14 March 1913, p. 28.
21. *JC*, 19 December 1913, p. 18.
22. See e.g. Rickie Burman, 'Middle-class Anglo-Jewish Lady Philanthropists and East European Jewish women' in Joan Grant, ed., *Women, Migration*

and Empire (Stoke-on-Trent, Trentham, 1996); Susan Tananbaum, 'Philanthropy and Identity: Gender and Ethnicity in London', *Journal of Social History* 30 (1997).
23. LSE MS WIC D2, Clubs' Industrial Association Minutes, 3 March, 14 July, 13 October, 1 December 1898, 6 July 1899. On Henrietta (Nettie) Adler, see Geoffrey Alderman's entry in *Oxford Dictionary of National Biography* (henceforth *ODNB*).
24. *JC*, 29 March 1912, p. 35. This was written before the formation of the JLWS, as was the Girls' Club resolution; see TWL microfiche 9/01/0965 (abstract): Mr William Burdett-Coutts to Miss Lily Montague [*sic*], 14 November 1911.
25. JLWS manifesto, *JC*, 8 November 1912, p. 19; letter of Percy Cohen of Princelet St (an unremitting anti-suffragist), *JC*, 15 November 1912, p. 19.
26. *JC*, 14 March 1913, p. 28.
27. Letter from Miss Lily Landstone, *JC*, 29 November 1912, p. 25. See also E.J. Bristow *Prostitution and Prejudice: the Jewish Fight against White Slavery 1870–1939* (Oxford, Clarendon Press, 1982)
28. *JC*, 15 March 1912, pp. 17–18. Kuzmack, *Woman's Cause*, p. 230 reference 42, errs in dating this news item November 1912 (after the formation of the JLWS) and the error has frequently been replicated. Leonard Woolf's sister, Flora Sidney Woolf, wrote the following week that the woman would not have been thought dirty had she been a customer—and that the views of 'a negligibly common man' were of little importance: *JC*, 22 March 1912, p. 40.
29. *JC*, 20 December 1912, p. 19.
30. Phoebe Rickards was a student at Bedford College.
31. Pankhurst, *Suffragette Movement*, Book VII, Ch. 2; Mary Davis, *Sylvia Pankhurst: a Life in Radical Politics* (London, Pluto Press, 1999), Ch. 3.
32. The Church League for Women's Suffrage *Bulletin* (*Church League*), February 1912, p. 8; March 1912, p. 15; July 1912, p. 61; January 1913, p. 91; March 1914, p. 56.
33. TWL MS 2LSW/C/7/36, reports on Whitechapel and St George's, November 1909.
34. *JC*, 22 November 1912, p. 36; 2 May 1913, p. 26; 16 May 1913, p. 18.
35. *JC*, 2 January 1914, p. 30.
36. *JC*, 31 October 1913, p. 48; 7 November 1913, p. 33; this was perhaps a distraction from the catastrophic state of his business affairs: see Bernard Wasserstein, *The Secret Lives of Trebitsch Lincoln* (Harmondsworth, Penguin, 1988), Ch. 5.
37. This statement in Kuzmack, *Woman's Cause*, p. 139, is unsubstantiated in the author's reference 37, p. 230.

38. See Pankhurst, *Suffragette Movement*, pp. 464–5, 497–8.
39. International Institute for Social History, Amsterdam, Pankhurst Papers, Microfilm Reel 26, item 229.
40. TWL MS 2LSW/A/3/3/03, Reports on the East End from Miss Bagenall, June 1913; TWL MS 2LSW/A/8, Whitechapel Committee minutes, 17 March 1914.
41. TWL MS 2LSW/A/8, Whitechapel and St George's branch minute book.
42. Rosa Waugh, *The Life of Benjamin Waugh* (London, T. Fisher Unwin, 1913), pp. 234–5.
43. Reminiscences of Alice Franklin are to be found in several recorded interviews with former activists in the interwar women's movement: see TWL 8SUF/B. Henrietta Adler and Miriam Moses have entries in *ODNB*; Ida Samuel's career is summarised in *The Woman's Who's Who* (1934–5) and in her obituary, *JC*, 30 September 1949, p. 8.
44. TWL MS 2LSW/E/04/68, Whitechapel correspondence file, Templar Printing Works to Miss Strachey, 12 April 1913.
45. *Church League*, August 1913, p. 259.
46. *The Free Church Suffrage Times* (henceforth *Free Church*), November 1913, p. 72.
47. *Church League*, October 1913, p. 304; November 1913, p. 320.
48. *Church League*, November 1913, p. 320; December 1913, p. 333; *Free Church*, December 1913, p. 84.
49. *Free Church*, January 1914, p. 10.
50. *Free Church*, March 1914, p. 31.
51. *Church League*, March 1914, p. 59; *Free Church*, April 1914, p. 50; *JC*, 8 May 1914, p. 18.
52. *Free Church*, December 1913, p. 84.
53. *Church League*, June 1914, p. 112; *JC*, 19 June 1914, p. 44.
54. Elizabeth Crawford, *The Women's Suffrage Movement*, p. 310.
55. W.R. Matthews, *Memories and Meanings* (London, Hodder & Stoughton, 1969), p. 128; Lawrence Barmann, 'Confronting Secularisation: Origins of the London Society for the Study of Religion', *Church History* 62.1 (1993). Other founding members included the Cambridge academic Israel Abrahams, the Reverend Simeon Singer of the New West End Synagogue, the liberal Congregationalist John Hunter, Reverend George Ernest Newsom of King's College London, the Unitarian J. Estlin Carpenter, soon afterwards Principal of Manchester College, Oxford, and Francis Crawford Burkitt, subsequently Norrisian Professor of Divinity at Cambridge. Burkitt was later a strong supporter of the Society of Jews and Christians.
56. See Chap. 8.
57. *JC*, 25 April 1913, p. 15: 'As a first step, resolutions to this effect were to be proposed at as many Synagogue meetings next May as possible'.

58. Sheila Fletcher, *Maude Royden* (Oxford and Cambridge, MA, Basil Blackwell, 1989), pp. 138–9. It is not known to what extent, if any, this was a response to activities of the Church League; however, several bishops sympathetic to these post-1914 developments had also supported the League.
59. *JC*, 10 July 1914, p. 19.
60. *JC*, 8 May 1914, p. 20.
61. Tony Kushner, "Sex And Semitism: Jewish Women in Britain in War and Peace" in Panikos Panayi, ed., *Minorities in Wartime: National and Racial Groupings in Europe, North America and Australia, During the two World Wars* (Oxford, Berg, 1993), p. 125, note 20, referencing Executive Minutes 22 September 1919.
62. *JC*, 18 July 2014, p. 12.
63. *JC*, 14 May 2010, Community Supplement, p. 1.
64. Fletcher, *Maude Royden*, Ch. 9; Lizzie Hands, *Some Legal Difficulties Which Beset the Jewess* (printed for private circulation, 1920). Hands was involved postwar with both the Council for the Amelioration of the Legal Position of the Jewess and the Jewish Peace Society, and was Hon. Sec of the Union of Jewish Literary Societies.
65. For an account of the most recent attempts to alter Jewish divorce law, see Geoffrey Alderman, *British Jewry since Emancipation* (Buckingham, University of Buckingham Press, 2014), pp. 417–19.
66. Todd M. Endelman, *Radical Assimilation in English Jewish History, 1656–1945* (Bloomington, Indiana University Press, 1990), pp. 81–5, and Paula E. Hyman, *Gender and Assimilation in Modern Jewish History: the Roles and Representation of Women* (Seattle, University of Washington Press, 1995), p. 22, espouse the view on 'feminisation' which is not supported here, but which may well be borne out in the USA, where Reform and Liberal Judaism have long been far more widespread than in Britain. Rickie Burman, 'Women in Jewish Religious Life: Manchester 1880–1930' in J. Obelkevich, L. Roper and R. Samuel, eds, *Disciplines of Faith: Studies in Religion, Politics and Patriarchy* (London, Routledge and Kegan Paul, 1987), pp. 51–2, attempts to square the circle: domestic religion and women's religious role had greater salience when these were visible aspects of a newly minority population, but 'the increased centrality of their [women's] role in religion did not result in a corresponding increase in communal stature or authority. For religion no longer represented a major avenue to social status, and the focus of male aspirations had changed'. However, twentieth- and twenty-first-century Anglo-Jewish institutional history shows that men have continued to prize religious status, even while the social range of male aspirations increased.

67. The author Amy Levy had published forcefully on the 'oriental' subjugation of Anglo-Jewish women, although her tragic death took place before she herself could weave this theme into Jewish suffragist discourse: see e.g., Alex Goody, 'Passing in the City: the Liminal Spaces of Levy's Late Work' in Naomi Hetherington and Nadia Valman, eds, *Amy Levy: Critical Essays* (Athens, Ohio University Press, 2010), p. 175. See also Paula E. Hyman, 'Does Gender Matter? Locating Women in European Jewish History' in Jeremy Cohen and Moshe Rosman, eds, *Rethinking European Jewish History* (Portman, Littman Library, 2009), p. 62.
68. *JC*, 27 September 1901, p. 19; Gertrude Spielmann, 'Woman's Place', p. 35.
69. Melissa R. Klapper, *Ballots, Babies and Banners of Peace: American Jewish Women's Activism 1890–1940* (New York, New York University Press, 2013), pp. 31–3; E. Ethelmer (E.C. Wolstonholme Elmy), 'Feminism', *Westminster Review* January 1898, p. 56; Florence Farr, *Modern Woman: Her Intentions* (London, Frank Palmer, 1910), pp. 8, 10, 12.
70. *JC*, 25 April 1913, p. 15; *JC*, 29 March 12, p. 35; see also 21 March 1913, p. 36.
71. *JC*, 20 December 1912, pp. 18-19; 23 May.1913, p. 19.
72. *JC*, 14 March 1913, p. 28.
73. Henrietta Leslie, *More Ha'pence than Kicks* (London, Macdonald, 1943); Bentwich, *If I Forget Thee*.
74. Central Zionist Archive (henceforth CZA) A 120/623, E. Pethick Lawrence to Zangwill, 13 March 1907.
75. Lily H. Montagu, *My Club and I* (London, Neville Spearman Ltd & Herbert Joseph Ltd, 1954), p. 14.
76. E. Pethick-Lawrence, *My Part in a Changing World* (London, Victor Gollancz, 1938), p. 124.
77. Pankhurst, *Home Front*, p. 371.
78. *JC*, 11 October.1912, p. 19; 18 October 1912, p. 25.
79. See reference 10.
80. Lilian H. Montagu, *The Faith of a Jewish Woman* (London, Allen & Unwin, 1943), and *My Club and I*; Monk Gibbon, *Netta* (London, Routledge and Kegan Paul, 1960).
81. Kuzmack, *Woman's Cause*, p. 142.
82. In a telephone conversation about the research resources of the Liberal Jewish Synagogue at St John's Wood, London, a (male) librarian indignantly rebutted my suggestion that Lily Montagu had had any connection with the suffrage movement.

PART II

Friendship in Private and Public, 1890s–1930

CHAPTER 6

'A Dear Good "God-Mother" to Her': Margaret MacDonald and Lily Montagu

On 2 July 1896, Margaret Ethel Gladstone, who was about to announce her engagement to the socialist politician James Ramsay MacDonald, wrote:

> I really know so little & care still less what my dogmatic beliefs are now ... You told me you were a Unitarian. I daresay I am—I leave out the earlier sentences about Christ in the creed if I think about it. But I know that whatever I do believe is only a small & distorted part of the real truth, & it never has troubled me much what it was at any particular time, so long as I had a practical working faith & thank GOD [*sic*] I can generally keep hold of something of that. I can worship just as well with R-Cs [*sic*] or Jews, as with any Protestant, so long as whoever they are seem to be in earnest, & I can get spiritual good from the writings of Buddhists or Atheists or anyone who looks beyond the superficial life. I never now regularly read the Bible or kneel down regularly to pray, except in family prayers night & morning ...[1]

She was protesting a little too much and, as we shall see, revising her autobiography as one is often wont to do on falling in love with someone whose personal history is profoundly different from one's own. But in one particular, her relationship with Jews and the Jewish faith, there was neither exaggeration nor revision. Some of the longest-lasting friendships of Margaret Gladstone MacDonald's life were with Jewish women. With one in particular, Lily Montagu, both friendship and social and political

© The Author(s) 2017
A. Summers, *Christian and Jewish Women in Britain, 1880–1940*,
Palgrave Critical Studies of Antisemitism and Racism,
DOI 10.1007/978-3-319-42150-6_6

work were closely intertwined. Margaret never failed to appreciate the central importance of religion in every aspect of her friend's life and, as time went on, increasingly acknowledged the role of religion in her own commitment to socialism.

Margaret was born in 1870; her mother, the daughter of a clergyman with aristocratic connections, died shortly afterwards. Her father was a Professor of Chemistry and Fellow of the Royal Society, whose inherited wealth eventually enabled him to devote his professional time to research. However, John Hall Gladstone's original vocation was for the ministry: he played an active part in the early years of the Young Men's Christian Association and other initiatives to bring religious thought into the practice of everyday life. In many ways his strong faith and social conscience made him a Christian mirror image of Lily's father Samuel Montagu, the Liberal MP for Whitechapel who combined a reforming secular politics with profound religious belief and observance. Like Montagu, Margaret's father was a Liberal in politics (though not related to Prime Minister W.E. Gladstone); he had been persuaded to stand (unsuccessfully) for election to Parliament a few years before she was born.[2] There was no particular friendship between the Christian man of science and the self-educated Jewish banker, but it was a different matter for the younger generation. Margaret grew up in London, and was educated alongside the daughters of Samuel Montagu at Doreck College in Bayswater, a school associated with the founding of the Froebel movement in education.[3]

It may seem surprising that a man of Montagu's unbending Orthodoxy, which would have kept his family from sharing a table at which non-kosher food was served, or travelling to social events on a Saturday, should have strong views on the value of Jewish integration into British society. As Lily was later to write, 'he preferred children of all denominations to be educated together. Such education was, he conceived, the best training for good citizenship. ... [and] ... in recreation people of all creeds should meet and learn to understand one another'.[4] His and his children's households were welcoming and sociable. Despite subsequent disagreements over religious belief and practice, their father's example in this instance was one which his daughters were to carry on throughout their adult careers.

Thus Margaret's friendship with the family continued without interruption after all the daughters had left school. Ethel Montagu had been her greatest friend to begin with, and they remained close after Ethel's marriage to Henry D'Arcy Hart in 1892.[5] Margaret's correspondence and diaries in her late teens and early twenties are full of references to luncheon, tea and dinner with the Montagu and Hart families. They also show how closely she worked with them in the Liberal interest in Whitechapel, where Samuel Montagu was MP. Entries such as 'Drive with Montagus to Whitechapel Women's Liberal Assn [*sic*] committee & back' (21 June 1894), 'Committee of Whitechapel Women's Liberal Federation at Lady Montagu's' (29 May and 11 June 1895), 'Off to Whitechapel to write for Sir Samuel Montagu' (5 July 1895) and 'Writing for Montagus at Whitechapel Investigation Committee' (8 July 1895) are typical (Figs. 6.1 and 6.2).[6]

Very gradually her relationship with Lily, three years her junior, became more significant. Her diary recalls 'Lily Montagu in to see me' (6 September 1894), 'Calling on Lily Montagu' (6 December 1894), 'Out with Lily Montagu to Soho. Calling on some of her girls & seeing over empty houses' (31 May 1895).[7] The initial link between the two lay in their respective activities as youth workers, as we should now term them. Margaret had taught a Sunday school class at St Mary Abbott's,

Fig. 6.1 Portrait of Margaret MacDonald, 1895 (Courtesy of the British Library Board)

Fig. 6.2 Portrait of Lily Montagu, 1895–1900 (Courtesy of the Jewish Museum, London)

Kensington since the late 1880s, and took on the additional commitment of a boys' club linked to the church on a weekly basis. Whilst also taking on visiting work with a district nursing association in East London, she maintained these church commitments throughout 1895—the year in which she met her future husband.[8] He chose to play down this aspect of her life, or rather, to 'left-angle' it, in his memoir of her. Margaret, he claimed, had written to her curate in 1889 (the date later revised to 1893) saying how hypocritical she felt at not teaching the boys the true social message of Christ;[9] the ordinary reader, and subsequent biographers, would infer that her club and Sunday school activities did not continue beyond this point, which her diaries reveal was certainly not the case. Similarly, Margaret's declaration to her fiancé in July 1896 that 'I never now regularly read the Bible' was almost certainly true, but the word 'regularly' was probably significant: most of her daily diary entries for the whole of 1894 had contained the phrase 'Read B.', so any falling off was from a high point.[10]

The religious beliefs and practices which constituted a potential obstacle in the way of Margaret's marriage to a leading member of the Independent Labour Party (ILP) placed no barrier between her and her Jewish friends. Lily's interest in finding new directions for Jewish liturgy and observance was a subject discussed as easily with Margaret as any of their shared concerns in social work. In a single letter of July 1895, Lily canvassed the possibility of their both becoming Poor Law Guardians; deferred their disagreement over the Independent Labour Party (which Margaret was to join the following April) until they had the chance of discussing it face-to-face; mentioned the piling up of paperwork for her Girls' Club; and added 'My prayers were well reviewed in last week's Jewish Chronicle'.[11] As Lily's ideas developed further away from the strict Orthodoxy in which she had been brought up, the emotional costs of forging a new path were fully appreciated by Margaret, who compared Lily's familial experience to her own decision to abandon her father's Liberal allegiance, and the political conservatism of other relatives, for the socialist ILP.[12]

Lily always insisted that it was Margaret's example and advice which had encouraged her to take up youth club work, though her activities within the Jewish community also steered her in that direction. Having begun to hold Sabbath children's services at the New West End Synagogue—in many ways the equivalent of Margaret's Sunday School class—she was asked to organise 'happy evenings' and 'happy Sunday afternoons' for young working girls, who themselves suggested the possibility of a more ambitious project.[13] This took institutional form in 1893, when premises were found in Soho where young Jewish garment workers could meet and enjoy a programme of supervised activities.[14] Soon afterwards Margaret, while continuing with club work on a religious basis, began to extend her social welfare concerns into a more secular context. In 1894 she became a founder member of the Women's Industrial Council (WIC). Here she joined women such as Clementina Black, Margaret Bondfield and Emmeline Pethick Lawrence in investigating conditions of women's employment and recommending changes in official economic, social and labour policies. Within two years, Lily and her sister Netta Franklin had followed her into the WIC.[15] The organisation was later to experience many divisions of opinion but, as will be seen, Margaret was always able to count on Lily's support there.

In that same year, Lily joined the Visiting Committee of the Jewish Board of Guardians, but there was no question of her confining her energies to the Jewish community. By 1897, both Lily and Margaret were active in the National Union of Women Workers, Lily on the Girls' Club Committee and Margaret on the Industrial Committee. In 1898 Lily was elected the first Honorary Secretary of the Clubs' Industrial Association, an offshoot of the WIC which sought to inform young working girls of their rights in the workplace, and give them the means to redress abuses of the law. Working on parallel lines which often contrived to meet, both Lily and Margaret were members of the NUWW Executive by the end of 1902.[16] That the two might occasionally have fun together, as well as earnest shared conversation and labour, is delightfully acknowledged in a letter of Ramsay MacDonald to his wife during an NUWW conference: 'How do the girls look? (Flo, Lily and the rest I mean) What do you talk about? Which of the waiters has captivated your hearts?'[17]

One area into which Lily did not follow her friend was the ILP. Although she was to strike a path away from her father's religious Orthodoxy, Lily was still loyal to his Liberal party politics. She was always more concerned to promote class conciliation than class conflict; however, she was not, as she has sometimes been portrayed, hostile or indifferent to working-class organisation. In a memoir published in 1954 she wrote of her 'deep regret that with a few exceptions our girls have not identified themselves closely with trade organisations. ... Perhaps, ... because of persecution, most of our parents are individualistic. ... Again and again we have tried to inculcate a wider point of view, and to explain the advantages of belonging to unions. The results have been rather sporadic and not very successful'.[18] She did not feel that she, Margaret and Ramsay were taking opposing sides over the big issues, but she was rarely confident in pronouncing on major political issues. She may have felt, in retrospect, that the narrow views of some of her coreligionists had once been her own. Later she was to recall of Margaret: 'it was she I think who helped me to see the connection between so-called philanthropic and industrial work. ... I used often to tell her I should have remained a tinkerer only, if she had not widened my horizon, and she thought my work among individuals supplemented her rather bigger work'.[19]

* * * * *

Lily remembered Margaret as having always been at her ease in male company,[20] unlike herself, an awkward teenager 'quite incapable of contributing small talk at any social gathering'.[21] At the time of Margaret's engagement she herself was nursing an unrequited affection for the widowed scholar Claude Montefiore, her mentor in the development of a progressive Judaism. But her joy at her friend's happiness was unfeigned and unbounded. 'You have won the love of a really splendid girl' she wrote to Ramsay in July 1896. 'I have always been anxious that she should marry someone worthy of her & thus find the happiness she so richly deserves'. To Margaret she wrote of her conviction that the happy couple would help each other to fulfil 'a splendid life of usefulness'—a phrase which may now sound like old-fashioned moralising, but which then meant a great deal to the three friends.[22]

Social networks, shared political interests or sheer chance might well have thrown them together. Although Margaret had written to Ramsay in May 1895 to make a financial donation to his Southampton election campaign,[23] the MacDonalds always insisted that it was through Lily's agency that they met in person. Margaret's diary for 13 June 1895 records: 'Had Montagus & S. D'Avigdor to tea. Pioneer Club. Tom Mann on Independent Labour Party, Mr Macdonald & others in discussion'; and elsewhere she noted 'First saw him, Pioneer Club, June 13, 1895'.[24] The club had been established by radical and progressive women in 1892; Lily's sister Netta Franklin was an active member, and men were encouraged to contribute to discussions of the great issues of the day. A few days later, Margaret met Ramsay again at a party at the Montagus.[25] Husband and wife ever after referred to Lily as their 'God-mother'.

Margaret and Ramsay lived life at a furious pace. They created a home in Lincoln's Inn Fields for a family of six children and an unending stream of co-workers and comrades from all over the country and the rest of the world. In 1902 Lily published a novel, *Broken Stalks*, in which she painted an affectionate portrait of her friends: 'Joan Carey', a young artist who has no interest in fashionable society (and while there was an element of self-portraiture here, Margaret too was, indeed, remembered as having gone out in clothes buttoned back to front); and 'Richard Ellis', a temperance campaigner of whom the Carey family initially disapprove. The intensity of their life after marriage is evoked in this extraordinary passage:

> [Richard] burns always—always, and always gets more fuel and is never satisfied with his flame. What drives him on, I wonder? He knows no limit, he has no fixed standard. He uses Joan's love and sympathy, the world's approbation, his own success, for fuel. They make the flame to burn stronger and stronger, and the altar of humanity can hold all of it. There is no rest, no rest, little Joan, for either of you. The flame is licked up, more fuel is added, and the burning must go on for ever.

Broken Stalks was published in 1902. The resolutely unfashionable female protagonist is not denied the happy ending of a romantic marriage,[26] but in this case Lily's life did not mirror her art. In that same year Claude Montefiore married a gentile woman friend who now converted to Judaism. Lily may not have known that Montefiore, widowed in 1889, had wanted to marry Florence Ward as far back as 1895, but that his mother's objections had obliged him to put the relationship on hold. His new engagement was not announced until after his mother's death.[27] Lily was now nearly thirty. She continued to value Montefiore as a figure crucial to the future of a Liberal Judaism, and as a collaborator in many of her religious initiatives; and she gave up all thoughts of marriage to anyone else. She subsequently shared a home with her sister Marian, who was devoted to Lily and supported her in all her undertakings. Lily described Marian as 'the closest relation in my life'[28] and dedicated *Broken Stalks* to her. The year was as significant in Lily's public career as in her private life, for in 1902 her earlier initiatives culminated in the formation of the forward-looking Jewish Religious Union. Despite all the changes in observance which the development of progressive Judaism was to bring in its train, Lily was always to cherish the rest which accompanied the orthodox Jewish Sabbath. However, after the inauguration of the JRU, her life was very nearly as hectic as Margaret's.

Throughout the first decade of the new century, Lily was helping to organise experimental and supplementary services in synagogues in the East and West Ends of London, and struggling to make the progressive movement in Judaism as inclusive as possible despite the differing positions adopted by participants who were orthodox or members of established Reform congregations.[29] At the same time she was assiduous in her attendance at the West Central Jewish Girls' Club which she had founded, and in her wholly secular work in the NUWW and the Clubs' Industrial Association. 'My present responsibilities' she was to write circa 1912, 'take 16 hours a day',[30] and this is likely to have been the case throughout this period. Margaret, meanwhile, whose sixth child was born in December 1910, can hardly have had time to sleep: not only did marriage, motherhood and world travel do nothing to reduce the public commitments she had taken on in the 1890s, but she found more and more opportunities to work in and for the labour movement. In 1905 she helped to organise a march of unemployed women in Whitehall and the following year helped to found a new organisation, the Women's Labour League, which sought improvements in workplace and domestic conditions for working-class women, as well as the involvement of more women in Labour politics. Unlike the NUWW and the WIC, this was an overtly party-political organisation, and Lily initially remained outside it, while continuing to work alongside Margaret in the two former organisations.

* * * * *

Between June and October 1909 the Jewish Religious Union 'came out' and constituted itself as a specifically Liberal Jewish congregation. Orthodox members had long since been pressured into resigning, and the sticking point for Reform had been the insistence of Lily and her closest associates that men and women should be permitted to sit and stand together in public prayer, a radical break with the practice of the rest of Anglo-Jewry. It was now impossible for Lily and her sisters Netta and Marian to gloss over their religious disagreements with their father. He had, after all, been the founding President of the Federation of Synagogues, which considered the practices of the mainstream United Synagogue and Chief Rabbinate to be altogether too anglicised to be authentically orthodox. Liberal Jewish practices included not just mixed seating: the early liturgy largely dispensed with Hebrew, expunged all reference to Temple sacrifice and the return to Jerusalem, and even included non-Trinitarian Anglican hymns. These were, simply, anathema to him, as to many others.[31]

Although Lily herself maintained the traditional Sabbath and dietary observances, the sisters had finally crossed the Rubicon; they would no longer defer to their father's authority in matters of belief and practice, and relations were irreparably damaged. From this moment onwards, Lily recalled, she 'cried inside'.[32] A few months later, Margaret and Ramsay suffered a crueller blow. In February 1910, their son David, not quite six years old, died of diphtheria. This time of emotional anguish and physical stress (Margaret's sixth pregnancy began soon afterwards) was the prelude to a series of distressing events within Margaret's circle of social reformers. They compounded her unhappiness, and may have played a part in shortening her life. Throughout this traumatic time, she and Lily remained united in their public decisions, and in their loving friendship.

Margaret's participation in the Women's Industrial Council had often taken a contentious turn. In the early 1900s there had been disagreements over the best way to protect the interests of 'sweated home workers'. Clementina Black briefly resigned as President over the opposition of Margaret and other members to the establishment of trade boards to establish minimum wages. The measure, which eventually passed into law, had been opposed on the grounds that it would consolidate low fixed rates in a trade.[33] A subsequent dispute concerned the waged work of married women: Black and others wished them to have more financial support, while Margaret argued, taking the fundamental trade union position of the time (and of subsequent eras) that mothers should stay at home while the wages of male workers were increased.[34] In this Margaret was, in essence, following the party line of the Labour movement without saying so: the WIC was supposed to be entirely free of either religious or party creeds. Unspoken sources of tension, between working-class and middle-class members and staff, and between socialists and Liberals, also simmered throughout this period. But the tragedy of little David's death produced a sincere outpouring of grief and sympathy from Margaret's WIC colleagues, as it did throughout the entire labour movement.

Both Clementina Black and the WIC Secretary, Lucy Wyatt Papworth, wrote to Margaret immediately, purely on an individual basis—the latter, indeed, sent three personal communications.[35] There was also a letter from her on behalf of the WIC Executive which was anything but official in tone:

> and I think you know that the Council takes a kind of special interest in you who have so largely helped to make it what it is, & whom it has seen marry & gather such a happy group of little people together. All the reminiscences of many years go into the feeling of their heartfelt sympathy ....[36]

These strong declarations of sympathy and solidarity make it difficult to understand why the definitive split in the WIC took place in the summer of 1910. The split has always been narrated within a political frame, and related to the policy disputes of previous years. Their more personal, and less dignified aspects have never been exposed, nor have they been related to the private tragedy in the life of Margaret, their main protagonist.[37]

The WIC Secretary was a Somerville graduate, daughter of the architect Wyatt Papworth. She had been in post since 1903, but complaints about her work were in the air: she had taken an unexpectedly long holiday on full pay; she was said to have bullied another employee;[38] she was thought by some to be unsympathetic to the labour movement. Margaret felt these dissatisfactions particularly strongly. As she returned to public life, she allowed them to come to the surface. Early in April she deputed Lily to attempt to clear the air. It was, Lily wrote, 'a very difficult interview and I daresay I have done no good', but she begged Margaret to talk things over with the Secretary face-to-face.[39] Margaret's experience of 'line management' was almost certainly non-existent; she was still in the throes of bereavement. Instead of seeking a meeting, she wrote a long and entirely tactless letter, listing every formal cause of complaint, adding that the Secretary's knowledge of industrial affairs was inadequate, as was her cooperation and communication with the Executive. Naively, Margaret wrote 'I apologise for saying all these horrid things, but perhaps they did more mischief still when bottled up.' Even more naively, she wrote that this was 'a private letter between you and me'.[40]

Lucy Wyatt-Papworth did not crush easily. Without acknowledging the letter, she immediately showed it to Clementina Black, who circulated a typed copy, with some names excised, to the whole Executive.[41] Margaret wrote to Black expressing her shock at being given no prior warning of the move, and in a letter to another member attempted, somewhat unfairly, to shift some of the responsibility onto Lily: 'I explained my opinion to Miss Papworth in response to an urgent request from Miss Montagu …'.[42] Lily reminded Margaret that she herself had wanted Margaret to sit down and talk things over in person: 'Your letter makes it look as if I *knew* that you would write this violent epistle'.[43] But their fundamental solidarity held: Lily made it clear that she approved of Margaret's rebuke to Clementina Black, and would support her position.

The Executive agreed to hold a special meeting at the beginning of May to discuss the matter. Margaret enlarged on her original list of complaints to include not only the secretary's 'overbearing ways', but also her 'undue extravagance in stationery'. Disingenuously, and rather riskily, she also played the neutrality card: 'Miss Papworth has hinted to various people that this difference of opinion has something to do with party politics. As the non-party character of the Council is essential to its work, it would be disloyal, if any of us allowed such considerations to influence us, and I, for one, deny that I am disloyal. I do not know what Miss Papworth's party politics are, nor whether she has any'.[44] The matter was referred to yet another meeting, for which Lucy Wyatt Papworth prepared a letter of resignation. This contained the counter-assertion that 'owing to the predominance of one political party, the Council is losing that non-political and non-party character which it formerly possessed'.[45] Confusion reigned throughout June and July. The executive's two-person committee of enquiry could not reconcile the conflicting narratives.[46] Margaret, Lily and others announced that they would resign if the Secretary stayed;

Clementina Black and others riposted that they would resign if she left.[47] At the 'Adjourned Ordinary Meeting' of the Council on 15 July at which Margaret was submitted to bruising criticism, the Papworth-Black axis, by a small majority, carried the day.[48]

A secession was now inevitable. Contrary to all subsequent accounts of the split, Margaret confided to a sympathetic friend: 'If we had split on policy or principle I should be sorry, but I should feel we had fought about something worth fighting about, but it is only about miserable personal distrusts & insinuations'.[49] Bearing the double burden of her bereavement and her new pregnancy, she was perhaps unwilling or unable to admit that the personal had also been political: that tectonic clashes between the new politics of socialism and trade unionism and an older Liberal reformism could hardly be avoided; that making changes within an organisation required the exercise of political skills with a small 'p' as much as, if not more than, the development of policies and principles.

What is extraordinary about the episode is the display of religious sectarianism which accompanied it. After the denouement of the Ordinary Meeting, Margaret reported that one of her allies had made 'rather a good point in reading a paragraph from the "Tablet" an R.C. [*sic*] paper which made out that the whole Council & its work was a R.C. piece of activity under the blessing of the R.C. archbishop, because Miss Papworth is an active R.C. Of course Mr Mackereth & Co ... said they could not be responsible for newspaper reporters & hardly let her explain that that was exactly her point & that they were attributing the Council's work to the Labour party in exactly the same wrong way'. Margaret added 'The Trained Charwomen are being taken over temporarily by an R.C. friend of Miss Papworth's ... I expect really the R.C. church has a good deal to do with Miss Papworth's attitude'.[50] Lily herself, in private, picked up the refrain, telling Margaret that 'Miss Streeter, a Roman Catholic lady, has written to ask my reason for resigning as Miss Papworth wants her to join the W.I.C. I cannot believe she does not know. I think we must be very careful about what we put in writing'.[51]

Perhaps it is not, after all, too surprising that the WIC's official versions of the story papered over such massive cracks. In all, fifty-six members of the organisation resigned, of whom ten were members of the Executive Committee. The report in the WIC's quarterly publication, *Women's Industrial News*, stated merely that 'This serious step is taken with great sorrow and reluctance by the workers concerned, but they consider it is rendered necessary in consequence of the position created by the vote of those members of the Council who attended the meeting on July 15th'.[52] From September 1910 Lucy Wyatt Papworth added to her responsibilities as Secretary and Treasurer of the Council those of Honorary Secretary of the Publications Committee and Honorary Editor of *Women's Industrial News*.[53] Previously, Publications had been a sub-committee of the Education Committee, of which Margaret had been the Chair. Existing literature on MacDonald and on the WIC states that 'arguments about how to handle a publication ... split the WIC'[54] but this was not, of course, the case. It has been justly said that history is written by the victors; it is also written by those who take the minutes.

Lily agonised over the injury to Margaret, wished she had never asked her to intervene with the Secretary in any way, and insisted on the supreme value of their friendship: 'they will rue the day they lost you & Ramsay. ... I think I admire & care for you both more than ever now'. A little later, she wrote more playfully: 'Miss Black told someone my affection for you had led me astray—Humph!'[55] For her, the immediate practical aftermath was relatively straightforward. She and Margaret had agreed a plan to withdraw the Clubs' Industrial Association from the WIC and affiliate it to the NUWW. As she had belonged to both organisations, was on the Executive of the latter, was known as the national authority on working girls' clubs, and remained the Secretary of the Association, she was able to facilitate this, and in 1911 assisted in a further transition into a new body, the National Organisation of Girls' Clubs.[56] At the end of 1910 Margaret's third daughter was safely delivered. She and Lily would continue to work together on the NUWW Executive, and within its Industrial Section. It would seem that a calmer and happier time of usefulness beckoned.

* * * * *

In January 1911 Samuel Montagu died. Lily's grief at having been unable to effect a reconciliation with the father she adored was not allowed to be a purely private matter. Baron Swaythling's will was published in March, and it specified that his considerable bequests to his ten children were dependent on their maintaining the Jewish religion, and not marrying non-Jews. The definition of the Jewish religion was, of course, his own. As the *Jewish Chronicle* put it, 'A notable clause in the will has reference to the "movement known as Liberal Judaism" and the connection therewith of certain members of his family'.[57] His trustees had been ordered to withhold three-quarters of his children's share of his estate if they continued to promote the Liberal tendency. But Lily, Marian and

Netta had no intention of reverting to Orthodoxy, or of pretending to do so. Indeed, their efforts contributed to the formal establishment of the first Liberal Jewish Synagogue in Britain later that year. In this they showed considerably more integrity than their brother Edwin who, with no attachment to Judaism, nevertheless valued the independent income derived from his father's fortune, which facilitated a political career at the highest level of government. In 1915 he married the non-Jewish Venetia Stanley at the Reform synagogue in London's Upper Berkeley Street; Lily was, apparently, supportive, saying that Venetia need commit to 'nothing but the avowal if *challenged* that you have adopted citizenship of our citadel and a steadfast refusal to propose yourself a Christian'.[58]

Lily's frugal habits, and the material support of her other siblings, ensured that she and Marian would in fact be able to live comfortably in their shared home while devoting themselves to voluntary work. However, the exposure of the family rift to the whole Jewish community was a painful experience, and the provisions of the will even fuelled an antisemitic diatribe accusing Montagu of hostility to the gentiles among whom he had amassed his wealth.[59] Lily dealt with this time of difficulty at an unconscious as well as a conscious level. Some time after her father died she dreamed that she was in his presence, receiving a document from him, and that there had been a 'revival of trust' between them.[60] Thenceforward she would continue on her chosen path in the conviction that the sympathy between them had been restored. Ironically perhaps, Lily was very much her father's daughter; he was to her the embodiment of goodness and the love of God and man.[61] She did not, of course, accept his literal interpretation of biblical texts, or his belief in the spiritual value of ritual practice; but she shared his disdain for show, his capacity for unwavering loyalty[62] and his utter commitment to the continuance of the Jewish community. She decided to write a life of her father for private circulation, a project which she completed by 1912; and she maintained her existing undertakings, both religious and secular, with unflagging determination.

While Lily was dealing with the shock waves of the will, Margaret was coping with a further bereavement. In April 1911 her closest colleague in the Women's Labour League, Mary Middleton, died of the cancer which had afflicted her for the previous two years. Margaret felt that the most appropriate memorial to her comrade should be one of practical utility which embodied the ideals of the WLL. She began to recruit support for a Baby Clinic to be set up in the North Kensington district of London, the much poorer neighbour of the Kensington proper in which Margaret and

Lily had grown up. Like Lily, and often alongside her, she soldiered on with all her other work. In March and in June, Margaret chaired meetings of the Industrial Section of the NUWW, whose minutes were signed by Lily. These minutes may be the last documentary evidence of their shared endeavours.[63]

The holiday period started, and at the end of July Lily was at the family country home near Southampton when she heard of Margaret's illness. She wrote begging her to be a good patient, 'not to worry about anything … for the present consider only yourself'[64]—advice she knew Margaret would find hard to follow. Over the next few weeks there was little improvement. Lily wrote to Ramsay explaining that she had to take a Club group on a summer holiday at their hostel near Littlehampton—would his secretary let her know further news?[65] She and all the Montagu clan sent telegrams with increasing frequency, the message always 'How is Margaret'. Margaret died, of septicaemia, on 8 September. The prayers of a huge circle of family and friends had been unavailing. Five children were motherless, as Margaret herself had been. The Baby Clinic would now be dedicated to Margaret MacDonald as well as Mary Middleton.

*****

'Don't mourn: organise!' might have been the coinage of Margaret's circle. Before September was out, Ramsay was planning a biographical memoir to supplement his own, privately printed, eulogy; by the middle of November, the Baby Clinic had opened to the public. Lily was heavily involved in both projects. She joined the Clinic's sponsoring body, the Women's Labour League,[66] was the first Chair of the Clinic's Committee and ensured that her wider kinship networks supported its work in cash and in kind.[67] She conferred frequently with Ramsay over the memoir which was published in 1912, and which underwent many reprintings, with a sixth edition published in 1929. He had originally asked Lily to compile it, which she declined to do,[68] but she supplied him with many of Margaret's letters to her, and wrote reminiscences which were quoted both in Ramsay's work and in biographies subsequently published by other authors.

These projects could function as displacement activities, certainly as a way of diverting a sense of loss into something productive and positive. But painful facts had to be confronted. An immediate task, in which Ramsay enlisted both Lily and her sister Netta, was to plan for the future care of the MacDonald children. Here the fact of Margaret's absence was unavoidably real. Early in 1912, after a visit to Lincoln's Inn Fields, Lily told Ramsay: 'I enjoyed the children but I was impotent with Joan & I came away with a great longing and a sense of failure. The home itself without Margaret is so unutterably sad to me for I have not yet braced myself to that'.[69]

Neither Lily nor Netta, of course, would allow grief to overcome a sense of duty. Ramsay turned to Netta, a pioneer of progressive home education through the Parents' National Education Union,[70] to find a suitable governess. Throughout October, sensitive to this family's special needs, she was interviewing candidates. One who 'read nothing' and had no political interests was unsuitable. A young woman from the Netherlands who 'sees to the full the honour and the responsibility of helping to train your children', who 'speaks the same language as we all do' and was possessed of 'breeziness & a little Bohemianism' was her final recommendation. Miss Byvoet joined the household, and the appointment was a lasting success.[71] Ramsay needed of course to select legal guardians for the children should he, too, die prematurely. He asked Lily to accept the role, in a sign of his affection and trust, which she feared might not be justified: she was considerably more confident around teenagers than in the handling of small children. Her loyalty to her friends was paramount, however, and her response unequivocal: 'I should gladly do anything you trusted me to do as regards your children. It would probably mean altering my whole life because my present responsibilities take sixteen hours a day but I would not fail you if you needed me'.[72]

What makes people friends is as mysterious as what makes people lovers. Prosaic factors—common interests, geographical proximity—are usually indispensable. Shared values and emotional complementarity take these bonds to a deeper level. 'I always wondered at her happiness—for she was motherless', Lily wrote after Margaret's death.[73] She herself suffered from anxiety and depression in her adolescence, overcoming them through a regenerated religious faith which took her life in many new directions. Margaret's own religious formation was reborn in her politics, as Ramsay's memoir of his wife makes clear: she regarded socialism 'as a religion binding its converts, not like a political association, but like a Church'.[74] The memoir has been described as 'sentimental' by modern writers, and this may be a reaction to the religious references in the text.[75] Margaret was no saint, as Lucy Wyatt-Papworth might attest, but she was not in the avant-garde of secularism. In her biography of Margaret, published in 1924, Lucy Herbert asserted that 'it is impossible to write of

Margaret Gladstone without dwelling upon her religious experiences',[76] and the girl was mother to the woman. When Ramsay MacDonald wrote of his wife's socialism that 'it was a dream of the City of God wrapt in peace',[77] he knew of what he spoke. These shared dream-lives were profoundly important to both Margaret and Lily. When Lily wrote to Ramsay that 'on the last day of her life she told me I had always been a dear good "God-mother" to her',[78] the reference may not have been solely to Lily's matchmaking role, but also to the now rock-like faith which she embodied and which had helped to make her such a loyal, understanding and unselfish friend.

* * * * *

Lily and Netta remained friends and supporters of Ramsay throughout his political career, despite their disappointments with him in the 1930s. They were not dismayed by his decision to form a national government with non-socialists: their correspondence with him related to Netta's pacifist concerns, and his unwillingness to pronounce publicly against the persecution of Jews in Germany. In these areas he did not differ greatly from the majority of office-holding British politicians, though the sisters had hoped it would be otherwise. The MacDonald children received Christmas presents from Lily well into adulthood, and to the end of her days addressed her as 'Dear Aunt Lily'.[79] It is, therefore, puzzling that her autobiographical publications reveal almost nothing of the depth of these relationships. *The Faith Of A Jewish Woman* (1943) and *My Club and I* (1954), slim volumes which appeared late in her life, do not, indeed, refer to any of her political involvements. The communications which she allowed Ramsay to use in his memoir of Margaret showed the extent of her personal feelings and social engagements in the early 1900s. But in these later volumes, neither the Women's Labour League, the Jewish Peace Society nor the Jewish League for Woman Suffrage, all of which she joined soon after Margaret's death, are mentioned, and there are very few references to Margaret herself.

It seems that by the time of her later publications, there had been something of a shift in Lily's perception of her relations with the gentile world. Throughout the interwar period she undertook secular responsibilities as a Justice of the Peace, but her overwhelming devotion was to nurturing the Liberal Jewish synagogue and its new understanding of Jewish identity. The congregation aspired to be seen as English men and women 'of the Jewish persuasion'. They stood aloof from the growing interest in the Zionist movement within Anglo-Jewry as a whole, even as horrific events unfolded in Nazi Germany. In the 1920s Lily used the still fledgling synagogue as a platform from which to pioneer the first national interfaith organisation, the Society of Jews and Christians, hoping to increase mutual theological understanding and find common ground on social questions. Its fortunes were mixed, and respect was not wholly reciprocal, as will be shown in Chap. 8. In these undertakings, she may have tested the limits of cross-denominational communication and, at a conscious and subconscious level, acknowledged the obstacles in the path of social assimilation.

However, it may also be the case that as a young girl, Lily did not realise how much her family's wealth and standing protected her from the prejudice and dislike vented against more recent Jewish immigrants; and as she matured, she may have continued to locate herself and them in different compartments of British society. From the vantage point of World War II she certainly saw herself as part of the wider picture. In 1943 she recalled:

> In the social work of an undenominational character in which I was engaged I was always conscious that on account of my religion I was *different* from my fellow workers. ... In the Women's Industrial Council and the National Union of Women Workers (later National Council of Women), and in all the work which I did with the Central Association for the Employment of Women during the last war, I was naturally always accepted on exactly the same footing as my colleagues. ... I did, nevertheless, feel a certain sensitiveness which is hard to define, and a considerable degree of responsibility. Both these feelings were increased as antisemitism acquired a greater hold.[80]

This statement does not entirely square with the evidence of, for example, her first will, made in 1917: in this she made small bequests to such colleagues as Emily Janes and Norah Green of the National Council of Women, 'as a small token of gratitude and in order that they may each buy some small remembrance of me', and specified that if she outlived her executors she would 'leave to my nephews and nieces including the children of Mr J Ramsay Macdonald to make what selection of my personal possessions they think fit'.[81] As early as 1894, indeed, the twenty-four-year-old Margaret had jotted down notes for a will including 'Lily Montagu. Girls' Own Annual & anything else suitable for her Girls' Club. If she & Marian would like books or engravings or anything for themselves let them have them'.[82] The interweaving of young idealistic lives, the mutual warmth of

Lily and her family's friendship with Margaret Gladstone and the man she married, the unequivocal trust which Margaret's widower placed in her, and Lily's sustained relationship with the MacDonald children: it was as if, in 1943, these barely registered.

Had antisemitism, indeed, increased so greatly since Lily's schooldays? Since the 1930s she had been able to see how state-sponsored racism in Germany had conferred a kind of legitimacy on expressions of antisemitism among some of her compatriots. This might have brought into a sharper focus certain incidents from the past in which she might not, at the time, have felt personally targeted. One such was the day in 1907 when a meeting of the Women's Industrial Council took place at London's Guildhall where she, Charlotte Despard and Elizabeth Cadbury were among those present. 'One of the speakers Mrs. Graves raised a storm of hisses by saying that if they kept foreigners out of the country they could find more work for English men and women. It was the foreigners who reduced the wages. She was an Englishwoman (hisses, and cries of "Shame")'.[83] As social and political circumstances changed, Lily may have re-evaluated such episodes: the 'cries of "Shame"' may have counted for less in her memory than the venom of the speaker.[84] Similarly, she might have winced at Ramsay's published reminiscence of a visit to South Africa immediately after the Anglo-Boer War, where he and Margaret encountered 'some of those who were patriotic in broken English and was taught by them how our national reputation had become a mere thing to traffic with by aliens and blackguards in the market-place'.[85] Yet it cannot be doubted that Margaret's presence, her encouragement and comradeship, had been crucial in enabling the painfully shy Lily to enter so fully into the world of gentile women's activism, and to know that her contribution to it was highly valued. For some years Margaret's memory sustained her there. As the loved image gradually faded, she may have found that world a less easy place to live in.

Notes

1. The National Archives (henceforth TNA) PRO 30/69/778, Margaret Ethel Gladstone to James Ramsay MacDonald, 2 July 1896.
2. Information on John Hall Gladstone from the article on Margaret MacDonald in *Oxford Dictionary of National Biography* (henceforth *ODNB*) by June Hannam.

3. Friedrich Froebel (1782–1852) was the originator of the kindergarten movement, stressing the importance of play and self-expression of the individual in child development. It was in the home of the Principal of this school, Beata Doreck, that the Froebel Society was founded in Britain. For the influence of similar ideas on Netta Franklin née Montagu, see Chap. 7.
4. Lily H. Montagu, *Samuel Montagu, First Baron Swaythling* (London [for private circulation only, 1912), pp. 49–50.
5. Henry D'Arcy Hart was a barrister and artist; his and Ethel's eldest son Philip was a distinguished medical researcher and member of the Socialist Medical Association: see his obituary in *The Independent*, 24 August 2006. He lived to the age of 106.
6. Margaret MacDonald Diaries, TNA PRO 30/69/919, 1894; PRO 30/69/921, 1895. It is not clear to what the 'writing' refers: minute-taking is a possibility.
7. The same.
8. Hannam on Margaret MacDonald, *ODNB*; TNA PRO 30/69/921, 1895.
9. J. Ramsay MacDonald, *Margaret Ethel MacDonald, 1870–1911* (privately printed, 1911), p. 41, gives the date as 1889; in J. Ramsay MacDonald, *Margaret Ethel MacDonald* (London, Hodder and Stoughton, 1912), pp. 96–7, the resignation date is given as the end of 1893.
10. TNA PRO 30/69/921, 1895.
11. TNA PRO 30/69/886, Lily Montagu to Margaret Gladstone, 29 July 1895.
12. J. Ramsay MacDonald, *Margaret Ethel MacDonald* (1912) pp. 108–9, quoting a letter from Margaret to Lily of 22 March 1911.
13. Lily Montagu, *The Faith of a Jewish Woman* (London, Allen & Unwin, 1943), pp. 14–17; Montagu, *My Club and I* (London, Neville Spearman Ltd & Herbert Joseph Ltd, 1954), pp. 18, 22–3.
14. Montagu, *My Club and I*, p. 25 *et seq.*
15. Jean Spence, 'Working for Jewish Girls: Lily Montagu, Girls' Clubs and Industrial Reform 1890–1914', *Women's History Review* 13.3 (2004), p. 504.
16. National Union Of Women Workers (henceforth NUWW), *Women Workers* [Conference Report for 1897] (1897–8), pamphlet in British Library; London Metropolitan Archive (henceforth LMA) ACC/3613/05/001, NUWW Conference Programme 1902; London School of Economics and Political Science (henceforth LSE) WIC D2, Clubs' Industrial Association Minute Book I, February 1898–May 1905.
17. Jane Cox, ed., *A Singular Marriage: a Labour Love Story in Letters and Diaries; Ramsay and Margaret MacDonald* (London, Harrap, 1988), p. 267.
18. Montagu, *My Club and I*, p. 64.

19. MacDonald, *Margaret Ethel MacDonald* (1912), p. 19. This may be compared with Ramsay's comment on Margaret's life during the 1880s, that she 'came dangerously near to that useless life of pottering about in ecclesiastical matters, from decorating churches on holy days to dispensing charity to "the poor", as a superior person': the same, p. 47.
20. Lucy Herbert, *Mrs Ramsay MacDonald* (London, Women Publishers, 1924), p. 9.
21. Montagu, *My Club and I*, p. 15.
22. TNA PRO 30/69/782, Lily Montagu to J. Ramsay MacDonald, 17 July 1896; the same, Lily Montagu to Margaret Gladstone, 12 July 1896.
23. J. MacDonald, *Margaret Ethel MacDonald, 1870–1911* (London, Women Publishers, 1911), p. 5.
24. TNA PRO 30/69/921, 1895; MacDonald, *Margaret Ethel MacDonald* (1912), p. 105. 'S. D'Avigdor' may have been Sylvie D'Avigdor, then a young writer interested in the progressive movement in Judaism: see Ellen M. Umansky, *Lily Montagu and the Advancement of Liberal Judaism* (New York, E. Mellen Press, 1983), p. 107; Meri-Jane Rochelson, *A Jew in the Public Arena: the Career of Israel Zangwill* (Detroit, Wayne State University Press, 2008), pp. 109 and 259 ref. 20.
25. David Marquand, *James Ramsay MacDonald* (London, Cape, 1977), p. 44, referencing his own interview with Lily Montagu.
26. The main female characters of her previous novel, *Naomi's Exodus* (London, T. Fisher Unwin, 1901), do appear, however, to be vehicles conveying Lily's own experiences of disappointment and loneliness: see, in particular, a passage on p. 95.
27. University of Southampton Library (henceforth USL) MS 363, A3006, 3/2/3, Waley Cohen Correspondence; letter of Claude Montefiore to Julia Matilda Cohen, n.d., unsigned.
28. Montagu, *Faith*, p. 64.
29. Umansky, *Lily Montagu*, pp. 7, 111, 112, 173.
30. TNA PRO 30/69/806, Lily Montagu to J. Ramsay MacDonald, 23 February, n.y.
31. For a detailed history of the movement, see Lawrence Rigal and Rosita Rosenberg, *Liberal Judaism: the First Hundred Years* (London, Union of Progressive and Liberal Synagogues, 2004).
32. Montagu, *Faith*, p. 36.
33. Ellen F. Mappen, 'Strategists for Change: Social Feminist Approaches to the Problems of Women's Work' in Angela V. John, ed., *Unequal Opportunities: Women's Employment in England 1800–1918* (Oxford, Blackwell, 1986), p. 252; Christine Collette, *For Labour and for Women: the Women's Labour League 1906–1918* (Manchester, Manchester University Press, 1989), pp. 46, 118–19.

34. See Mappen, 'Strategists for Change', p.251, and the entry on the Women's Industrial Council by June Hannam in *ODNB*.
35. TNA PRO 30/69/802, Part I, Large envelope, 'Mementoes of David', printed card, n.d., from Lucy Wyatt Papworth; File, 'David's death, correspondence 1910 M-P', her letter to Margaret MacDonald of 13 February 1910; PRO 30/69/802, Part II, 'David's Death Correspondence 1910 R-Z', her letter to Margaret of 4 February 1910.
36. TNA PRO 30/69/802, Part II, 'David's Death Correspondence 1910 R-Z', letter on behalf of WIC to Margaret MacDonald, 16 February 1910.
37. My principal source for this episode has been the MacDonald archive deposited at the National Archives (then the Public Record Office) in 1976 by David Marquand, whose biography of Ramsay MacDonald was published a year later. The papers cited were, at the time I consulted them, placed in two large envelopes, but not arranged chronologically. They do not seem to have been consulted by other scholars. In 1989 Christine Collette described them as 'largely unsorted': Collette, *For Labour*, pp. 44–5.
38. TNA PRO/30/69/1390, Papers on the resignation of L. Wyatt Papworth, Envelope 2, Typed (duplicated) notes for the WIC Executive meeting of 5 May 1910; the same, Annie Hicks to Margaret MacDonald, n.d.
39. The same, Lily Montagu to Margaret MacDonald, n.d. and 21 April 1910.
40. TNA PRO/30/69/1390, Papers on the resignation of L. Wyatt Papworth, Envelope 1, Margaret MacDonald to Lucy Wyatt Papworth (typed copy), 7 April 1910.
41. TNA PRO/30/69/1390, Papers on the resignation of L. Wyatt Papworth, Envelope 2, Clementina Black to Margaret MacDonald, 18 and 19 April 1910.
42. The same, Margaret MacDonald to Clementina Black, 20 April 1910; to Mrs Minnie [Philip] Nodin, 20 April 1910.
43. The same, Lily Montagu to Margaret MacDonald, 21 April 1910.
44. The same, typed (duplicated) notes for the WIC Executive meeting of 5 May 1910.
45. The same, Printed Minutes of Council meeting; letter of resignation dated 1 June 1910.
46. The same, Printed Report of Committee of Inquiry (Edith C. Harvey and George P. Gooch).
47. The same, typed (duplicated) letter of Margaret MacDonald, Lily Montagu, M. Macpherson, Mrs F. J. McCrosty, Mrs Nodin, Mrs Bernard. Player and Florence Potter, 11 July 1910; the same, printed letter of Clementina Black and Henry Bazett, 12 July 1910.
48. The same, letters of G.P. Gooch, Lily and Marian Montagu to Margaret MacDonald, 15 July 1910, after the WIC meeting of that date.

49. The same, Margaret MacDonald to Rosalind Countess of Carlisle, 5 August 1910.
50. The same.
51. The same, Lily Montagu to Margaret MacDonald, 16 August 1910.
52. *Women's Industrial News*, July 1910, p. 1. October 1910, p. 20; Women's Industrial Council, *Annual Report* for 1909–1910, pp. 17–18.
53. Women's Industrial Council, *Annual Report* for 1909–1910, p. 21; *Annual Report* for 1910–1911, p. 45.
54. This was the conclusion of Ellen Mappen, in her introduction to the republication of Clementina Black, *Married Women's Work* (London, Virago 1983), p. viii, and followed by Collette and Hannam; Mappen adds that there were further concerns over a proposed incorporation of the Council which might give the Executive more power, and also states 'there is some indication that there was dissension over the role of the secretary of the Council'.
55. TNA PRO/30/69/1390, Papers on the resignation of L. Wyatt Papworth, Envelope 2, Lily Montagu to Margaret MacDonald, 15 July 1910; the same, 15 September 1910.
56. Women's Industrial Council, *Annual Report* for 1910–1911, pp. 31–2; Spence, 'Working for Jewish Girls', p. 492.
57. *Jewish Chronicle* (henceforth *JC*), 10 March 1911, pp. 9–10.
58. Naomi B. Levine, *Politics, Religion and Love: the Story of H.H. Asquith, Venetia Stanley, and Edwin Montagu* (New York, New York University Press, 1991), pp. 315–16, 322. Edwin Montagu, who died in 1924, was Secretary of State for India, 1917–22.
59. *JC*, 31 March 1911, p. 14.
60. Montagu, *Faith*, p. 36.
61. As a child, her night terrors were soothed by her mother telling her 'that my father was too good for God to let him be hurt as badly as he would be if his little daughter were taken from him': Montagu, *Club*, p. 19.
62. Montagu, *Samuel Montagu*, pp. 70–1: her father 'always remembered gratefully the practical sympathy which [Liberal Party leader] Mr Gladstone shewed towards the oppressed Jews, and, in his turn, assisted with vigorous protests against the Armenian atrocities when his leader held meetings to denounce them', to the extent that, although he 'entertained a personal feeling of kindness towards Turkey for her fair treatment of the Jews', he was prepared to support a boycott of Turkey by all European governments.
63. LMA ACC/3613/01/063, National Union of Women Workers, Minutes of the Industrial Section, 30 March and 12 June 1911.
64. TNA PRO30/69/803, Lily Montagu to Margaret MacDonald, 30 July 1911.

65. The same, Lily Montagu to Ramsay MacDonald, 20 August 1911.
66. Lily joined the Women's Labour League almost immediately after Margaret's death: TNA PRO 30/69/733, Lily Montagu to J. Ramsay MacDonald, 8 October 1911. The League was absorbed into the Labour Party in 1918. Lily appears not to have joined the Labour Party.
67. This account of the Baby Clinic is drawn from correspondence, brochures and annual reports in TNA PRO30/69/734 and TNA PRO 30/69/811. Gaps in the annual report series have been supplemented by British Library holdings. Records of the Baby Clinic are also held at the Labour History Archives and Study Centre, Manchester, and the London Metropolitan Archives. See also Lara V. Marks, *Metropolitan Maternity: Maternal and Infant Welfare Services in Early Twentieth Century London* (1996), Chs. 4 and 8.
68. TNA PRO30/69/992, Lily Montagu to Ramsay MacDonald, 25 September 1911, explaining that she was at work on the memoir of her father and lacked the talent, as well as the time, for this task. She also suggested Ella, sister of Amy Levy, as a substitute.
69. TNA PRO30/69/803, Lily Montagu to Ramsay MacDonald, 23 February [1912?]. Joan was Ramsay and Margaret's fifth child.
70. See Chap. 7.
71. TNA PRO30/69/733, Netta Franklin to Ramsay MacDonald, 24 October 1911. The MacDonald children were still in touch with their governess over two decades later: see LMA ACC/3529/03/006B, Ishbel MacDonald to 'My dear Aunt Lily', 18 December 1935.
72. TNA PRO 30/69/806, Lily Montagu to J. Ramsay MacDonald, 23 February, n.y.
73. MacDonald, *Margaret Ethel MacDonald* (1912), p. 16.
74. MacDonald, *Margaret Ethel MacDonald, 1870–1911* (privately printed, 1911), p. 35.
75. Hannam on MacDonald in *ODNB*; Collette, *For Labour*, p. 45, writes that 'Margaret's husband eulogised her' and that Lucy Herbert's biography of Margaret is 'sycophantic'.
76. Lucy Herbert, *Mrs Ramsay MacDonald*, p. 10.
77. MacDonald, *Margaret Ethel MacDonald, 1870–1911* (privately printed, 1911), p. 37.
78. MacDonald, *Margaret Ethel MacDonald* (1912), p. 18.
79. LMA ACC/3529/03/006B, Ishbel MacDonald to 'My dear Aunt Lily', 18 December 1935; LMA ACC/3529/03/006D, Malcolm MacDonald to 'Dear Aunt Lily', 1 June 1955.
80. Montagu, *Faith* pp. 53–4.
81. LMA Microfilm X041/055, document dated 2 September 1917.
82. TNA PRO 30/69/810, document dated 6 October 1894.

83. William Purdie Treloar, *A Lord Mayor's Diary, 1906–7*, (London, T. Fisher Unwin, 1913), p. 213. Charlotte Despard was about to become one of the most militant of suffragists at this time; Elizabeth Cadbury was a Quaker whose interests in welfare, youth work and pacifism coincided with Lily's throughout the period covered by this book.
84. This might particularly have been the case if the 'Mrs Graves' in question were Beatrice Mary (Mrs Spencer) Graves, who was from 1910 the Hon. Treasurer of the London Society for Women's Suffrage, the non-militant wing of the suffrage movement with which Lily and Netta were in sympathy.
85. MacDonald, *Margaret Ethel MacDonald* (1912), p. 251.

CHAPTER 7

'We Fell in Love with Each Other at First Sight': Charlotte Mason and Netta Franklin

Henrietta 'Netta' Montagu, born in 1866, was the eldest of Samuel Montagu's ten children. Like her younger sister Lily, she was brought up in a deep religious faith, expressed in formal and informal practice, which in the Montagu household was allied to a strong sense of obligation to the unfortunate of all religious communities and none. Netta's name is linked with Lily's in many public arenas, notably the National Council of Women, the Women's Industrial Council, the Jewish League for Woman Suffrage, the Jewish Peace Society and the movement for progressive Judaism which emerged from the Jewish Religious Union. However, the cause with which she herself most strongly identified, and for which she is best known, was the Parents' National Education Union (PNEU) which originated in Bradford in 1887 (Fig. 7.1).[1]

A combination of circumstances drew her onto this path. Netta was strikingly handsome when young. In 1885, aged 19, she was married—one is inclined to write 'married off'—to another scion of a wealthy banking dynasty, her first cousin Ernest Franklin. She gave birth to three children within the next five years, and to three more by 1903. Her sudden plunge into maternal responsibility coincided with the rise of a new educational movement focused on parent-led home learning, led by an unmarried, childless, devoutly Christian teacher and writer named Charlotte Maria Shaw Mason. The strength of the friendship between these two women— which might at first sight seem improbable—ultimately propelled Netta

Fig. 7.1 Portrait of Netta Franklin, c. 1895 (By kind permission of the Franklin family)

into the secretaryship of the PNEU, and supported her through years of (as she later recalled):

> 'Getting to know members and giving them help and advice … talking to fellow-travellers in the train, always carrying a *Parents' Review* and lending it, leaving it in the consulting room of doctors and dentists, … [recruiting] people representing different sets … opening up new platforms for our lectures, luncheon clubs, women's institutes, Rotary Clubs, etc., Townswomen's Guilds, where I have often spoken … In early days too we arranged for study groups with courses of lectures on Miss Mason's books, nature walks for parents, health talks to "nannies" [now] an extinct animal! And so on'.[2]

Although Netta did not mention it, it is also very likely that her hospitality and financial generosity made a material difference to the Union's longevity.

The details of Charlotte Mason's early life have only recently been revealed;[3] her official obituaries mask a remarkable process of self-invention.[4] She seems to have been born in 1842, almost certainly the only child of her Irish Catholic mother, and she was orphaned and obliged to earn her living at the age at which the prosperous Netta Franklin would be entering marriage and motherhood. However, she had twelve older half-siblings by her Irish Quaker father's previous two marriages, and the reasons why she was not as closely embedded within her own extended family as Netta was within hers—indeed, her motives for airbrushing them entirely from her personal history—remain unclear. Her parents had married in an Anglican church, but were interred separately in Quaker and Catholic burial grounds. Their 'mixed marriage', and the fact that it took place only after Charlotte's birth, together with the successive failures of her father's business ventures and her parents' separation before their deaths in 1858 and 1859 respectively, were aspects of her autobiography which she determinedly suppressed as she made her way into the world.

Charlotte was educated in an Anglican 'National' school for girls in Birkenhead, where she was subsequently employed as a pupil-teacher, an indication at that period of lowly social status which she was, subsequently, increasingly careful to conceal. An early influence may have been a Birkenhead clergyman who, like a number of her half-siblings, had moved from the Quaker fellowship to the Anglican Communion.[5] Charlotte always defined herself as a member of the Church of England, but her intensely personal sense of religion evoked her Quaker ancestry; her mother's Catholicism would appear to have made very little impression on her. In 1859 she spent a year in London at the Anglican teacher-training institution of the Home and Colonial Infant School Society. Here she began to create an alternative family, in the network of male and female tutors, and female friends and colleagues, which eventually enabled her to achieve economic independence and intellectual influence.

For more than a decade Charlotte headed an Anglican institution, the William Davison Infantine School in Worthing. Subsequently, from 1874 to 1878, she lectured in the Bishop Otter Memorial College at Chichester; this was established to train middle-class women to teach in the new Elementary Schools established under the Education Act of 1870.[6] She left the college in the spring of 1878 and spent a period resting and travelling on the Continent, before beginning the research which led to the publication, in 1880, of a well-received guide to 'The Forty Shires'. In that year she moved north to Bradford to live with a 'Home and Colonial' friend, Mrs Lizzie Groveham, in whose school she taught part-time while continuing to research and write geography textbooks for elementary schools.

In 1885, as Netta Franklin engaged in her first struggles to manage a household, Charlotte Mason was formulating the educational theories which led to the creation of her own 'school' in the abstract as well as the concrete sense. She delivered a series of lectures in Bradford which were soon published as *Home Education*. Her original audience, at St Mark's parish church, formed the nucleus of the first eighty-strong Parents' Education Union set up in Bradford in 1887. The decision to constitute the society as the Parents' National Education Union was taken in 1888, after consultation with a number of educationists such as Frances Buss, Dorothea Beale and the headmaster of Rugby School; clerics, including the Bishop of London; and Cambridge academics to whom Anne Jemima Clough, Principal of Newnham College and herself a Home and Colonial alumna, provided introductions. In 1891 Charlotte moved to Ambleside, in the Lake District, in order to set up a 'House of Education' at Scale How to train future governesses and schoolteachers in her methods. Her contacts in the region were provided by another longstanding Home and Colonial friend, Selina Fleming née Healey, who had taken over the school originally founded at Eller How by Anne Jemima Clough. [7]

Charlotte's views on the early-years education of middle-class children were both derivative and critical of the new theories emanating from the Continent—from Pestalozzi and Froebel in particular. First and foremost she stressed that the young child was a person with inborn intelligence and abilities which should not be patronised and underestimated, and an individual for whom a one-size-fits-all curriculum could not be adequate. Her child-centred philosophy sought to avoid the regimentation which was likely to destroy all love of learning on the one hand, and the absence of discipline which she observed in many middle-class homes on the other. Children should find learning a joy, and at the same time acquire the self-discipline which emerged from the requirement to complete age-appropriate tasks and duties. She insisted that her philosophy and practice differed from that of her Continental predecessors because she was aware of the constant 'danger that a method, a *bona fide* method, should degenerate into a mere system', though in recalling a secession of some of her supporters in 1894, she stressed that 'the P.N.E.U. is designed as a tacit protest against the fundamental principles of the philosophers'.[8] The home-grown character of her thinking is indicated by her recollection of Anne Jemima Clough, who 'almost alone I thought amongst educationalists, had very strong sympathy with parents'; and as Selina Fleming would have known, Clough was as early as the 1850s giving each of her pupils an individual timetable.[9]

She laid great stress on daily excursions out of doors in all weather.[10] This was partly a counsel for physical health, but more as a foundational syllabus in nature study and the power of observation and notation. Charlotte elaborated a practice which she called 'narration', whereby children reported what they had just seen and heard, at first orally and in later years in writing. They were to develop their powers of attention and recall in this way, through a judiciously timed and varied daily learning schedule, in which great literature and the visual arts held a large place. Most importantly of all, perhaps, Charlotte declared herself opposed to secular education, while avoiding any specific church affiliation.[11] Her own Christianity was rooted in a deep sense of loyalty to the person of Christ, and she and many PNEU members stressed the importance of imbuing ordinary daily lessons with a sense of God's activity in the world, as opposed to requiring young children to learn formulaic prayers and ritualised behaviour. This approach ensured that her philosophy appealed to a very wide spectrum of middle-class families. (Currently her philosophies are being appropriated and adapted by evangelical Christian home-schoolers in Canada and the USA, and this new development must await its historian.)

Reading successive editions of *Home Education*, one cannot help wondering if parents felt more daunted than empowered by the huge range of educational and moral responsibilities proposed for them. Charlotte felt that she was restoring to the middle-class home—and to the mother in particular—a role which was in danger of being removed through what she considered a somewhat spurious process of professionalisation. She wisely observed what remains true to this day, that the lack of training for parenthood left many well-meaning families in a state of confusion and difficulty. But the mother-figure who emerges from her writings is a physical, mental and spiritual *perpetuum mobile* who in real life would have had rather little time and energy left for the social and familial duties of her class. Although Charlotte's instructions are leavened with her firm reiteration of the child's need to be allowed to play and learn without constant adult interference, this same freedom nevertheless needed to be highly organised and constantly supervised.

Occasionally these contradictions were addressed, if not very fully examined. While a child should not be consigned to 'an ignorant nursemaid', it was 'very likely' unsuitable 'for educated people to have their children always about them. The constant society of his parents might be too stimulating for the child; and frequent change of thought, and the society of other people, make the mother all the fresher for her children.

But they should have the *best* of their mother, her freshest, brightest hours …'.[12] In similar vein, Charlotte thought that a mother who had fully absorbed PNEU principles would be able to delegate much of the work successfully: 'Half an hour's talk of this kind with a sensible governess will secure a whole month's work for the children, so well directed that much is done in little time, and the widest possible margin secured for play and open-air exercise'.[13]

From 1890, she edited together with Mrs Emmeline ('Lienie') Steinthal the monthly *Parents' Review*, to which they and other PNEU members were enthusiastic contributors. A 'virtual school' was created, originally called the Parents' Review School and later the Parents' Union School, whereby home educators all over Britain and, ultimately, the Empire could use the same teaching materials prepared in Ambleside. Older pupils were also sent examination papers which were returned to Charlotte to be marked. However, while these teaching packages were greatly valued, parents, starting with Netta, initiated a move away from the home school-room. In 1894 she argued that boys in particular needed the discipline of an external environment, but that sending them to board away from home at a young age was not desirable. She then arranged for one of Charlotte's trainees to start a class in London for girls and boys aged from seven to ten, which her own children attended.[14] In 1902 another class was started in London, which became a school in 1910; in 1906 two more schools were founded; and by 1908 there were thirty-seven schools functioning under Ambleside headmistresses. Meanwhile, a 'Practising School' had come into being in Ambleside itself, where trainees taught, at first local boys and girls attending daily, and from 1900 older boarding-school pupils.[15]

* * * * * *

Long after Charlotte's death, Netta recalled: 'Only that it sounds silly I would say that we fell in love with each other at first sight'.[16] Her introduction to the PNEU appears to have come through drawing-room meetings in London around 1890: 'I at once felt that the P.N.E.U. was the one "cause" which appealed to me. Though still a young woman I had married so early that I already had quite big children, and I felt sorry that I had known of this rather late'. At her first opportunity, she made a 'pilgrimage' to Ambleside.[17] Netta told her own biographer that 'Miss Mason did say quite often that with my arrival she had found her long-awaited and predestined "chela". If that was true on her side, it was still truer on mine. I had found the "guru", or sage and teacher, of whom I stood so much in need'.[18] The word 'guru' is very familiar to the twenty-first-century reader; 'chela', less so. According to the *Shorter Oxford Dictionary* this entered English usage around 1883, from the Hindi word for slave, or servant; 'in esoteric Buddhism, a novice'.

The choice of language on both sides is intriguing. The Jewish woman in her twenties had been brought up in the strictest Orthodoxy, which was broadly maintained in her own household. She had not yet entered on the path of questioning and reform which her younger sister would blaze at the start of the new century. The Christian woman, who had reached her fiftieth year, was embarking, alongside her educational mission, on a lifelong writing project of verse meditations on the life of Christ, resulting in a six-volume work, *The Saviour of the World*, published between 1908 and 1914. Neither felt completely at home in the religious traditions of her upbringing, which in Charlotte's case included some very mixed messages, and in both cases emphasised the need for a formal ritual obedience. Each, in her search for fundamental truths about the nature of human beings, acknowledged at some level a failure in Western culture and morality. Children were not learning awareness of self and others; the natural world was insufficiently nurtured and understood; personal peace and social harmony were lacking.

Netta was of course ignorant of the concealed and conflicted aspects of her friend's upbringing which Charlotte suppressed from public consumption. Had she known the facts she might not, in any case, have been particularly sensitive to the nuances of High and Low Anglicanism, Quakerism and Catholicism which directly and indirectly contributed to Charlotte's self-recreation. But she may have had some instinctive understanding of the internal struggles which had made it possible for her 'guru' to forge her individual path. Charlotte's friendship certainly enabled Netta to make spiritual sense of both private and public life in the modern world, and gave her, too, a calling which was to underlay almost all her activities. When Netta wrote: 'I was determined to learn all I could and to help others to avoid those first mistakes which so often mean tears and sorrow', she perhaps unconsciously mirrored Charlotte's own experience and sense of mission.[19]

Netta's marriage was for many years reportedly stormy. Her bond with her sisters was strong, and like Charlotte, she also placed great importance on female friendship. She evinced the capacity to inspire intense love and loyalty from an early age. Her biographer records that at Doreck College Netta had a crush on 'her headmistress's partner, who taught her Latin', and this evoked a response. Like her sister Lily, Netta was taken out of school at fifteen, but the relationship continued, and 'after I was married, when this *grande passion*, if it were a *grande passion*, had come to be more on her side than mine', the lady tried to give up her weekly tea with Netta for Lent—but failed.[20] There was certainly something of the *grande passion*, or something passionately spiritual, in this new relationship. In May 1897 Netta wrote to thank Charlotte for her love and friendship: 'I feel I have got nearer to you this time than ever & I miss you very much. ... I can dedicate to you a life of loving, humble service in your work & a constant prayer that I may become worthier of *you* & *it*'. Charlotte replied the next day:

> 'you will find me very exacting, ... in the way of having you ever more and more God-fulfilled, ever more and more of your best beautiful self. I could not let you be less than yourself. Happily you are like me, a woman lover and you have lovely friends and one at least who holds you very close, but will probably not tell you so again, but will expect you always to trust her'.[21]

It is well to remember the very high value placed on same-sex friendship—among men as well as women—in the Victorian period and among those born towards its end. These relationships were respected and celebrated in public and private. A post-Freudian perspective inclines modern readers to see all such relationships as sexually charged, and indeed, as such interpretations acquired currency in the 1920s and 1930s, men and women became more reticent about their sentiments and domestic arrangements.[22] Devoted attachments between teachers and pupils, or teacher-figures and younger friends, were a recognised aspect of the Victorian emotional landscape, very applicable in Netta's case; but equally important, as women strove for economic or intellectual independence, or both, was the collegial support and understanding of women who shared the same ideals and could collaborate in wholly original endeavours.[23] What is striking about Netta's friendships is the fact that, no matter how intense or romantic her feelings may have been, they were not maintained in opposition to her family networks and obligations. On the contrary: the PNEU and its passions were, as will be seen, both absorbed into her home life and allowed to absorb it in turn.

After their first meeting in 1891, Charlotte, whose nickname for Netta was 'Lady Augustus', came to stay at the Franklins' London home every year until 1914. Another close friend who emerged from the same milieu spent part of every summer with the Franklins until her death in 1926. This was Dr Helen Webb, whom Charlotte nicknamed 'B.P.'—Beloved

Physician—and Netta, more obscurely, 'Wai'. (Helen almost certainly saved Netta's life in 1909, overruling the characteristic stoicism with which Netta bore chronic leg pain, and insisting on a biopsy. This revealed a carcinoma requiring immediate amputation of the entire limb. For the next fifty-five years Netta depended on a prosthesis, maintaining all her commitments with seemingly undiminished energies.)[24]) Helen's life was intertwined with the Franklins in many ways. A Quaker, in 1914 she gave moral support and reasoned advice to Netta's son Geoffrey, who joined the Friends' War Victims Relief Committee in France for the duration.[25] She had a Quaker funeral; but Lily, at Helen's previous request, spoke at the graveside, using prayers translated from the Hebrew liturgy.[26] A few years later Michael, Netta's youngest child, gave his own daughter the names Angela Wai Netta.

Netta and Charlotte's relationship contained many 'agreements to differ'. Despite the value Charlotte placed on Helen as a medical woman, much in demand at PNEU meetings, she was not anxious to promote the higher education of women. Netta herself had been known to deplore the 'excessive cleverness' of some young women,[27] and it has proved surprisingly difficult to discover where her daughters were educated, if not merely at home:[28] but one daughter read for a degree at Girton, and another, as will be seen, qualified as a doctor. Charlotte was mistrustful of state intervention and professionalism alike, and disapproved when Netta, flatly stating 'I believe less than you in "parents"', attempted to keep Ambleside alumnae in touch with new educational developments;[29] and Netta, as we have seen, departed from Ambleside doctrine in setting up her own, more formal, 'primary school' in London. It has been argued that Charlotte's determination to strengthen the role of mothers as home educators was a form of feminism, but she was in fact largely unsympathetic to the organised women's movements of her day, whether expressed in the social initiatives of the National Union of Women Workers, or in the political demands of the suffrage campaign. Netta's public engagements were in such outright contradiction to these attitudes that the continuance of the friendship seems miraculous, but continue it did. 'Now please don't make me waste time in talking politics again!!' Charlotte wrote on the eve of Netta's departure for the conference of the International Council of Women at The Hague in May 1913. 'Of course I care and care intensely. Also of course, reasonable persons are not carried away by every wind of doctrine. Also of course you are a darling'.[30]

* * * * * *

Of all Netta's children, Michael was most often to be found at her side at PNEU gatherings, but each sibling experienced Charlotte's philosophy in action to a greater or lesser degree. After their London primary schooling on Ambleside lines, the boys (but not, curiously enough, the girls) were sent to board at the progressive co-educational Bedales School in Hampshire, rather against their father's wishes. Sydney and Cyril subsequently entered the family firm Samuel Montagu & Co., but Sydney's heart was in settlement and youth work in the East End, to which he gave lifelong service. Geoffrey also took up youth work between 1910 and 1914 in Birmingham, where he displayed great respect for the reasoning power of working-class boys and encouraged them to take their own decisions in group activities.[31] Olive might be thought the apple to have fallen the furthest from the PNEU tree: she told Netta's biographer that 'we really saw very little of our mother. The house was full of domestics and governesses and bosom friends and protegés, and we were quite a little jealous of them'. She joined the Communist Party in 1937 and became an object of suspicion to H.M. Government. It is interesting to note that amongst her other activities she became a member of the Council of King Alfred School, a progressive coeducational day school in London; perhaps, after all, something of the Mason legacy was retained.[32]

However, it was Netta's eldest daughter, Marjorie, whose upbringing bore the strongest imprint of Charlotte's theory and practice. In 1897, soon after her ninth birthday, she was sent to live for a few months with Charlotte in the Ambleside training school. Since Netta had, on setting up a PNEU primary school in London three years previously, voiced her objection to the custom of educating young boys away from their homes, this episode remains an enigma. Clearly, the Franklin household was experiencing difficulties with 'Madge', and Netta felt unable to cope. Exporting the problem did not, in the short term, give her peace of mind. 'Please get the little girl off your brain', Charlotte wrote at the beginning of March, 'her fault is comparatively venial'. Five days later she wrote urging Netta not to 'take up the burthen of the sweet girlie at present'. Later the same month she wrote 'It is unfair that one failing should be allowed to cloud so much beauty and nobleness of character; so please don't scold the childie nor your beloved self any more'.[33]

Charlotte's letter the next day, 28 March, offers more detail:

> We read your beautiful letter every 'Sabbath' and while I read, Girlie makes good resolutions all to her self. ... We behave perfectly at table, and here I think I may have a hint to offer: I never say do or don't, or take any notice at all of what goes on. Once we went without dinner and I took no notice ... We go on charmingly for a week or so, life seems so smooth that we think we are having it all our own way and try to have our own way about something not allowed. If I see what is coming, I change the child's thoughts and we have no trouble. If it is too late for that, I say, 'No' firmly, and a screaming fit follows ... and we take no notice ... This reduces us to great meekness, for days afterwards.[34]

Charlotte's methods were certainly an improvement on those recalled (perhaps losing nothing in the telling) by young Mary Arnold (better known as the novelist Mrs Humphry Ward), who forty years earlier was a boarding pupil at Anne Jemima Clough's school in Ambleside. Visiting that school in later life, she showed a friend 'the damaged panel which I bashed in with my fists in my fury when I was locked into the cloakroom for punishment', and we are left still wondering as to the possible sources of Mary's fury and Marjorie's screaming fits.[35] Charlotte wrote an article on 'Authority' for the *Parents' Review* later in 1897, having assured Netta in advance that '"Maud" in the article is *not* Madge, but is hundreds of children who labour under such conditions'. Following the maxim of believing nothing until it is officially denied, it may be worth quoting at length from the article:

> ... there are many children of thoughtful parents whose lives are spent in day-long efforts of decision upon matters which it is their parents' business to settle for them. Maude is nervous, excitable, has an over-active brain, is too highly organised, grows pale, acquires nervous tricks [*sic*]. ... the parents are slow to perceive that it is not the soothing routine of lessons which is exhausting the little girl, but the fact that she goes through the labour of decision twenty times a day, and not only that, but the added fatigue of a contest to get her own way. Every point in the day's routine is discussed, nothing comes with the comforting ease of a matter of course; the child always prefers to do something else and commonly does it. No wonder the poor little girl is worn out.

The article ended on a note of optimism: it might be too late to inculcate the beneficent habit of routine obedience, but 'it is a happy thing that the "difficult" children who are the readiest to resist a direct command are often the quickest to respond to the stimulus of an idea'.[36]

It is possible that the behaviour identified in 'Maud', and individuals like her, was the consequence of overzealous application of some of Charlotte's own ideas on the autonomy and personality of the child; and these are not issues which any parental generation can claim to have solved and laid to rest. Relations between Netta and Marjorie may have been problematic, but relations between mother and daughter on the one hand and Charlotte on the other remained excellent. When she was eighteen, Marjorie returned to Ambleside to train as a teacher. On Marjorie's twenty-first birthday, a familiar note sounded in one of Charlotte's letters: 'your dear daughter … is sweet! So don't tell me any more ever about your children being failures. And this is your achievement! All we have done is to give her room and work—So please, Ma'am do you also give her *room*—let her think her thoughts, say her says, read her books, *without criticism* to me or anyone'.[37]

Marjorie did not, in the end, become a teacher, choosing instead to retrain in medicine. She qualified as a doctor in 1916, and at the end of World War I travelled to New York to train in psychiatry under Adolf Meyer. After a few years working in mental hospitals in England, she left again to undertake analysis and training under Sandor Ferenczi in Budapest. In the late 1920s she helped establish the Institute for the Scientific Study and Treatment of Delinquency (later the Portman Clinic) in London, where her colleagues included Edward Glover, Grace Pailthorpe and Melitta Schmideberg, the daughter of Melanie Klein. Marjorie devoted her greatest energies to troubled young people, often from the least privileged classes in society, and was concerned to explore the impact on mental illness of the patient environment. Within her profession she is remembered for developing the therapeutic concept of 'Planned Environmental Therapy': the therapeutic communities she set up in the 1930s were known as 'Q camps' (where Q presumably stands for Quaker), and worked in conjunction with the British Friends' Penal Reform Committee. It seems fitting that her therapy should be described as 'based on establishing non-authoritarian, loving and accepting relationships'.[38]

* * * * * *

How did Netta's Judaism mesh with her engagement in the PNEU? No matter how eclectic her interests and circle of acquaintance, her core identity and kin were Anglo-Jewish, and from the turn of the century she was heavily involved with her sister Lily in the development of the new Liberal synagogue. These two public projects seem to have been completely compatible. Lily summed it up towards the end of their lives:

'[Netta's] chief concern in religion lies in making Judaism to be understood and fairly reverenced by society in general'.[39] The seed seemed to have been sown on remarkably favourable ground: Charlotte had, apparently, 'often said how glad she was that the Bishop of London (at whose house the P.N.E.U. was launched) had altered the word "Christian" to "religious" in the Constitution. "Otherwise," he had said, "you would never get Jewish members".—she would add with a smile, and what would have happened if I had never had you?'[40] Marjorie's periods of residence at Ambleside, first as a schoolgirl and later as a student, were marked by careful arrangements for her observance of the Jewish Sabbath, together with that of a German-Jewish member of staff, Fräulein Hamburger.[41] Charlotte's devotion to the person of Christ presented no obstacle to her affection for her Unitarian friend and the extended Franklin family: *'you know, dearest, how utterly [Christianity] includes and reverences you and all good and wise persons who have ever lived ... We are all one and there is no middle wall of partition'*.[42]

Toleration and respect were mutual. Charlotte, in referring Netta to a passage in her opus *The Saviour of the World*, felt confident enough to write 'I know you too receive Jesus as "a teacher sent from God" and that is all the argument requires'.[43] In the early 1900s Netta was closely involved in developing religious teaching for children within the new Liberal Jewish movement. She did not ask pupils to discuss the life of Jesus, but she did use, on Charlotte's recommendation, Canon Paterson Smyth's series *The Bible for the Young* as one of her first textbooks. Charlotte had praised this work for preparing young children 'not [to] be startled to be told that the world was not made in six days; and, at the same time, they will be very sure that the world was made by God'.[44] (The broad-mindedness and modernity of this approach might give pause for thought to some of the current generation of Charlotte Mason's Christian admirers.) In 1921 Netta and Lily were preparing their own textbook for publication. They discussed *Daily Readings from the Old Testament* with Charlotte, who approved their biblical commentaries, made suggestions for different topic headings, and confirmed that it would be placed on the PNEU curriculum.[45]

All this left Netta utterly unprepared for the changed atmosphere at the House of Education after Charlotte's death in 1923, when a more narrow definition of Christianity, and of the role of religion in education, emerged as predominant. Charlotte was succeeded as head of the House by Ellen Parish, who was appointed vice principal in 1921. It is not impossible that her 'chela' felt slight pangs of jealousy and unease at the prospect that this was the 'guru's' new anointed: Charlotte wrote many letters to Netta singing Ellen Parish's praises around this time.[46] For close to a decade, between 1907 and 1917, Ellen Parish had worked in London as an organising secretary under Netta's direction, but the collaboration seems not to have been an entirely happy one: she lacked Netta's flair for enthusing recruits to the cause, and may have resented her own lack of social status and influence compared to that of Netta, daughter of a peer and sister of a Cabinet minister.[47]

It is equally likely, of course, that Ellen Parish herself resented the very great place which Netta occupied in Charlotte's affections. Her own devotion to preserving Charlotte's legacy in aspic extended as far as 'lying on a sofa and dressing like her gracious predecessor',[48] and she had inherited both her teacher's mistrust of higher education and her resistance to Netta's drive to increase the centralisation of PNEU organisation from London. However, Netta can have had little inkling of any change in her relationship to the House of Education when in April 1927 she wrote to Miss Parish (whom she never addressed by her first, or any diminutive name) recommending Fanny Marofsky, a pupil of Christ's Hospital, Hertford, for training at Ambleside. 'She is, as you see, a Jewess. She is willing, if you wish her to do so, to attend Church. She did it at school, and as a matter of fact, came out top in Divinity, Old and New Testament, but you will remember that Miss Mason excused Madge from doing this as she felt, and you will probably do too, it is not well to have among the congregation a non-worshipper. Still, it is for you to decide'.[49]

The response was a categorical refusal on all fronts. There had, perhaps, been a warning sign given four years earlier in Ellen Parish's contribution to the Charlotte Mason memorial volume: she had focused at length on her predecessor's series *The Saviour of the World*, and attempted to root the PNEU motto in 'the study of the Life of Jesus'.[50] (This motto was, from a religious viewpoint, the studiedly neutral 'I am, I can, I ought, I will'.) Now, in her respective replies to Netta and the candidate, Ellen Parish stressed that she was being as considerate of the student's feelings as of her own scruples. 'Miss Marofsky would be conscious that she was unable to comprehend what we were after because the keynote would be missing. It would be entirely unfair to her'; 'you would soon find yourself perplexed and isolated'. What stung Netta particularly, in the letter addressed to her, was the assertion 'I think all my colleagues here would feel this but perhaps I do so specially because I take Miss Mason's books with the students and we see daily that her philosophy is Christian philosophy and can only be taught as such'.[51] 'How can Miss Parish write that last paragraph', she wrote the next day to Horace West Household, a sympathetic member of the PNEU Council, 'when I, a Jewess, have expounded Miss Mason's philosophy for thirty-five years, spending money and strength on doing so? I have masses of letters from Miss Mason to her "Chela" expressing satisfaction in my understanding of her philosophy'.[52]

Netta immediately set about having typed copies made of much of her correspondence with Charlotte, particularly those letters where reference was made to Judaism and to the possibility of taking PNEU methods into (non-Christian) schools in India. These she shared with Household, who as Secretary to the County Education Committee in Gloucestershire had played a great part in disseminating the movement's philosophy in locally maintained schools; he was also anxious, as was Netta, to bring more graduates into education, and into the PNEU. Together they presented their case to sympathetic Council members, who agreed that at the forthcoming Annual Meeting in July a resolution should be moved from the Chair 'that it be an instruction to the Principal that no applicant for admission shall be rejected merely on the ground of her religion provided that she is willing to take the complete course'.[53]

Netta felt hugely exposed as 'Executor, Trustee, and member of the Governing Body of a College which should close its doors to my co-religionists, almost unique in so doing among schools and colleges in the British Empire'.[54] It can only have added to the strain of the situation that she was in an even more prominent public position at the time: this was the second year of her term as President of the National Council of Women. She was only the second Jewish woman to hold this office, and needed at all times to maintain her public composure and powers of rational judgment. 'It is very unpleasant to have to write thus about oneself' she confided in Household, 'but I don't feel that in loyalty to my co-religionists I can sit down under what amounts to an insult'.[55] But it was, of course, as much an insult to herself as to the Jews: a negation of decades of love and work. Her own daughter's attendance at Scale How was described as 'an exception'. Members of staff and Council were clear that Netta could not, in fact, have absorbed 'Miss Mason's real teaching'.[56] Neither Charlotte nor 'Wai' was alive to bear witness on her behalf. Possibly the most important friendship of her life was being obliterated from her personal history, as well as from that of an institution, and she had to place the truth of her own experience on record.

Dignity and calm were indeed required to face considerable obtuseness and insensitivity. From the Ambleside office Elsie Kitching, close enough to Netta to employ a nickname, 'Kit-Kat', wrote: 'It *is* a difficult question but I am sure it must be faced without personal feelings by any of us'. Even an ally, the Reverend Dr Harold Costley-White, headmaster of Westminster, who thought that 'a religious-minded girl recommended by yourself is just the kind of exceptional individual whom the community could well accept with advantage', urged Netta to believe that 'Miss Parish never realised what pain she was giving'.[57] Ellen Parish wrote that 'the matter is not a personal one. Please keep this constantly in mind'.[58] Frances Gibson, a Council member who supported the exclusion, added the almost inevitable proviso that 'I honour & respect the Jews most sincerely & have friends among them'.[59]

Naturally Netta could open her heart to Lily, who considered the matter 'nothing less than disgraceful', and asked 'if you will see your way to make an unholy row about it?'[60] The meek ways of their Victorian predecessors were not for the Montagu sisters: there might be diplomatic manoeuvres, but there was to be no question of 'not making trouble'. Netta and Household lobbied the individual members of the Council; Ellen Parish, predictably, made her own démarches to them at the same time. The Annual Meeting was, according to Netta, 'of a most painful nature in as much as it seemed to lead to rather medieval, narrow, prejudiced views, and hard hits were given'. At least one member of 'the opposition' presented the issue as one of clashing personalities rather than principles. In the end, the threat of a split following the probable resignation of two senior figures seems to have concentrated the minds of the majority: ten members voted for the Chair's resolution, and five against, 'Kit-Kat' abstaining.[61] The meeting closed with a fulsome vote of thanks to Mrs Franklin proposed by Household;[62] and on 8 July Fanny Marofsky was invited to renew her application to the House of Education. Netta thought that she might decline, but in January 1929, after her protégée had put careful financial arrangements in place, she arrived in Ambleside.[63]

The correspondence over the issue in 1927 demonstrated—as had much material in the *Parents' Review* over the years—that many adherents of the movement were not greatly interested in sectarian approaches to education. Dr Telford Petrie, a Council member at the College of Technology in Manchester, wrote that 'Miss Parish is so deeply steeped in the *Christian* faith that she confuses that with Religion in the broader sense ... After all we are not a theological college and even Jesus Christ put little children before himself'. Amy Pennethorne, a House of Education alumna who was on the PNEU staff and spreading the word in South Africa at the time of the crisis, insisted that 'every place where men try to realize the fathership of God is holy ground & not merely our own altar'. However, she also described the previous twenty years at Ambleside, when Charlotte's bad health had limited her engagement with the outside world, as a time when a formulaic and ritualised approach to Christian observance had become prevalent. She recalled that 'every sort of Nonconformist has always been welcome at Ambleside so long as they outwardly conformed & went to the English Church; though I know some in my time who felt *very* bitterly about this obligation'. Her recollection evokes an atmosphere of defensiveness which permeated some Anglican circles post-1918,[64] and which Netta's sister Lily had begun to experience in her cross-denominational activities.[65] It also suggests that some of the older sectarian controversies and hierarchies died hard in women's organisations.

Surviving records do not reveal how far the Council minority may have resented the prominence of a Jewish woman in their affairs, and the active role taken by members of her family and community. (Even the legal incorporation of the PNEU in 1918 was undertaken by, amongst others, a firm of solicitors employing one of Ernest Franklin's nephews[66]). Certainly Netta's work for the movement continued unabated, and she gave enthusiastic support to the PNEU's new ventures, trying to gain more influence in university teacher-training colleges, and in 1929 setting up a boarding school, Overstone, in Northamptonshire for girls of secondary-school age (a Junior Department was added during World War II).[67] These developments were often divisive, though not on explicitly sectarian grounds. As late as 1933 Elsie Kitching considered that the need for boarding schools for girls would 'pass away with much of the present highly academic education for women—which has already not only failed of its purpose but has been a considerable hindrance to the true education of the country'. Four years later, Netta wrote to a colleague of 'the folly and narrow-mindedness, chiefly of Miss Parish, which has prevented our being one united whole'.[68]

The serpent had truly entered Eden, and taken up permanent residence. Hitherto Netta had functioned in a female social world which had appeared to facilitate conversations across the religious divide. For many Jewish women they were, however, often unequal, dependent upon a certain meekness passing for consent. Netta's intimate and spiritual relationship with Charlotte had perhaps been, in this context, exceptional; her sister Lily's interwar initiative for a more balanced dialogue was to enjoy only qualified success.[69] Within the PNEU and Ambleside, the assertion of Jewish equality and 'making trouble' in a national organisation involved bruising experiences for Netta, even though the ultimate outcome was satisfactory. She remained an unwavering guardian of Charlotte's heritage, and if she was disappointed by its uses and misuses, her misgivings were not made public at this time. Increasingly, they were being overshadowed by vastly more disturbing developments on the international stage. It is noteworthy, however, that the Marofsky affair was one chapter in Netta's life which, unlike her involvements in suffragism and pacifism, was considered worthy of inclusion in her authorised biography, which was published more than thirty years after the case was closed.

Notes

1. There is as yet no published history of the PNEU. All information presented in this chapter is gleaned from the primary and secondary sources cited.
2. Armitt Gallery, Ambleside, Charlotte Mason Archive (henceforth CMA), CMC 102B, letter of Netta Franklin to Miss Cholmondeley, n.d. [c. 1927].
3. Margaret A. Coombs, *Charlotte Mason: Hidden Heritage and Educational Influence* (Cambridge, Lutterworth Press, 2015), from which all biographical information is taken unless otherwise referenced.
4. See e.g., *The Times*, 17 January 1923; and F.C.A. Williams, contributing to *In Memoriam Charlotte M. Mason* (London, Parents' National Education Union, 1923) pp. 56–7. Miss Williams was a clergyman's daughter who trained at Bishop Otter under Charlotte, and was her Vice-Principal at Ambleside 1898–1921.
5. Coombs, *Charlotte Mason*, pp. 64–5. This was the Revd Joseph Baylee (1807–83), an enthusiastic sponsor of Anglican schooling.
6. Most elementary schoolteachers came from a lower social class and, as F.C.A. Williams writes, *In Memoriam*, p. 57, 'At that time there was a movement among earnest people to induce educated women of the professional classes to take up teaching in elementary schools, and in order to further the cause The Bishop Otter Memorial College at Chichester was set apart for training such women'.
7. Kitching, in *In Memoriam*, p. 124; Blanche Athena Clough, *Memoir of Anne Jemima Clough* (London, Edward Arnold, 1897), pp. 90–2, 101–02; Gill Sutherland, *Faith, Duty and the Power of Mind: the Cloughs and their Circle, 1820–1960* (Cambridge, Cambridge University Press, 2006), pp. 56, 60, 66, 195.; Essex Cholmondeley, *The Story of Charlotte Mason*

1842–1923 (London, Dent, 1960), pp. 5–6, 16–22, 32, 36–7 (this author spells Healey as Heelis).

8. Charlotte M. Mason, *Home Education* (London, Kegan Paul, 1886), p. 4; ten years after the event, she wrote: 'Lady Isabel Margesson and some other members of the Committee left us in June 1894 because we could not receive their amendment pledging us to the "new" education as it is set[*sic*] Pestalozzi, Herbert Spencer, Froebel and other educational philosophers.'; CMA Box CM 44 CMC 309, Charlotte Mason to Netta Franklin, 12 February 1904.
9. The Editor, 'Recollections of Miss Clough and her connexion with the P.N.E.U.', *Parents' Review* 8 (1897), pp. 51–6; Sutherland, *Faith, Duty*, pp. 31, 56.
10. Netta recalled 'She introduced me to the delights of open windows and fresh air and of the country even when it rains': 'H.F.' [Netta Franklin], contributing to *In Memoriam*, p. 31.
11. Charlotte M. Mason, Preface to the *'Home Education'* series, Vol II, *Parents and Children* (London, Kegan Paul, 1904), p. xvii: 'We should allow no separation to grow up between the intellectual and 'spiritual' life of children'. (This is the earliest dating I have been able to find for this particular quotation.)
12. Charlotte M. Mason, *Home Education* (1886), p. 14.
13. The same, p. 126.
14. *Parents' Review* 5 (1894–5), pp. 475–6.
15. Cholmondeley, *Charlotte Mason*, pp. 43, 93–4.
16. Monk Gibbon, *Netta* (London, Routledge and Kegan Paul, 1960), pp. 36–7.
17. *In Memoriam*, p. 31. Letters of Charlotte Mason to Netta Franklin in CMA PNEU Box II Envelope 22, 1 July and 26 December 1891, show that they were well acquainted by this date; Cholmondeley, *Charlotte Mason*, p. 52, is incorrect in dating their first meeting to early 1894.
18. Gibbon, *Netta*, p. 37.
19. *In Memoriam*, p. 31.
20. Gibbon, *Netta*, pp. 7, 12.
21. CMA, PNEU Box 2 Folder 12, Netta Franklin to Charlotte Mason, 30 May 1897; CMA, Box CM 44 CMC 309, Charlotte Mason to Netta Franklin, 31 May 1897.
22. See Stephanie Spencer, '"Knowledge as the Necessary Food of the Mind": Charlotte Mason's Philosophy of Education' in Jean Spence, Sarah Jane Aiston, Maureen M. Meikle, eds, *Women, Education, and Agency, 1600–2000* (London, Routledge, 2010), p. 110: 'Mrs Groveham a fellow student of Mason's destroyed all their letters and Elsie Kitching destroyed more personal papers after Mason's death. One is left wondering why'; and

compare Pat Jalland, ed., *Octavia Wilberforce: the Autobiography of a Pioneer Woman Doctor* (London, Cassell, 1989), ref 21, p. xxvi: 'Many years later, when Octavia gave Mabel Smith the Graylingwell letters [to Elizabeth Robins], she insisted the handwritten originals be destroyed after Mabel had typed copies omitting the affectionate endearments. Octavia hated the thought that readers might misinterpret the terms used'.
23. See also discussions on this topic in Sutherland, *Faith, Duty,* pp. 200–3; Mary Beard, *The Invention of Jane Harrison* (London and Cambridge, MA, Harvard University Press, 2000), pp. 82–3; Susan Pedersen, *Eleanor Rathbone and the Politics of Conscience* (London, New Haven, Yale University Press, 2004), pp. 163–175, explores these themes in the interwar context.
24. Gibbon, *Netta*, pp. 50, 91–5.
25. *Geoffrey Franklin. Born May 11th 1890. Died September 11th 1930.* [Memoirs and correspondence printed for private circulation] (1933), pp. 5, 12.
26. 'In Memoriam Helen Webb', *Parents' Review* 37.3 (March 1926), p. 160.
27. *Jewish Chronicle* (henceforth *JC*), 16 May 1902, p. 14.
28. *Girton College Register 1869–1946* (Cambridge, privately printed for Girton College, 1948), p. 223, entry for Olive Franklin, reads: '*Educ.* Priv. classes and sch. in London; family in Dresden'.
29. CMA, PNEU Box 2 Folder 12, Netta Franklin to Charlotte Mason, 7 March 1900.
30. CMA Box CM 44 CMC 309, Charlotte Mason to Netta Franklin, [n.d.] May 1913.
31. Gibbon, *Netta*, pp. 42–3, 115–16, 156–7; *Geoffrey Franklin*, pp. 44, 47, 65–7.
32. Gibbon, *Netta*, p. 52; *Girton College Register*, p. 223; *Oxford Dictionary of National Biography* (henceforth *ODNB*), entry on Eva Reckitt; TNA webpage, 'Security and Intelligence History, Your Guide to Resources', Reference: KV 2/1983 Description: Olive Netta PARSONS, alias FRANKLIN: British. PARSONS was suspected of secret work for the British Communist Party and the COMINTERN.
33. CMA Box CM 44 CMC 309, letters of Charlotte Mason to Netta Franklin 3 March, 8 March, 27 March 1897.
34. The same, Charlotte Mason to Netta Franklin, 28 March 1897.
35. John Sutherland, *Mrs. Humphry Ward: Eminent Victorian, Pre-eminent Edwardian* (Oxford, Clarendon Press, 1990), pp. 13–15.
36. CMA Box CM 44 CMC 309, Charlotte Mason to Netta Franklin, 19 April 1897; *Parents' Review* 8 (1897), pp. 328–30.
37. CMA Box CM 44 CMC 309, Charlotte Mason to Netta Franklin, 17 December 1908.

38. Gibbon, *Netta*, p. 157; W. David Wills, 'An Appreciation of Marjorie E Franklin', *Studies in Environment Therapy* (1968):1, pp. 5–6; http://www.quakersintheworld.org/quakers-in-action/182; http://www.psychoanalytikerinnen.de/greatbritain_biographies.html#Franklin.
39. Gibbon, *Netta*, p. 66.
40. The same, p. 43.
41. CMA Box CM 44 CMC 309, letters of Charlotte Mason to Netta Franklin, 20 February, 28 March 1897; CMA CMC 81, the same, n.d., c. 1905.
42. The same, [n.d.] July 1905.
43. CMA Box CM 44 CMC 309, Charlotte Mason to Netta Franklin, 12 June 1911.
44. Lawrence Rigal and Rosita Rosenberg, *Liberal Judaism: the First Hundred Years* (London, Union of Progressive and Liberal Synagogues, 2004), p. 31; Charlotte M. Mason, '*Home Education*' series, Vol. I, *Home Education* (London, Kegan Paul, 1905), pp. 251–2. *The Bible for the Young. A Series for Schools and Families*, was published by John Paterson Smyth between 1901 and 1908.
45. CMA PNEU Box II Envelope 22, letters of Charlotte Mason to Netta Franklin, 9 and 11 November 1921, and n.d.
46. CMA PNEU Box 2a Envelope 48, letters of Charlotte Mason to Netta Franklin, 1920.
47. Coombs, *Charlotte Mason*, pp. 225, 236.
48. The same, p. 256.
49. CMA CMC 81, Netta Franklin to Ellen Parish, 22 April 1927.
50. E.A. Parish, contributing to *In Memoriam*, p. 61.
51. CMA CMC 81, Ellen Parish to Netta Franklin, 26 April 1927; to Miss Marofsky, 26 April 1927.
52. The same, Netta Franklin to Horace West Household, 27 April 1927.
53. The same, typed copy of draft letter to Parish, n.d.
54. The same, Netta Franklin to Mrs Parsons, 3 May 1927.
55. The same, Netta Franklin to Horace West Household, 27 April 1927.
56. The same, Elsie Kitching to Netta Franklin, 'Private & unofficial', 28 April 1927; Frances Gibson to Horace West Household, 20 June 1927.
57. The same, Elsie Kitching to Netta Franklin, 'Private & unofficial', 28 April 1927; the same, H. Costley-White to Netta Franklin, 13 May 1927.
58. The same, Ellen Parish to Netta Franklin, 3 May 1927.
59. The same, Frances Gibson to Horace West Household, 20 June 1927.
60. The same, Lily Montagu to Netta Franklin, 27 April 1927.
61. The same, Netta Franklin to H. Costley-White, 5 July 1927; to Mrs Foster, 5 July 1927.
62. *Parents' Review* 38 (1927), p. 494.

63. CMA CMC 81, Horace West Household to Ellen Parish, 7 July 1927; Netta Franklin to Ellen Parish, 7 July 1927; Ellen Parish to Netta Franklin, 8 July 1927; Unsigned typescript, 22 May 1929. Fanny Marofsky was born in 1910 and it is thought that she travelled to Lisbon in 1933. In 1937, in London, she married a Robert A. Godby; she died in 1974. I am most grateful to Clifford Jones, an 'Old Blue' volunteer in the Christ's Hospital archives, for this information.
64. The same, Telford Petrie to Netta Franklin, 19 May 1927; Amy Pennethorne to Netta Franklin, 20 May 1927.
65. See Chap. 8.
66. CMA PNEU Box 22, Letter concerning PNEU incorporation from solicitors Tamplin, Tayler & Joseph, beginning 'Dear Aunt Netta', signed F.G. Joseph, 27 June 1918.
67. CMA CMC 266, Netta Franklin to Elsie Kitching, 22 November 1933; *Geoffrey Franklin*, p. 12; Cholmondeley, *Charlotte Mason*, p. 167.
68. CMA CMC 266, Elsie Kitching to Netta Franklin, 20 November 1933; PNEU Box 21, Netta Franklin to Lady Helen Cassel, 30 April 1937.
69. See Chap. 8.

PART III

Continuity and Change, 1920s–1940s

Reflections: The World Between Wars

The fact of Hitler's advent to power in Germany in the spring of 1933 opens new chapters in the history of every European country. One such concerns the history of relations between Jews and non-Jews in British civil society. It is a chapter mired in controversy, anger, accusations and above all—the source, indeed, of all—grief. British antisemitism is alleged to have been increasing between the wars. This, it is implied, is the reason that governments did not do enough to help Jews flee destruction in Nazi Germany and Austria; and a timid and deferential Anglo-Jewry is accused of not doing enough for them either. Government policies restricted the number of Jews admitted as refugees both to Britain and to Palestine, which Britain administered under the League of Nations mandate; Anglo-Jewry's leading figures were unable to put sufficient pressure on the Home Office and the Foreign and Colonial Offices to modify these policies. Historians are castigated for congratulating Britain on its generosity to the pitifully few refugees who were allowed entry visas.[1]

There is truth in all of the above, but there are also other truths which deserve to be told, and other perceptions which are equally valid. Looking at the period prior to the 1933 watershed, it can plausibly be argued that antisemitism was not increasing: relations between Jews and non-Jews were following a trajectory of greater integration, with a progressive assimilation of the minority within the host community.[2] Netta Franklin was deeply wounded by the antisemitic prejudice manifested at the P.N.E.U. training school in 1927, but the majority of the organisation supported her position. Her sister Lily's perception of an increase in antisemitism by 1943 may have reflected a widening of her social experience rather than an intensification of feeling within the milieux with which she was familiar in the early years of the century. Formal anti-alien discrimination—for example, within the sphere of local authority allocations of housing and grants for education—was perforce declining as more Jews were born and educated in Britain and the generation disqualified through foreign birth passed away: it has been ascertained, indeed, that by 1930 fewer than 30 % of East End Jews were foreign-born.[3]

Moving wholly into the counterfactual realm, if the world had not been engulfed in economic depression—in particular, if the Great Crash of 1929 had not wrecked promising international efforts to stabilise the German economy—relative prosperity at home and the absence of external threats would have reinforced improvements in social relationships. Moreover, if the monstrous calumnies and atrocious violence of the German National Socialists had not been so openly legitimated by the German sovereign state, British antisemitism might never have been emboldened to develop its organised, uniformed incarnation under the leadership of fascists such as Oswald Mosley. Germany's example suggested that it could be legal and indeed respectable to injure and libel neighbours and fellow citizens, just as Italy in the 1920s had encouraged many to think that modern societies could be run more efficiently without democratic political institutions.

Antisemitism was not, however, always the most important factor in fascism's appeal. Looking at one subset of recruits, the small number of former suffragettes active in interwar extreme-right groups, one can surmise that, like many of their male counterparts, they were reacting to a postwar world which for them had become unrecognisable.[4] It wasn't Jews but flappers that so upset Mary Allen, the pioneer of women police forces in Britain who became an admirer of Hitler and joined the British Union of Fascists (BUF). Her publications of the 1930s rail against youthful materialism, birth control, nudism, the cinema and Bolshevism, and hardly mention the Jews. Similarly, BUF member Yolande McShane thought Mosley's antisemitism not 'very important, compared with the promise of "equal opportunities for all"'.[5] Organisations like these offered a framework for broader anxieties, and their rhetoric was adopted without necessarily having been fundamental in these female recruits' personal formation. It is interesting to note that the suffragette Flora Drummond, whose unpleasant remarks about Herbert Samuel have been noted in Chap. 5, established the Women's Guild of Empire after World War I, but actually opposed the BUF in London County Council Elections in 1937.[6]

Any discussion of this topic returns us to the issue of the subjectivity which inflects our selection of evidence and our judgement of what we see and read. As the historian Laura Tabili has written, with reference to German and Scandinavian migrants to the north-east of Britain, 'Notorious episodes of conflict continue to capture scholars' imagination, to the neglect of community formation and internal dynamics, or even daily interactions between migrants and natives'.[7] Violent scenes and hateful remarks do not necessarily reveal the 'true' character of a society; they need not be considered more representative than periods of peaceful coexistence. The evidence available for making such assessments is, undoubtedly, perplexing and equivocal. The famous 'battle of Cable Street' of 1936 can be taken to represent a general East End solidarity in the face of native fascism or, more exclusively, the principled stand of a significant minority who were politically organised on the left at that time; and it has, indeed, been ascertained that BUF membership actually increased in the East End following the affair.[8] In a retrospect of the decade 1920–30, the East End social worker Edith Ramsay saw her own cordial relationships with the councillor Ida Samuel and the doctor Hannah Billig mirrored in good feeling between Jewish and Catholic neighbours: 'Never once did I hear … a criticism on racial grounds'. But in 1940 she was writing that her job as principal of a women's evening institute was 'dominated by antagonisms between my Jewish and non-Jewish members, stirred up by Mosley propaganda'.[9] Her biography suggests that harsher times, and unemployment among the young, hardened at least some hearts over that decade.[10]

Not the least of the benefits of exploring this period through the prism of some women's organisations and friendships is that of gaining the perspective of 'ordinary' citizens, or at least those not striving to follow any particular 'party line', on the events of the times. It enables us to escape some of the historical traps set for us by hindsight. Our own retrospect, inevitably dominated by personal, familial or national memories of World War II, can make it hard to understand why everyone did not see the threat posed by Nazism to Jews, Christians and the peace of Europe. The minutes of voluntary organisations remind us that public-spirited adults were faced with wholly new dilemmas; could war really be averted by supporting disarmament under the aegis of the League of Nations? Would it strengthen or weaken the cause of peace if the Communist Party were to play a leading role in arousing public opinion? Was it more important to boycott Germany or Japan, to succour the children of German Jews or the children of Spanish Republicans? Opinion within many organised feminist groups ranged widely, from seeing Nazism principally as a defeat for the German women's movement, to a continuing commitment to pacifism which overrode all other considerations in world politics.[11] And as women's committees up and down the land pondered these questions, there was always someone insisting on keeping the possible cruelty to imported tortoises on the monthly agenda.[12]

The way Jewish and Christian women dealt, together and separately, with the growing crisis is approached here through narratives illustrating the continuities and discontinuities between their pre- and post-1914 concerns. The 1930s are not treated as an entirely distinct era of national life. Tabili's claim for the study of 'even daily interactions' is validated by an approach which is chronological as well as thematic: we are able to see individuals reacting to events as they unfold, and it is my hope that this will help us to avoid prejudging their motives. Some patterns of action can of course be distinguished and traced through these decades. It was inevitable that, with the historical exception of members of the Society of Friends, women in the Jewish community would react more immediately to the rise of Nazism than their Christian colleagues, and that their energies would begin to be channelled into organisations set up to deal with the new emergency. But even as some forms of cooperation decayed, new bridges and new identities were being built. One historian, indeed, concludes that 'by late 1939, the Jewish identity of the refugee organisations had become diluted and Anglicized' and that 'through its work for the refugees the Jewish community also contributed to its own assimilation'.[13] These are not conclusions supported by the following chapters, from which a more nuanced picture of 'living with difference' emerges.

NOTES

1. For a recent restatement of some of these views see Geoffrey Alderman, *British Jewry since Emancipation* (Buckingham, University of Buckingham Press, 2014), pp. 273–80, 284–7. Further bibliographical references are to be found in Chap. 10.
2. The difficulty of characterising social relations in this period is evidenced in a recent major work, Anthony Julius's *Trials of the Diaspora: a History of Anti-Semitism in England* (Oxford, Oxford University Press, 2010). It is stated, p. 305: 'By the mid-1920s, the purchase that the notion of an international Jewish conspiracy had on the public mind weakened, and these committed, preoccupied anti-Semites were forced to resume their practice of talking mostly to themselves and to each other'; but he then adds that because of 'the open channels between the fascist and Conservative Right … "the everyday kind" [of anti-Semitism] … was also somewhat sharper, and more menacing in its implications, than in previous decades'.
3. Tony Kushner, 'Jew and Non-Jew in the East End of London: Towards an Anthropology of "Everyday" Relations' in Geoffrey Alderman and Colin Holmes. eds, *Outsiders and Outcasts: Essays in Honour of William J. Fishman* (London, Duckworth, 1993), p. 51, reference 52.
4. Julie V. Gottlieb, *Feminine Fascism: Women in Britain's Fascist Movement 1923–1945* (London, I.B. Tauris, 2000). See also the following essays in Tony Kushner and Kenneth Lunn, eds, *The Politics of Marginality: Race, the Radical Right And Minorities In Twentieth Century Britain* (London, Cass, 1990): Martin Durham, 'Women and the British Union of Fascists, 1932–1940'; Julie Wheelwright, '"Colonel" Barker: a Case Study in the

Contradictions of Fascism'; Tony Kushner, 'Politics and Race, Gender and Class: Refugees, Fascists and Domestic Service in Britain, 1933–1940'.
5. Mary Sophia Allen and Julie Helen Heyneman, *Woman at the Crossroads* (London, Unicorn Press, 1934); Mary S. Allen, *Lady in Blue* (London, Stanley Paul, 1936). Yolande McShane is quoted by Julie V. Gottlieb, 'Women and Fascism in the East End' in Kushner and Valman, eds, *Remembering Cable Street: Fascism and Anti-fascism in British Society* (London, Vallentine Mitchell, 2000) p. 39. Gottlieb's essay does, however, cite many overt expressions of antisemitism by female fascists.
6. Gottlieb, *Feminine Fascism*, pp. 169–70.
7. Laura Tabili, *Global Migrants, Local Culture: Natives and Newcomers in Provincial England, 1841–1939* (Basingstoke, Palgrave Macmillan, 2011), p. 6.
8. Thomas P. Linehan, 'Fascist Perceptions of Cable Street' in Kushner and Valman, *Remembering Cable Street*, p. 23.
9. Tower Hamlets Archives, Edith Ramsay papers, P/RAM/5/9, 'Life in Stepney 1920–1930' (typescript, 1980), pp. 1, 4, 5; University of Southampton Library (henceforth USL) MS 60, 18/1/9, Edith Ramsay to James Parkes, 8 March 1940. Edith Ramsay was the daughter of the Revd Alexander Ramsay of the Presbyterian Church of England; he was a member of the Society of Jews and Christians, discussed in the next chapter.
10. Bertha Sokoloff, *Edith and Stepney: The Life of Edith Ramsay* (London, Stepney Books, 1987), pp. 79–80. For a discussion of differing memories of the East End in the 1920s and subsequently, see Kushner, 'Jew and Non-Jew', pp. 42–4.
11. Julie V. Gottlieb, 'Varieties of Feminist Responses to Fascism in inter-war Britain' in N. Copsey, and A. Olechnowicz, eds, *Varieties of Anti-fascism: Britain in the Inter-war Period* (Basingstoke, Palgrave Macmillan, 2010).
12. See, e.g. London Metropolitan Archives (henceforth LMA) ACC/3613/01/012, Minutes of the National Council of Women Executive Committee, 1938–40 *passim*.
13. Louise London, 'Jewish Refugees, Anglo-Jewry and British Government Policy 1930–40' in David Cesarani, ed., *The Making of Modern Anglo-Jewry* (Oxford, Blackwell, 1990) pp. 189–90.

CHAPTER 8

False Start or Brave Beginning? Lily Montagu and Interfaith Initiatives

As has been seen, the religious suffrage leagues were short-lived, as the demand for the vote was suspended in 1914; but something of their ethos could be felt in interfaith initiatives emerging soon after the war, when pacifism replaced suffragism as a unifying focus. Lily Montagu, Netta Franklin, Ethel Behrens, Edith Ayrton Zangwill and other members of the Jewish League for Woman Suffrage (JLWS) had become part of a wider national campaign for peace as early as June 1914, when they helped to found the Jewish Peace Society (JPS). Within weeks, fearing accusations of disloyalty to their host community, they felt compelled to declare their conviction that the military triumph of the British Empire over German aggression would make the world a better place. In 1916 they were, indeed responsible for a bitter disagreement within the National Peace Council, founded over a decade previously; when Ethel Behrens proposed a resolution declaring the war a 'righteous' one, the resolution was blocked and several member organisations subsequently withdrew from the Council.[1]

The JPS remained, nevertheless, fully part of the national peace movement, with Lily in particular being forthright in support of conscientious objection to military conscription. Remarkably, by the end of the war its President was the Chief Rabbi, Dr Joseph Hertz (he was also a Vice President of the National Peace Council) while the Vice Presidents of the JPS included, in Lily and Netta, two pillars of the Liberal Synagogue, with the Committee containing suffragist ministers inclined to the progressive

© The Author(s) 2017
A. Summers, *Christian and Jewish Women in Britain, 1880–1940*,
Palgrave Critical Studies of Antisemitism and Racism,
DOI 10.1007/978-3-319-42150-6_8

wing of Judaism, to all of which Hertz's Orthodoxy was implacably opposed. In November 1918 the JPS proposed 'a League of Religions for the promotion of world peace'. This was taken up at a conference of the National Peace Council in May 1919.[2] The League was formed under JPS auspices in November 1919.[3] Among its supporters were the Bishop of Southwark, the Dean of Durham and the Master of Balliol College, Oxford.[4] By 1922 this League had been subsumed into the Religions and Ethics Committee of the League of Nations Union,[5] but the JPS and a plethora of individual Christian and secular peace societies survived, supportive of the League of Nations and increasingly vocal on issues of disarmament and arbitration.

With hindsight, the 1919 peace movement may have been a high-water mark for interfaith collaboration before World War II, involving as it did leading figures within almost all strands of the Jewish and church communities. To many in Anglo-Jewry, this apparent continuity between pre- and postwar interfaith activity demonstrated a growing national acceptance of, and respect for, the traditions, teachings and congregations of British Judaism. There were, however, indications that, while Christians might on occasion respond to Jewish initiatives, parity of esteem was more apparent than real; or, at least, somewhat ad hoc and instrumental. This was of particular concern to the Liberal Jewish movement with whose fortunes Lily Montagu was so deeply concerned. In an anonymous editorial, with which she would certainly have sympathised, the *Bulletin* of the progressively oriented Jewish Religious Union noted at the beginning of 1918:

> By Royal Proclamation, a Day of National Prayer will be observed in the Churches on January 6th; the Synagogues, we presume, will have the Service on the preceding Saturday. We may be permitted to say, in passing, how much we wish the proclamation had made mention of the Jews and called upon them to join in prayer for the nation in their Synagogues on their Sabbath. That to us would have meant more than the declaration in favour of a Jewish state in Palestine. It would have shewn that our religion is accepted as one of the facts and influences in the life of the nation.[6]

The writer was, presumably, unaware that a day of prayer for 'the clearsightedness and strength necessary to the victory of our cause' had been proclaimed to forestall a less politic request for one commemorating the 400th anniversary of the Protestant Reformation. It had nothing to do with either the British army's occupation of Jerusalem or the Balfour Declaration concerning a national home for the Jewish people. Moreover, the Chief Rabbi's signature was among those appealing for the proceeds of collections on that particular date to be donated to the Red Cross and the Order of St John;[7] and the holding of synagogue services in sympathy with the royal proclamation was subsequently reported in the national press.

While orthodox Jewish congregations received some official recognition through the institution of the United Synagogue of Great Britain and the Empire and the representative figure of its Chief Rabbi, progressive Judaism in Britain was a little-known and relatively tiny sect. Liberal Judaism was not yet a ten years' growth in Britain, and its expectations were unrealistic. However, its willingness to adapt to British society through experiment with non-Jewish forms of worship and practice made it particularly sensitive on the subject of its standing within the host community. A decade later, the *Bulletin* again proclaimed its aspiration, which, as this chapter will show, was unlikely to be fulfilled:

> The 'Times' review of the year devotes two columns to religion. Three quarters of this space is given to the Church of England; half a column to Non-conformity, Roman Catholicism, and all other religions. … Islam and Buddhism get a small paragraph between them; Judaism not even a sentence. … It all shows another part of the task of the Liberal Jewish movement—to give Judaism a place of influence in the national life.[8]

There was at least one occasion in the 1920s when these particular concerns of Liberal Judaism were shared and articulated in the wider Jewish community. This was in April 1924, when a Christian organisation subsequently known as COPEC—the Conference on Politics, Economics and Citizenship—held its first conference. Jewish observers may have been unaware that COPEC was born out of a new postwar spirit of dissension within the established church. Striving to apply in peacetime the lessons learned in the hard school of battlefield chaplaincy, many Anglican clergy wished to extend wartime cross-denominational collaboration, develop greater outreach to the urban working classes, and promote the ideas of such prewar organisations as the Christian Social Union on intervention in the nation's social and economic life. This was sufficiently controversial to move the Archbishop of Canterbury, as head of the Church of England, to refuse the conference his official sanction.[9]

What the Jewish community saw, however, was that, like the prewar religious suffrage leagues and the ongoing religious peace movement—with whom COPEC shared several members—this new movement wished to develop and assert religious responses to social problems; but unlike its predecessors, this ecumenical grouping did not invite Jewish membership. Both traditional and progressive wings of Anglo-Jewry felt the snub, and were vocal in their disappointment. Passover sermons alluding to their exclusion were given by two orthodox ministers, the Reverend Livingstone at Dennington Park Road Synagogue, London, and Rabbi Dr Salomon of the Great Synagogue, Manchester. The Dean of Manchester, the Very Reverend Joseph Gough McCormick, delivered a sermon in riposte: there was nothing to stop Jews organising a conference of their own, he said, and they would surely have something to contribute on the subject of economics. Less tartly, he stated that after the Jewish community had done so, 'it may be that we shall discover much common ground, and may even be able to proceed to common action'.[10]

It was Liberal Judaism which accepted McCormick's challenge, by founding the organisation which became known as the Society of Jews and Christians. As Lily was to write in 1927 to her old friend Ramsay, 'We found it necessary to start these conferences because our people could not join the C.O.P.E.C., as the basis of that organisation is definitely denominational.' Many years later, the memory was still strong: 'The Society was in a measure called into being because organisations, established to raise the standard of English citizenship by harmonising civic with religious ideas, were based on definitely Christian conceptions, and therefore could not admit the co-operation of Jews'.[11]

Lily may have felt a particularly personal sense of exclusion from the COPEC of 1924, because a significant number of close pre-1914 Christian colleagues were actively involved: these included Mrs Arnold Glover, active in the Girls' Clubs movement, Mrs Dorothy Wise, a member of the Church League for Woman Suffrage, and Constance Smith of the National Union of Women Workers and the Women's Industrial Council, who had collaborated with Lily in investigations into women's employment.[12] Lily later succeeded in getting several of these women to participate in the Society and its conferences, but her principal colleagues in her new endeavour—originally known as 'the Interdenominational Conference Committee'—were initially a Mrs Irene McArthur of St John's Wood Liberal Synagogue's Social Service Committee and the Liberal Rabbi Israel Mattuck.[13] The original suggestion to hold a conference is attributed to Mrs McArthur, and it took place in November 1924, on the topic of 'Religion as an Educational Force'—a choice of subject reflecting Montagu's own social work experience, and a relatively uncontroversial one with which to launch a potentially controversial endeavour.[14] 'The Society of Jews and Christians' was formally constituted in 1927, with sixty-two Christian and forty-two Jewish members. Within two years membership had reached 250.[15]

Over time Lily succeeded in bringing a formidable cohort of women into the organisation, as committee members or conference participants. The contacts from her prewar activities in social work, Liberal politics and the women's movement included Constance Smith; municipal councillors such as Ida Samuel, Miriam Moses and Nettie Adler; her sister Netta, at the height of her activity in the National Council of Women and the Parents' National Education Union; Clara Collet, an employment expert at the Board of Trade; and Maude Royden, a Christian thinker and activist who had been a leading figure in both the religious and the secular suffrage movements. In 1929 the Society constituted an additional Advisory Council of notable figures, to meet annually; by the early 1930s the non-Jewish women on this Council included Royden, Ishbel Lady Aberdeen (President of the National Council of Women and of the Parents' National Education Union), and Dame Elizabeth Cadbury, the Quaker philanthropist who shared Lily's concerns with girls' clubs, the National Council of Women and the magistracy.[16]

The Society kept in touch with other sympathetic groups bringing Christians and Jews together, such as those assembled by Nettie Adler to improve communal relations in Clapton and Stoke Newington. It responded to requests for speakers on Jewish religious subjects from groups of young Christians and of Free Church ministers. Although predominantly London-based, it was always looking to extend its reach, and had over thirty provincial members by 1930. Activities were promoted in Stoke-on-Trent, Brighton, Bristol and Leeds; however, provincial branches as such did not materialise as hoped.[17] We cannot know, of course, how greatly these activities contributed to understanding between communities. A certain degree of enlightenment might be expected given that, as a Christian member of the Society, a Miss Lorel Goodfellow, observed in 1933, 'many Christians had never met a Jew'. However, some hint of the challenges speakers had to meet is conveyed in Lily's rueful reminiscence: 'I remember once giving an address on the teaching of Liberal Judaism to a Church Society, and being asked at the close: "Why, with all those fine doctrines, are Jews always twisters?" I had to explain that here and there Jews were at fault, not Judaism'.[18]

Throughout this time, Lily was navigating between Scylla and Charybdis. From the start the bulk of the mainstream Jewish community was unremittingly hostile to the Society. The *Jewish Chronicle* gleefully reported after the first conference that Mrs McArthur was a recent convert from Christianity to Liberal Judaism; that an invited participant was the conversionist Father Day, of the Catholic Guild of Israel; that 'A Voice' had interpolated 'Get rid of the Alien' to a response of 'Laughter'; and that the conference commenced and concluded with the singing of (non-Trinitarian) Anglican hymns.[19] The Jewish organisers were accused, at best, of naïveté and of a snobbish disdain for the company of their coreligionists; at worst, of wanting to destroy Jewish identity by assimilationist practices and flirting with conversionists. These were already standard polemics against Liberal Judaism, which can only have been reinforced by such episodes as Mrs McArthur's suggestion that the Liberal Synagogue should use Kipling's 'Recessional' as a hymn, but that the author should be asked to offer replacement lines for 'Such boastings as the Gentiles use, / And lesser breeds without the law'.[20] There were orthodox Jews, such as Nettie Adler and Hannah Hyam, who supported Lily's interfaith work as individuals; but collectively, the Society was largely shunned.

In 1933 the Society's social and theological concerns had to take on the added dimension of foreign policy. The executive sent to the German embassy and leading dailies a resolution passed at a public meeting deploring the situation of Jews in Germany, which was published in the *Manchester Guardian*;[21] the following year a letter to the *Times* appealed for 'those many Christians who have shown sympathy in one way or another with the sufferings of the Jewish community of Germany' to join the Society.[22] No specific practical measures were being urged in respect of German Jews at this stage, as the issue of large-scale refugee migration had not yet arisen. However, these interventions produced many letters of support and expressions of sympathy, prompting a renewed attempt to found more branches in the provinces.[23] At the same time, the Society took up the JRU's suggestion to contact church leaders and Sunday school teachers concerning the portrayal of the Crucifixion. After circularising a number of clergy, invitations to address meetings, held mainly in London and the home counties, were received from Anglican, Congregational, Baptist and Free Church ministers, the YWCA and the Dean of Gonville and Caius College, Cambridge.[24] Even if, as Lily Montagu had found, such engagements could elicit disobliging responses, these letters and invitations were a heartening sign of progress.

The letter to the *Times* had stressed that Society 'expressly excludes any attempt at proselytizing; nor is it the intention of members to promote a common religion'.[25] Here the Society was alluding to a very sore point. Its formal constitution explicitly forbade members to proselytise, but there were repeated attempts to do so. If Father Day was the first conversionist to see an interfaith conference as an opportunity, he was not the last. The Anglican Vicar of Holy Trinity Shoreditch, Reverend Paul Levertoff, attended the 1925 conference and spoke from the floor, despite being known to preside over a conversionist 'Jewish Christian Union'.[26] In 1928 a Mr MacGregor 'distributed cards of invitation of a missionary nature' at one of the Society's meetings; being advised that he appeared 'to have misunderstood the purpose of the Society to which he must conform in letter and in spirit', he and his wife resigned.[27] Early in 1933, when the Baptist Union's new representative wrote that 'as Chair and Treasurer of one of the Baptist Jewish Missionary Societies, he felt that his presence on the committee might not be acceptable', the Committee, gratefully, agreed.[28]

Missions to the Jews may not have been high on the priorities of the churches of interwar Britain,[29] but the Society acted as a magnet to those still committed to the cause. Several strands within the churches considered these missions more urgent than those directed at other unbelievers: Jews had to be brought to see that Christianity was the fulfilment of the Jewish covenant, and that theirs was the husk of an outworn creed; this might even be the precondition of the Second Coming. While there were many sectarian differences of emphasis, as late as 1942 the Archbishop of Canterbury reiterated that the conversion of the Jews was a fundamental Christian obligation.[30] The currency of this obligation is indicated in a letter of Jean Miller, Secretary of the Auxiliary Movement (the extension of the Student Christian Movement), which was affiliated to the Society, writing in 1928 to a Miss Marshall of the Church Mission to the Jews: 'our Jewish friends ... fully realise that we are still free to carry on missions among Jews even while we undertake not to use the Society ... for any kind of missionary work'.[31]

By 1934 Israel Mattuck had as good as thrown in the towel. He wrote to a fellow committee member, the Anglican Reverend James Parkes,— who did not accept his argument—that although the Society offered no platform for proselytisation, given that 'Christianity considers missions essential to its practice ... if we were to adopt an attitude of hostility to missionary work, the position of some of the Christians on our Committee would probably become difficult'.[32] In 1942, the Society actually accepted onto its Executive a member of the British Society for the Propagation of the Gospel among the Jews.[33] This level of compromise fell far short of the status of civic and spiritual parity that Liberal Jews had been seeking from the host society since 1917. A community willing to be regarded as merely Christians-in-waiting could hardly expect 'a place of influence in the national life'. One wonders what Lily Montagu and Israel Mattuck would have made of a private communication from a member of the Society's Advisory Council, Reverend A. Herbert Gray, to his fellow Christian James Parkes. Gray revealed a remarkable indifference to the aims of the Society's Jewish founders, writing that 'When all repression ceases and education is really offered to them all will not Judaism certainly die? And when it is dead will not a very large degree of assimilation be possible?'[34]

If the friendship of conversionist members of the Society might be considered at the very least double-edged, worse was to come as the international situation deteriorated. Former colleagues in the peace movement such as Maude Royden at first appeared to share the anxieties of the Anglo-Jewish community over events in Germany. But often such colleagues perceived Jews principally as the source of potential conflict in the Middle East. Some pacifists found reasons to blame Jews (and even the British government) for the rise of antisemitism on the Continent.[35] While large numbers of churchmen and -women denounced Nazism, many pacifists succumbed to the anti-war agitation of Nazi sympathisers. In July and August 1939 as the writer Ethel Mannin (a former analysand of the Jewish psychologist and Zionist David Eder, and now closely linked to the Quaker community), spoke in *Peace News* of 'world Jewry's' campaign to get support for an anti-Nazi war.[36] The previous spring John Beckett, latterly of the No More War movement, had founded the British Peace Party, pointedly 'open to all adults of British descent'.[37] Its Council included Royden, who was still a member of the Advisory Council of the Society. The British Peace Party announced a campaign against 'war and usury'—the latter term a familiar synonym for 'Jewry'. It established the British Council for a Christian Settlement in Europe: a spokesman, only recently associated with the Society of Friends, endorsed Hitler's right to invade Poland.[38] Royden signed this Council's request to the government to participate in peace negotiations, as did Ruth Fry, a well-known Quaker and supporter of interfaith activity.[39]

Perhaps we should not be surprised that biographical writings by or about Lily and Netta carry no trace of their involvement in the peace movement. It had not, after all, been any kind of a success in their lifetimes; and it had latterly brought them up hard against the limits of non-Jewish sympathy for Jews. It is a little more surprising that neither they nor any other participants placed on record the pioneering work of the Society of Jews and Christians. Its membership rose as events abroad took on a more terrifying aspect;[40] and one of its members, James Parkes, was inspired to take the Society's work to a higher level. Parkes had long been developing a radical theology of the relationship between Christianity and its parent faith. He believed that it was no part of God's plan that Judaism should 'certainly die'. From an early stage he had seen the threat that Nazism posed to Christianity as well as to the Jewish community, and his strenuous lobbying over many years within the established church hierarchy ultimately made it possible for the leadership of all Jewish and Christian denominations to commit in 1942 to a stronger and more equal form of interfaith partnership in the Council of Christians and Jews (CCJ).[41]

The level of spiritual equality initially achieved should not be exaggerated; Parkes's theology on its own could not prevail against the longevity of the conversionist persuasion. His colleague the Reverend William Wynn Simpson later recalled the difficulty of negotiating in the early days 'between Jewish friends who feared that the organization was merely a veiled form of proselytizing and Christian friends who were afraid it was not!' As late as 1947 he was attempting to recruit the Church Mission to the Jews to the CCJ by claiming that it had never been proposed 'either to oppose missionary activity or to place any sort of condition in this respect on members of the Council in connection with any activities with which they may be engaged outside those specifically connected with the Council'.[42]

The formation of the Council of Christians and Jews was not a foregone conclusion, but it has survived to this day. The Society gave up its ambition to become a national organisation, and now functions as the London Society of Jews and Christians.[43] There was perhaps considerable chagrin for Lily in the recollection that the orthodox Jewish community, ever aloof from a Society originating in the Liberal Synagogue, was (with, admittedly, much hesitation) willing to accept the overtures, orchestrated by Parkes, of the Archbishop of Canterbury. Liberal Judaism's vanguard role counted for very little in conversations between the big battalions; and that Parkes's initiative came to fruition at all depended heavily on its being launched from within the established church. Moreover, it may not have been entirely by chance that a Society of 'Jews and Christians' was replaced by one for 'Christians and Jews'. The sequence of words had significance. Jewish hopes notwithstanding, relations between a majority and a minority faith could never be wholly equal. The philosemitism which these organisations had, on one side at least, hoped to engender, remained for some time of a highly equivocal character.

If Jews and Christians could not be religious equals, nor could men and women. The official hierarchies of Jewish and Christian congregations during this period were, of course, overwhelmingly masculine. If the Society's origins in Liberal Judaism weakened its position nationally, the fact that women were so strongly represented in its membership ensured that it would lack the prestige of its successor body. The Society was not only superseded but, as the feminist catchphrase has it, 'Hidden from History'.[44] Parkes's autobiography, in which the Council for Christians and Jews figures largely, contains no reference to the Society and very few to female colleagues: none at all to Lily Montagu, who had died six years before the autobiography was published. The Society did not wholly live up to Lily's expectations, and in many cases must have disappointed them bitterly. Her reticence on the subject of her own contribution may be understandable. It is easier, certainly, to understand than Parkes's signal failure to acknowledge her pioneering role.

Notes

1. Ruth Abrams, *Jewish Women and the International Woman Suffrage Alliance 1899–1926* (Ph.D., Brandeis University, 1996), pp. 183–4, 186; Martin Ceadel, *Semi-detached Idealists: the British Peace Movement and International Relations, 1854–1945* (Oxford and New York, Oxford University Press, 2000), p. 197.
2. *Jewish Chronicle* (henceforth *JC*), 29 November 1918, p. 20, letter of Ethel Behrens; Ceadel, *Semi-detached*, p. 197; *Manchester Guardian*, 17 May 1919, p. 10.
3. London Metropolitan Archives (henceforth LMA) ACC/3121/E1/54, Jewish Peace Society, *Report 1919–1922*; however, Revd J. Tyssul Davis, *A League of Religions* (London, Lindsey Press, 1927), p. 121, refers to a 'Presiding Bishop'.
4. *Manchester Guardian*, 17 May 1919, p. 10.

5. LMA ACC/3121/E1/54, Jewish Peace Society, *Report;* Tyssul Davis, *A League*, p. 121.
6. Unsigned editorial, JRU *Bulletin*, January 1918, pp. 4–5.
7. *The Times*, 17 November 1917, p. 7.
8. JRU, *Bulletin*, February 1929, p. 4.
9. On COPEC and its wider context, see Edward Shillito, *Christian Citizenship: the Story and Meaning of C.O.P.E.C.*, (London, Longmans, 1924); Alan Wilkinson, *The Church of England and the First World War* (London, Society for the Propagation of Christian Knowledge, 1978); John Kent, *William Temple: Church, State and Society in Britain, 1880–1950* (Cambridge, Cambridge University Press, 1992); Matthew Grimley, *Citizenship, Community and the Church of England: Liberal Anglican Theories of the State between the Wars* (Oxford, Clarendon Press, 2004), pp. 6, 16–19, 40; and Mark Rowland's essay at http://www.davidalton.com/rowland2.html.
10. *JC*, 2 May 1924, p. 21. Revd McCormick died in August that year.
11. TNA PRO 30/69/1437 (2), Lily Montagu to Ramsay MacDonald, 18 March 1927; Montagu, 'Jewish Christian Relations', *The Jewish Bulletin* 8 (April), 1942/5702, unpaginated.
12. COPEC *Commission Reports* II–IV, VIII (London, Longmans Green, 1924).
13. Lily Montagu, *The Faith of a Jewish Woman* (London, Allen & Unwin, 1943), p. 53.
14. JRU, *Bulletin*, November 1924, p. 8.
15. LMA ACC/3686/ /01/01/001, minutes of the Society of Jews and Christians, 17 May 1927; 7 June 1927; 16 January 1930. Some of the 250 subscriptions were admitted to be overdue at the latter date.
16. The same, minutes 21 March, 22 April, 17 May, 20 June, 23 October 1929. By the early 1930s the Advisory Council also included the Archbishop of York, the Bishop of Kensington, the respective Deans of Manchester, Exeter and St Paul's, and the historian R.H. Tawney.
17. The same, minutes 16 February 1928; 15 November 1928; LMA ACC/3686/01/01/002, minutes 26 April 1938; 17 May 1938; 21 June 1938.
18. The same, Society meeting 16 November 1933; Montagu, *Faith*, pp. 53–4.
19. *JC*, 5 December 1924, pp. 8, 13–14.
20. JRU, *Bulletin*, October 1924, p. 6.
21. LMA ACC/3686/01/01/002, minutes 25 May 1933; resolution proposed by the Revd Simms, Rural Dean of Marylebone, seconded Dr Alexander Ramsay.
22. *The Times*, 8 February 1934, p. 10, letter signed by the Society's Advisory Council.

23. LMA ACC/3686 /01/01/002, minutes 2 February.1934; 22 March 1934.
24. Ibid., minutes 14 December 1933; 22 March 1934.
25. As reference 21.
26. *JC*, 14 November 1924, p. 8. Rather feebly, in 1938, the Society asked Levertoff if he would mind changing the name of his organisation as it could cause confusion; he refused. LMA ACC/3686 /01/01/002, minutes 17 May 1938; 21 June 1938.
27. LMA ACC/3686 /01/01/001, minutes, 16 March 1928; 23 April 1928.
28. LMA ACC/3686 /01/01/002, minutes 19 January 1933.
29. Andrew Chandler, 'A Question of Fundamental Principles. The Church of England and the Jews of Germany 1933–1937', *Leo Baeck Institute Yearbook* xxxviii (New York, Leo Baeck Institute, 1993) pp. 223–4.
30. Lambeth Palace Library MS William Temple 31, correspondence of James Parkes and William Temple 8 and 11 May 1942.
31. Bodleian Library, Oxford, MS Dep. CMJ 68/14, Jean Miller to Miss Marshall, 4 July 1928.
32. University of Southampton Library (henceforth USL) MS 60 17/8, Israel Mattuck to James Parkes, 20 February 1934.
33. LMA ACC/3686/01/01/003.
34. USL MS 60 17/8, Gray to Parkes, 6 April [1930?].
35. *Peace News*, 10 October 1936, p. 7; 17 October 1936, p. 4; 22 January 1938; USL MS 60 18/1/9, correspondence between Maude Royden and James Parkes, 25 June, 18 July 1942. Royden was President of the Peace Army, which sent visitors to Palestine from 1937 onwards.
36. Tony Kushner, 'Beyond the Pale? British Reactions to Nazi Anti-semitism, 1933–1939' in Kushner and Lunn, eds, *The Politics Of Marginality: Race, The Radical Right and Minorities in Twentieth Century Britain* (London, Cass, 1990), p. 152; Martin Ceadel, *Pacifism in Britain, 1914–1945: the Defining of a Faith* (Oxford, Clarendon Press, 1980), pp. 282–3 and n. 6.
37. *JC*, 30 June 1939, p. 22.
38. Ceadel, *Semi-detached*, pp. 380–1, 393, 404. This spokesman was Beckett's principal colleague Ben Greene, formerly active in the Society of Friends and the Peace Pledge Union. Sent by the Friends to observe the aftermath of Kristallnacht, he later helped to facilitate the Kindertransport. He could, clearly, compartmentalise his responses to Jewish distress: see Lawrence Darton, *An Account of the Work of the Friends Committee for Refugees and Aliens, first known as the Germany Emergency Committee of the Society of Friends, 1933–50* (FRCA, duplicated text, 1954), p. 53; Sybil Oldfield, '"It is usually She": the Role of British Women in the Rescue and Care of the Kindertransport Kinder', *Shofar: An Interdisciplinary Journal Of Jewish Studies*, xxiii (2004), p. 60. Greene was interned by the British government in 1940.

39. *JC*, 13 October 1939, p. 12. Royden subsequently renounced her pacifism: Richard Griffiths, *Patriotism Perverted: Captain Ramsey, the Right Club and English Anti-semitism, 1939–40* (London, Constable, 1998), p. 182. Comparable disappointments with the pacifist movement were experienced by American Jewish feminists: see Klapper, *Ballots, Babies and Banners of Peace: American Jewish Women's Activism 1890–1940* (New York, New York University Press, 2013), Ch. 5.
40. Early in 1941 'subscriptions were coming in daily': LMA ACC/3686/01/01/003, minutes 19 December 1939; 13 June 1940; 13 February 1941.
41. James Parkes, *Voyage of Discoveries* (London, Gollancz, 1969). For a more detailed account of the transition from the Society of Jews and Christians to the Council of Christians and Jews see Anne Summers, 'False Start or Brave Beginning? The Society of Jews and Christians, 1924–1944', *Journal of Ecclesiastical History* 65.4 (October 2014).
42. W.W. Simpson, 'Jewish-Christian Relations since the Inception of the Council of Christians and Jews', *Jewish Historical Studies* xxviii (1981–2) p. 93; Bodleian Library, Oxford. MS Dep. CMJ 68/15, W.W. Simpson to Revd D.M. Lynch, 10 February 1947, typed extract.
43. This is based at the Liberal Jewish Synagogue in St John's Wood, London, of which Lily Montagu was the 'founding mother'.
44. The coinage is Sheila Rowbotham's: see her *Hidden from History: 300 Years of Women's Oppression and the Fight against It* (London, Pluto Press, 1973).

CHAPTER 9

Separatism Without Separation: Rebecca Sieff, Englishwomen and Zionism

Lily Montagu's initiatives constituted one strand among many in the attempt to reconcile difference with acculturation. The Society of Jews and Christians was intended to create new relations of mutual respect and equality between distinct religious traditions; as has been shown, this was not something which could be achieved where the initiative was taken on the Jewish side of the relationship, and certainly not where only a minority within the religious minority was involved. The Liberal Judaism which she promoted could justifiably be described as assimilationist in its early years, when it shed non-English custom and practice and much of the Hebrew liturgy, and discarded all prayers for the restoration of the Jewish people to Zion. Ironically, perhaps, this 'progressive turn' coincided historically with the rise of what would appear to be the diametrically opposed current of modern Zionism.

At Zionism's core stood a desire to construct a new, independent national identity for Jewish people. In the early 1900s the movement derived much of its urgency from realistic fears for the physical future of the Jewish populations of Eastern Europe; and while traditional religious longing and Messianic expectation were its cultural underpinning, they were not at the forefront of organisation and propaganda. From this movement Lily and Liberal Judaism stood determinedly aloof. A nationalist Judaism seemed to her a contradiction in terms, negating the legacy of centuries of spirituality. She was also one of many Jews, grateful for the degree of legal equality and social acceptance which they had found in Britain, who feared that the new movement would discourage further progress, if not indeed reverse it.

While Zionism did not immediately become the mainstream commitment of Anglo-Jewry, the movement rapidly became prominent within communal cultural and political affairs, making constant and energetic efforts to 'convert' the Jewish majority. At the same time and, it might seem, paradoxically, it could succeed only by reaching out to non-Jews and making its aims acceptable to them. What was just one aspect of progressive Judaism's mission was a core function of the new Jewish nationalism. The issuing of the Balfour Declaration of 1917, and the subsequent granting of the League of Nations mandate for Palestine to Britain in 1922, were the foundation stones of the hoped-for future state. The new movement had to maintain momentum by engaging with each successive British government, with all political parties, and with many different social and intellectual constituencies. Nowhere was the engagement with non-Jewish civil society more evident than in the activities of organised women Zionists.

Ever since the first international Zionist congress, convened by Theodor Herzl in 1897, women as individuals and in a variety of small groups had been part of the movement. The drive to unite the different British women's organisations was particularly strong in Manchester.[1] Chaim Weizmann, a university lecturer in chemistry who would become the first President of the modern state of Israel, had settled there in the decade before World War I with his doctor wife Vera. In 1905 they met their MP Arthur Balfour briefly, through the chair of the local Conservative Party, Charles Dreyfus, Alsace-born and distantly related to Captain Alfred Dreyfus. Only in 1916 was the acquaintanceship renewed, with the momentous result of the Balfour Declaration of 1917. More immediately important for communicating Zionist ideas among liberal opinion-formers and the Jewish community was the Weizmanns' absorption into an intellectual circle around C.P. Scott, the editor of *The Manchester Guardian*, which included the journalist Harry Sacher; he in turn was linked through marriage to Simon Marks and Israel Sieff, who were at that time engaged in turning the firm of Marks and Spencer into an immensely prosperous concern, and who became enthusiastic Zionists after meeting Weizmann.[2]

Israel Sieff's wife Rebecca Marks (1890–1966) was to become the leading figure in the (British) Federation of Women Zionists (FWZ), whose founding conference was held in 1919, and the Women's International

Zionist Organisation (WIZO), founded a year later. This lifelong engagement was not in any way a tame following of a male initiative, and was indeed bound up with an equally strong commitment to post-suffrage feminism, though the 'f-word' was sometimes disavowed in public pronouncements. Rebecca Sieff became the FWZ's first president, and among the founding members were an earlier generation of suffragists, including Alice Model, Nina Davis Salaman, Edith Ayrton Zangwill and Lizzie Hands. Women Zionists maintained the concern over the unequal status of women within their own religious congregations, which had been a key issue for the Jewish League for Woman Suffrage. Lizzie Hands, long a stalwart of the Union of Jewish Literary Societies, and a tireless speaker for the Council for the Amelioration of the Legal Position of the Jewess, presented a paper on 'Some Legal Difficulties Which Beset the Jewess' at the first conference of WIZO, held in London in 1920. This detailed the unequal treatment of women in Jewish religious law, particularly in regard to divorce. Some of the issues she highlighted remain unresolved at the time of writing.[3]

The religious establishment's obduracy was one factor in strengthening the resolve of Zionist women to push for female political suffrage and social equality in the putative future state. They were also convinced that organising separately from the male-dominated movement was essential to defend the moral and material interests of women and children already living in Palestine, as well as those who would be encouraged to settle there in the coming years. These elements were combined in Rebecca's address (as reported in the *Jewish Chronicle*) to the FWZ annual conference in June 1920: 'Women Zionists were often described as Feminists—they were not—feminists thought men were inferior. The Women Zionists thought that men were superior in some things, and inferior in others. Mrs Sieff hoped that their work would help to raise the women from the inferior status that the Jewish religion gave them. She herself had not been allowed to make a speech in a synagogue'.[4] Rebecca's Zionist project began at home, in the 'conversion' of the Anglo-Jewish community, in which she would often have to proceed cautiously, and not assume an immediate sympathy with her secular opinions; nevertheless, there were to be times when she would not mince her words.

Rebecca Sieff was fortunate in growing up in a time and place where middle-class Jewish parents did not consider a mere year or two of secondary schooling as sufficient for their daughters' needs. Indeed, given that her own mother, Hannah Marks, was barely literate, her parents' concern for their daughters' education is particularly noteworthy. All four sisters attended the non-denominational Manchester High School for girls, whose headmistress, Joan Burstall, an active suffragist, seems to have bequeathed a feminist legacy to many of her pupils. Rebecca's youngest sister Elaine recollected that 'in my second year, she [Burstall] took part in a protest demonstration from Manchester to Stockport, riding in the back of a lorry'.[5] Burstall established strong relations with Manchester Jewry, which were maintained and strengthened by her interwar successor, Mary Clarke, who wrote of the 'large contingent of Jewish girls who had traditionally an important place in our school community' many of whose parents 'were generous benefactors of the School' (Fig. 9.1).[6]

From Manchester High School Rebecca proceeded to the Women's Department of Manchester University. Here she studied Mathematics and English Literature; in a 1940 interview she stated that she gave up the former subject for Domestic Science. No practical application of this subject was ever likely to be required of her, even if marriage and domesticity

Fig. 9.1 Portrait of Rebecca Sieff 1915 (Courtesy of The Marks & Spencer Company Archive)

were imminently in her sights. It appears that she had long before set her heart on marrying Israel Sieff, a fellow student at the university and her brother Simon's best friend: she withdrew from her degree course, and the wedding took place in 1910. In retrospect she described her education as taking place outside formal teaching institutions: 'my real school was *The Manchester Guardian*, Halle Concerts' as well as the men and women associated with the *Guardian* and its editor to all whom her brother-in-law Harry Sacher introduced her and other members of her family.[7] The closeness of these connections by 1918 is revealed by the publication of a book of essays on the restoration of a Jewish state: written by a *Guardian* journalist, Herbert Sidebotham, it was dedicated to Rebecca Sieff and Sacher's then fiancée, her younger sister Miriam.[8]

Following the occupation of Palestine by British troops under General Allenby in December 1917, a Zionist Commission had been despatched to investigate relations between Jews and Arabs, with Weizmann at its head and Israel Sieff as its Secretary. A clear indication of the difficulty that Rebecca encountered in her early years as an activist within her own community is revealed by the treatment of this episode in the autobiography of her sister Elaine Blond. Elaine perceived Rebecca's passionate desire to see Palestine for herself, and her disappointment that neither she nor any other women were included in the first Zionist Commission as 'mental torture for Becky, who saw it as her natural right to be at the centre of the action'. With the war's end 'the pressure was then put on in earnest for [Sieff] to share the limelight'.[9] Fortunately Rebecca had sympathetic female colleagues who shared her concerns: these included Dr Vera Weizmann and Edith Eder, wife of the psychoanalyst and fellow Zionist David Eder. Between September 1919 and April 1920 she was able to visit Palestine for the first time in a party which included them and her husband. Their investigations covered every aspect of training and education for girls, from lace schools to agricultural colleges, as well as the functioning of maternal and infant welfare centres and a 'housewives' co-operative guild'; they came home determined to raise funds for all these facilities.[10] On their return, they held the founding conference of WIZO; however, while valuing the support of an international women's movement, the FWZ founders prioritised the task of bringing existing Jewish women's groups in Britain under their umbrella. A punishing regime followed of travelling to centres of Jewish population all over the country, organising fundraising events, and planning the programmes that would enable the women they had seen living in poverty and squalor in Palestine to earn decent livelihoods there.

A new phase in Rebecca's public life opened after 1926, when she, Israel and their children moved to London. She entered the world of the *Times* 'Court Circular' as a hostess and philanthropist. In the 1930s the fashionable Syrie Maugham was commissioned to design the interior of the Sieffs' new apartment in Mayfair.[11] Rebecca became a Vice President of Queen Charlotte's Hospital, was presented to the Prince of Wales in December 1931, and presented at Court the following June.[12] But she had not lost her sense of purpose. It has been perceptively observed that her aim at this time was 'to make "the Jewish question and Zionism normal subjects"'.[13] In the early 1930s, charity balls and gala performances were organised in aid of women and children in Palestine as well as of Queen Charlotte's Hospital, with the patronage of titled women such as Lady Emily Lutyens, Lady Clementine Waring, Lady Iris Chalmers and Lady Irene Mountbatten, Marchioness of Carisbrooke.[14] Some had links to the Jewish community. Violet Lady Melchett was the non-Jewish widow of Sir Alfred Mond, who had been an enthusiastic Zionist. Lady Lily Fitzgerald (née Bischoffsheim) was a granddaughter of Baron Hirsch, an early supporter of Jewish settlement in Palestine; her daughter Nesta, wife of the second son of the Duke of Wellington, brought her sister-in-law, the Marchioness of Douro, into Rebecca's circle. Viscountess Snowden, wife of the Labour Chancellor of the Exchequer who was ennobled in 1931, was a non-Jewish supporter with whom Rebecca had perhaps socially more in common. Born Ethel Annakin, the daughter of a nonconformist building contractor in Harrogate, she had been a keen suffragist, was now active in the Labour Party and was on friendly terms with the Weizmanns.[15] Rebecca's existing links to the Anglo-Jewish community were also maintained and extended. She raised funds for the London Hospital in Whitechapel; she supported the Jewish Peace Society; and there were more visits to Palestine.[16]

Neither the Marks nor the Sieff families were overly committed to the conventional practice and beliefs of Judaism. A gathering at the Passover table, and the 'once-a-year' tribute of synagogue attendance over the High Holy Days marked the extent of their observance. Zionism could be said to have become their religion and their mode of connection with the Jewish community, but, as can be seen, this did not equate to an impulse to ethnic separatism. Moreover, this was not solely due to the need to cultivate social and political links with the Mandate power, but rather a sign of a strong engagement with, and concern for the wider British society. There was substance in Rebecca's description of her father, Michael

Marks, as 'a fine Liberal and great humanitarian' and of the *Manchester Guardian* as her 'second bible'.[17] Simon Marks and Israel Sieff set out to be model employers in the tradition of the Rowntree, Cadbury and Courtauld dynasties, and were deeply in sympathy with the progressive activists of their generation who were trying to repair the ravages of the post-1918 economic depression. Thus these years of targeted social climbing also saw the development of a personal and political relationship which at first sight seems improbable.

Israel and Rebecca became close friends of the socialist politicians Jennie Lee and Nye Bevan. Neither Sieff could at that time be described as leaning to the left: their activities were rooted in a culture of philanthropy rather than one of collectivisation or state direction of the economy. But they were patriotic citizens: Marks and Spencer, famously, gave the vast majority of their contracts to British manufacturers. They were also, of course, committed to the creation of an entirely new state for the Jewish people, and of necessity acquiring larger perspectives on social action. As a newly successful businessman, Israel was soon being drawn into a ferment of discussion between economic, social and political reformers in Britain. One of the most important of their groupings was the organisation known as PEP—Political and Economic Planning—of which he was a founder member, soon becoming chair. PEP attempted to think outside governmental and party parameters, and brought like minds into intellectual collaborations which could develop into close friendships. In the respective memoirs of Israel Sieff and Jennie Lee, there are touching accounts of the times these couples spent together at Lane End, Brimpton Common—a Berkshire cottage purchased first by the Bevans and then by the Sieffs, with the pattern of use by both couples remaining unchanged throughout.[18]

Jennie, one of a small band of women elected to the House of Commons between the world wars, may have understood the challenges in the way of Rebecca's activism better than most. 'Becky was born before her time', she wrote. Her male relatives and coreligionists 'accepted the Victorian and Jewish conventions where women were concerned. Becky never surrendered ... She could be awkward, talk out of turn, shout to be heard when she found soft words led nowhere. ... With Nye and with me, there was never any of this defiant behaviour. There was no need. She would be relaxed, her true lovable, rational self, for she knew we accepted her not as her husband's wife or her brother's sister, but as a person in her own right'.[19] Rebecca never became a socialist, and Jennie, in turn, could never accept her friend's arguments for the overriding importance of returning women MPs to Westminster, which will be discussed below. But in her published memoir *My Life with Nye* Jennie paid tribute to that determined feminism with the (possibly unique) index entry 'Sieff, Israel, husband of Rebecca'. Rebecca's index entry stands alone, without marital epithet.

Not all was harmony, and the two women had often to take different paths through the tormented political landscape of the 1930s. The year 1933 was not the political and campaigning watershed for Jennie that it was for Rebecca. In all Jennie's published memoirs, it is the betrayal of Republican Spain by the British government and the Labour Party which is presented as the unforgivable failure of the international community and Western socialism. Her *Tomorrow is a New Day*, completed a few months before the outbreak of World War II, is very revealing of the emotions of her political circle, which was 'sorry when Vienna fell. Sorrier than about Germany'.[20] She felt more sympathy for a former socialist municipality than for the liberal individuals going into exile who should, she thought, have done more to defend democracy and the working class in Germany. Confessing her 'conflicting emotions', her words for these exiles make unpleasant reading:

> damn you, poor folks can't run like you. Why should you expect *me* to help you? ... Some of you have contrived to get your wealth, or part of it, out ahead of you. Others of you are now as nakedly poor as the German unemployed worker whose shadow darkened your door through all your comfortable years if only you had had eyes to see him, heart to pity him, camaraderie enough to make common cause with him ...[21]

Leaving aside the analytical lacunae in this attribution of responsibility for the rise of Nazism, and in her subsequent statement that 'the victims of poverty and fascism are one and the same',[22] it is interesting to reflect on the difficulties facing the campaign for German Jewish refugees which such passages expose. Jennie also had words for those of her friends involved in this struggle:

> I ran by your side, campaigned and collected with you—while wanting to say 'what about *my* folks' ... It was not that I was less concerned than you about the suffering of Hitler's victims. But ... nothing was too much trouble if it was on behalf of German refugees. But you had sometimes difficulty in disguising your impatience when asked to give your serious attention to sufferers nearer hom.[23]

It is hard not to read these comments as applying to the Sieffs' circle, and to wonder if they provide the key to the comment, in Jennie's obituary of Rebecca, that her 'generosity of spirit ... brought her closer to many of us in the Labour Movement than other members of her family'.[24]

This is not, of course, to say that Nye and Jennie were indifferent to their Jewish friends' concerns. In 1935, Nye and others in the House of Commons attempted to move a 'statement of disquiet' at German treatment of 'some of its citizens', and in 1938 asked the Home Secretary not to turn refugees away on grounds of poverty.[25] Both were, also, sympathetic to the Zionist project.[26] But they could imagine that German antisemitism was politically epiphenomenal, an aberrant means to an end, a temporary episode. For them, the all-consuming tragedies were Spain, and the internecine conflicts within the British and European left. Many Jewish socialists, certainly those in places of prewar safety, would have endorsed their priorities. It was different for Israel and Rebecca and their peers. While no one in the 1930s could have foreseen the full horror waiting to be born, Jews of Eastern European descent like the Sieffs knew the meaning of the word pogrom. Rebecca in particular felt that she had now to throw herself into a new engagement—which she would meld with her existing commitments to Palestine—to raise funds and create new lives for refugees from Germany. It is worthy of note that when *Tomorrow is a New Day* was republished by Jennie in 1963 as *This Great Journey*, not one word of the passages I have quoted from the former edition remained in the text.

* * * * *

Hitler's assumption of power in Germany at the beginning of 1933 prompted the creation of a plethora of refugee committees in Britain, some of whose work is described in the next chapter. The earliest were the Central British Fund for German Jewry and the Jewish Refugees Committee for refugee resettlement, both set up in March that year; and the Quaker organisation, the Germany Emergency Committee (originally the Joint Committee on the German Situation), which began meeting the following month. The organisation of a boycott of Jewish shops in Germany on 1 April 1933 was widely publicised by Anglo-Jewry, and was followed by further protests on the part of Jewish and non-Jewish voluntary and civic bodies.[27] A few months later the Federation of Women Zionists and the Union of Jewish Women were discussing the formation of a joint Women's Appeal Committee for German-Jewish women and children, as a section of the Central British Fund.[28] This was chaired by Rebecca, with leading roles taken by her sister Elaine and the late Alfred Mond's daughter Eva Isaacs, Viscountess Erleigh. The president, Yvonne de Rothschild, was the wife of Anthony de Rothschild, a founder of the Central British Fund. The Women's Appeal Committee raised nearly £25,000 in its first year, another £75,000 by the end of 1937 and a further £150,000 by the end of 1940.[29]

These sums could not match those raised by the Central British Fund, which brought in sums variously estimated as £100,000 and £250,000 in its first year;[30] nevertheless, they represented a huge investment in time and energy on the part of the women involved, who included representatives of the Union of Jewish Women, B'Nei Brith, the FWZ and WIZO and many smaller societies. There were, inevitably, dissensions between the collaborating organisations. The Women's Appeal Committee's aims were 'the support of schemes in Great Britain and Palestine for the relief of German Jewish women and children',[31] and it was possible to disagree over where the money could best be spent. Rebecca's priorities were to provide training for resettlement (preferably agrarian) in Palestine; the Committee as a whole had a wider remit, including helping refugee children with school fees and holiday accommodation in Britain, and providing young women with nursing or secretarial training. Following the *Anschluss* of March 1938, the commitment expanded to include the Jews of Austria, and concern grew over the fate of Jewish communities in neighbouring lands. There were soon very few Anglo-Jewish women activists who were not involved in one scheme or another for refugees; the FWZ found that, while the women attending their meetings now needed little persuading that emigration to Palestine was a cause deserving of support, Zionism as a project in itself mattered less to them than the work of relief and rescue.[32]

Despite this—or perhaps because of this—the FWZ in this period expanded its outreach work within the non-Jewish community. If Rebecca had been concerned to make Zionism a 'normal' current of opinion within Britain before the rise of Hitler, it had become a much more urgent task now. Society ladies were no longer an important target, especially as 'in the present disastrous times, it would be unsuitable to hold showy functions, such as balls'.[33] The veteran activist Lizzie Hands headed the FWZ's external propaganda committee, which made approaches to the National Peace Council and the Countrywomen of the World, the Women's International League for Peace and Freedom, the British Commonwealth League and the National Council of Women; its representatives attended meetings of the Friends' Germany Emergency Committee and the Women's Advisory Council of the League of Nations Union. Speakers addressed the Women Transport Workers' Union, the Women's Citizens' Association, a 'Luncheon Club of Catholic women', a Unitarian group in Wandsworth and numerous schools.[34] They were also sent on many occasions to branches of the Women's Co-operative Guild (WCG).[35] Most bizarrely, the Council was asked 'to endeavour to establish contact with the Women's Section of the British Union of Fascists and ask them to have a speaker', but there is no record of this engagement's having taken place.[36] Between January and mid-June of 1937, it was reported that forty-two non-Jewish meetings had been addressed, an average of seven per month.[37]

Within this plethora of approaches to the voluntary associational world of women, two organisations were of particular importance. The first was the British Commonwealth League (BCL). Like the WCG, this was a feminist initiative. It was formed in 1923 by a group of former suffragettes from Britain and the Dominions who wanted to extend and promote equal rights for women throughout the Empire, and to maintain the links between them. Clearly, its founders had much in common with those of WIZO. Margery Corbett Ashby was the BCL's first President, and by the mid-1930s she and Rebecca were sympathetic colleagues. It would be possible to see Rebecca's attitude to the Empire as purely instrumental—Britain was, after all, the trustee of the Palestine Mandate, as well as the originator of the Balfour Declaration in favour of a Jewish homeland, and it seemed conceivable that a Jewish state might one day be part of a British Commonwealth of Nations. However, that would be to misunderstand the determinedly dual nature of her identity as an Englishwoman as well as a Jewess. Rebecca believed passionately in the goodness and decency of the society to which her parents' generation had migrated. She told young people training to farm in Palestine that they would bring with them 'the special advantages they had from being English'.[38] She reminded Zionists who were angry with the government for what they saw as bias and weakness in the face of Arab uprisings in the Mandate of 'the community of ideals which animated the British and the Jewish people', and warned that this would soon be needed to 'once more stand before the world as a bulwark which would prevent civilisation from being entirely swept away'.[39] Rebecca was not a simple-minded advocate of Empire, and she supported the movement for Indian independence;[40] it is well to remember that her conceptual framework was bounded on the one side by family experience of Tsarism and on the other by the pressing realities of the Third Reich.

The requirement to understand the context in which political perceptions were formed applies particularly to the early history of the Zionist movement. Many Jews and Gentiles did not believe that the interests of Jews and Arabs were irreconcilable. Josiah Wedgwood MP, speaking in 1934 at a BCL meeting also addressed by Margery Corbett Ashby and Rebecca, rejoiced in the ousting of the Ottoman Empire's political establishment from Palestine, and declared Zionist achievements 'nothing but an unmixed blessing for the people of that country, whether poor or rich'.[41] In 1936, Margery Corbett Ashby told a meeting of the FWZ that 'as an internationalist and a representative of Arab Women's Societies, she hoped that women would be enabled to find a bridge over the difficulties that at present divided the Arab and Jewish peoples in Palestine'.[42] Giving a 'well received' speech at the 14th annual conference of the BCL in 1938, Rebecca pointed out that 'it was in Palestine that by far the greatest increase in the Arab population had taken place in the past few years. So far from pushing the Arabs into the desert, the Jewish effort was turning the desert into gardens and plantations, and in those spots were working thousands of Arabs'.[43] As much of the world drew inexorably closer to conflagration, Palestine still seemed a place where one need not abandon hope.

The second organisation with which the FWZ formed a significant relationship was the Women's Co-operative Guild. Lizzie Hands was assiduous in cultivating links with the Guild; however, given that it was not just the Labour Party, but 'Labour and Co-operative' MPs who represented socialist and working-class interests in Parliament, the many visits to Guild meetings invite speculation as to whether a 'Sieff-Lee Axis' might also have been at work here. There was already considerable sympathy within the left for the experiments in cooperative economy and collective living practised among the pioneer Zionists. Former Labour MP Susan Lawrence compared the kibbutz (collective farm) to the Utopia of William Morris's socialist classic *News from Nowhere*.[44] The Co-operative Wholesale Society traded with and visited fruit cooperatives in Palestine, and reported on the kibbutz experiment in its press. By March 1936, both the Co-operative Wholesale Society and the Women's Co-operative Guild had headquarters in the East End, in Leman Street and Great Prescott Street respectively.[45] In November that year Lizzie Hands reported that some branches of the Guild had agreed to distribute leaflets published by the Jewish Board of Deputies to combat antisemitic propaganda in the locality.[46] Official links between the Zionist and Labour movements have in the past been attributed to the activities of male politicians on both sides.[47] The patient work of the Federation of Women Zionists may also have contributed substantially to this relationship, normalising the concept of the Jewish national home in hundreds of Labour-voting households.

In some respects, however, the WCG might be thought to offer stony ground. The organisation was resolutely pacifist, to the point of seeing moral equivalence between British preparations to resist Nazi aggression and the Nazi regime itself. Military conscription was categorised by Rose Simpson as 'the thin end of the wedge of Fascism here … the ruling classes desire to mould and discipline our youth as the youth of Germany and other dictatorship countries have been moulded and disciplined'. If city children were evacuated to camps in an emergency this would be a sign that 'The Government want to make them akin to the young Brown Shirts of Germany'.[48] The answer given by a woman asked what she would do if requested to take her children to a gas-mask trial—'I think I would rather put my head in a gas oven'—may have come back to haunt her.[49] Nevertheless, despite their many inconsistencies and illogicalities—one absolutist pacifist even saw fit to denounce 'the terrible consequences of appeasement'[50]—Guild members do not seem to have succumbed to the temptation to speak in terms of a 'Jewish war'. The propaganda work of Rebecca and her colleagues had, indeed, had significant 'side-effects'. For the FWZ to lecture on the settlement of Palestine in the 1930s was to make connections, and plead for sympathy, for all Jews, and to make a powerful case for asylum. As Guild members felt the 'nervous strain' of resisting the inevitable catastrophe of war, they were reminded that 'there is immense service needed for refugees'.[51] The response of non-Jewish women as the crisis deepened—it has been remarked that Britain 'seems to be the only country where non-Jews organised support locally for refugees'[52]—almost certainly owes more to the intervention of Rebecca and her colleagues than has hitherto been appreciated.

* * * *

With the outbreak of World War II in 1939, it soon became impossible for refugees to reach British or any other shores. While WIZO and FWZ did not cease to denounce persecution and mass murder on the Continent, new strategies were called for. Shortening the duration of the war was a priority, and once the Nazi-Soviet pact had been shattered, Rebecca was prominent in campaigns to support Britain's new ally. She was on the Executive of the Women's Anglo-Soviet Committee, which sent supplies to the Red Cross, and parcels to Soviet soldiers via the embassy in London, and aimed to establish good relations more generally with Soviet women. The Committee also called for a military 'Second Front' to reinforce Soviet resistance to the German invasion. Jennie Lee recalled that an 'active element in this campaign were influential Jewish families. They were frenetically concerned to defeat Hitler' and Rebecca was 'one of the most militant' of these Jewish advocates.[53]

Yet another wartime project was to direct Rebecca's attention to a postwar world, and the role of women in a future British society. This was not, however, the original intention of those sponsoring the project. In December 1939 a scheme emanating from the Ministry of Information established the Women's Publicity Planning Association (WPPA). This brought together representatives of organisations including the Women's Freedom League, the National Council of Women, the National Council of Girls' Clubs, the National Union of Societies for Equal Citizenship, the Townswomen's Guild and the Women's Co-operative Guild, in order 'to inform people, especially the women of other countries, including Latin-America, what we were doing and thinking during this period of War, to create a better understanding between them and us, and to make and maintain contacts from the point of view of publicity and propaganda which would be useful to maintain after the War'.[54] A committee in which Rebecca and Margery Corbett Ashby were the leading members set about finding suitable topics and writers, taking advice from, amongst others, Mass Observation's Tom Harrison.[55] Growing critical of the Ministry's plan to syndicate articles to quite different readerships, they decided to publish a journal of their own. All arrangements were in place to publish 'The New Challenge' when concerns over paper shortages caused the Ministries of Information and Supply to forbid the publication of any new periodicals. Within hours of the edict the committee had escaped the ban by amalgamating their proposed organ, 'The New Challenge', with the extant *International Women's News*.[56]

Throughout the war the project was entirely funded by Rebecca, her family and friends. In mid-April 1940, as Vice Chair of the Association, Rebecca agreed to guarantee the new journal for at least six months, subscribing an initial £1000. Later that month she volunteered a further £2000, and undertook to canvass her friends for further contributions: she hoped to succeed despite being clear with them that they would almost certainly receive no return on their investment. In May it was agreed to set up a private limited company to finance and manage the publication, with

Rebecca as Chair. June saw the decorators arrive at office premises which had been found in Westminster: 'Mrs Sieff had most generously promised them some furniture ... [they] went to Harrods and chose desks, lamps, tables, cupboards, cushions and a carpet etc. from Mrs Sieff's store there'.[57] It had been agreed that she would chair the Business and Finance Board of the new publication, and that Margery Corbett Ashby would chair the Editorial Board. Through this arrangement Rebecca was kept abreast of the complexities of the international women's movement, with her editorial colleague explaining that as there were many Catholic members of the International Women's Suffrage Alliance, a 'controversial' subject (such as, presumably, birth control) could be broached in an editorial comment but not as a statement of official policy. It was also explained that *International Women's News* 'had relations with a very fine paper called the "Egyptian Woman" and suggested that if, for example, there was an article on Palestine a note should be put at the foot saying that they hoped this would be followed by an article showing the Arab or the Egyptian point of view'.[58]

WPPA quite rapidly moved into overtly feminist campaigning on home ground. It joined the agitation for Equal Compensation for War Injuries in 1941, and sponsored Vera Douie's survey of conditions of life and work for women, published in 1943 as *The Lesser Half*. In 1942 it set up a sub-committee, Women for Westminster, which soon became an independent organisation. This initiative owed much to Dr Edith Summerskill, who had been elected as a Labour MP in 1938, and was convinced that a male-dominated Parliament would remain biased against women's demands for social and legislative equality.[59] As well as supporting women parliamentary candidates in wartime bye-elections—Rebecca brought a contingent of canvassers to Bristol on behalf of Jennie Lee in 1943[60]—Women for Westminster considered means by which legal anomalies could be removed and the struggles of the pre-1914 generation be completed. The solution which Women for Westminster proposed was the Equal Citizenship (Blanket) Bill. The text, prepared by Dorothy Evans with a foreword by Rebecca, set out the changes required in more than thirty pieces of legislation, covering marriage and divorce as well as the workplace and matters relating to war service and injuries. Even though Dorothy Evans was a former suffragette, and an active member of the Six Point Group and the London and National Society for Women's Service, her colleagues in these and other feminist organisations did not collectively support Women for Westminster's strategy. Some women trade unionists feared the consequences of abandoning protective legislation, and in the intensely partisan atmosphere building up to the first general election since 1935, the overall project of a non-party, woman-focused campaign was not thought likely to succeed.[61]

It is possible that women in other, longer-established groups may have disliked Rebecca's 'management style', and perhaps her 'Society' connections; they may have considered her a relative newcomer to feminist politics. As Jennie Lee's memoirs indicate, and those of Elaine Blond express more blatantly, Rebecca's personality was one which aroused strong negative as well as positive reactions. Nevertheless, it is clear that she was a deeply thoughtful political animal, whose ideas on feminism as well as on colonial emancipation were in constant evolution throughout World War II. In 1941 she published a prescient reflection on the differences between the limited goals of professional women 'high-flyers' and the immensely broader politics of change which earlier feminist struggles had embodied.[62] Within that last circle of British, non-Jewish women with whom she collaborated closely, the verdict was unequivocal. Norah Jeans, the editor of *International Women's News*, wrote in 1940: 'I wish that I could thank you for all that you are doing and attempting to do for women. Some day maybe I shall find the right words. Meanwhile never doubt it'.[63] Three years later Dorothy Evans told 'dear Becky' that 'in these two years we have moved forward further than in all the 25 [*sic*] years since women won the vote'.[64]

On Rebecca's death in 1966 Margery Corbett Ashby described her as 'one of the few people with a flame in her soul. Intensely alive to other people's sufferings she never spared herself'.[65] In 1948, when the former mandate was formally recognized as the state of Israel, Rebecca Sieff made it her home; her life thereafter belongs to a different narrative. Her native land still awaits a legislature in which women representatives are so numerous, and their presence so normal, that they are not mocked for the shape of their bodies or the lightness of their voices, and do not have to struggle for parity of esteem. In 1980 the '300 group' was founded to campaign for a House of Commons in which 50 % of MPs are female, but dissolved some twenty years later without achieving its objective. The Women's Equality Party was founded in 2015 to take forward the feminist agenda in the parliamentary sphere. It is evident that Women for Westminster's work has proceeded only by fits and starts; one may well feel that Israel's gain was Britain's loss, and wish that circumstances had conspired to make Rebecca Sieff retain her dual identity for longer.

Notes

1. Rosalie Gassman-Sherr, *The Story of the Federation of Women Zionists of Great Britain and Ireland, 1919–1968* (London, Federation of Women Zionists, 1968), pp. 5–7.
2. Chaim Weizmann, *Trial and Error* (London, Hamish Hamilton, 1949).
3. *Jewish Chronicle* (henceforth *JC*), 6 January 1933, p. 9; 27 January 1933, p. 27; 7 April 1933, p. 40; 21 April 1933, p. 29; 10 November 1933, p. 31; 17 November 1933, p. 37; 24 November 1933, p. 31; 15 December 1933, p. 38; 30 November 1934, p. 34; 11 January 1935, p. 34; 1 March 1935, p. 32; 10 July 1936, p. 47; 18 December 1936, p. 46. She was also Hon. Sec. of the Jewish Peace Society: University of Southampton (henceforth USL) MS 122, 4/5, printed pamphlet, n.d.; *JC*, 21 April 1933, p. 28.
4. *JC*, 4 June 1920, p. 28.
5. Elaine Blond with Barry Turner, *Marks of Distinction* (London, Vallentine Mitchell, 1988), p. 15. The three Pankhurst daughters had attended the school.
6. Mary G. Clarke, *A Short Life of Ninety Years* (Edinburgh, Astrid and Martin Huggins, 1973), p. 58.
7. Marks and Spencer Company Archives (henceforth M&S) R/1/3, biographical notes on Mrs Sieff, 1949; *International Women's News* 35 (October–November 1940), p. 11.
8. Herbert Sidebotham, *England and Palestine: Essays towards the Restoration of a Jewish State* (London, Constable, 1918)
9. Blond, *Marks of Distinction*, p. 25.
10. *JC*, 12 September 1919, p. 20; 9 January 1920, p. 28; 2 April 1920, p. 20.
11. This was in Park Lane, in a block owned by Edwina Mountbatten. Sir Edwin Lutyens's son Robert also contributed to the decor. Enemy bombardment in 1940 led to the subsequent demolition of the building: Pauline C. Metcalf, *Syrie Maugham: Staging Glamorous Interiors* (New York, Acanthus Press, 2010), pp. 221–4, 280.
12. *JC*, 18 December 1931, p. 7; 1 July 1932, p. 9. Her sponsor was Katherine (Mrs Reginald) Coke, whose husband was half-brother to the 3rd Earl of Leicester.
13. M&S R/1/3, biographical notes on Mrs Sieff, 1949, p. 16.
14. *The Times*, 22 January 1932, p. 13; 24 March 1932, p. 15; *Morning Post*, 24 March 1932, and unidentified press cuttings in M&S R/1/1/4.
15. Article on Ethel Snowden by June Hannam in *Oxford Dictionary of National Biography* (henceforth *ODNB*); Weizmann, *Trial and Error*, p. 410.
16. *JC*, 26 February 1932, p. 12; M&S R/1/1/1, envelope containing letter of thanks from Queen Mary, 17 November 1933. The WIZO conference of spring 1934 took place in Palestine.

17. *International Women's News* 35.1 (October-November 1940), p. 11.
18. Jennie Lee, *My Life with Nye* (London, J. Cape, 1980), pp. 149-50; Israel Moses Sieff, *Memoirs* (London, Weidenfeld & Nicolson, 1970), pp 194-6.
19. Lee, *My Life*, pp. 143-5.
20. Jennie Lee, *Tomorrow is a New Day* (London, Cresset Press, 1939), pp. 195-6.
21. Lee, *Tomorrow*, pp. 252-4.
22. The same, pp. 256-7.
23. The same, pp. 254-5.
24. Obituary contribution by Jennie Lee, *Jewish Woman's Review*, February 1966: press cutting, n.p., in M&S R/1/1/3.
25. *JC*, 24 May 1935, p. 38; 25 March 1938, p. 30.
26. Cecil Bloom, 'The British Labour Party and Palestine, 1917-1948', *Jewish Historical Studies* 36 (1999-2001), p. 171, states that when Bevin announced the delaying tactic of the Anglo-American Committee of Enquiry on Palestine in 1945, Nye 'contemplated resignation from the Government' on the issue.
27. Central British Fund For Jewish Relief And Rehabilitation, *Report* for 1933-43, p. 3.
28. London Metropolitan Archives (henceforth LMA) ACC/4175/01/01/002, Minutes of the Council of the Federation of Women Zionists (henceforth FWZ), 30 May 1933; USL MS 129 AJ 26/B/7, Minutes of the Executive of the Union of Jewish Women (henceforth UJW), 27 June 1933.
29. UJW, *Annual Report*, November 1934; Council for German Jewry, *Report*, 1938; Amy Zahl Gottlieb, *Men [sic] of Vision: Anglo-Jewry's Aid to Victims of the Nazi Regime, 1933-1945* (London, Weidenfeld & Nicolson, 1998), pp. 32-3; R. Stent, 'Jewish Refugee Organisations' in W.E. Mosse, ed., *Second Chance: Two Centuries of German-speaking Jews in the United Kingdom* (Tübingen, J.C.B. Mohr, 1991), p. 594.
30. Louise London, 'Jewish Refugees, Anglo-Jewry and British Government Policy 1930-40' in David Cesarani, ed., *The Making of Modern Anglo-Jewry* (Oxford, Blackwell, 1990), p. 173. The higher sum is given in Pamela Shatzkes, *Holocaust and Rescue: Impotent or Indifferent? Anglo-Jewry 1938-1945* (London, Vallentine Mitchell, 2002), p.26.
31. LMA ACC/4175/01/01/002, Minutes of the Council of the FWZ, 2 November 1933.
32. LMA ACC/4175/01/01/005, Meetings of Honorary Officers of FWZ, 30 March and 13 June 1938.

33. LMA ACC/4175/01/01/002, Minutes of the Council of the FWZ, 16 November 1938.
34. The same, 26 April, 5 July, 22 November 1933; 3 January, 14 March, 9 May, 20 June, 18 July 1934; 9 January 1935.
35. In addition to the above references, see *JC*, 4 February 1938 p. 33, and 31 March 1939 p. 38.
36. LMA ACC/4175/01/01/002, Minutes of the Council of the FWZ, 31 January 1934.
37. The same, 17 June 1937.
38. *JC*, 23 October 1936, p. 22.
39. *JC*, 8 April 1938, p. 57.
40. *International Women's News* 35.3 (1940), p. 59.
41. *JC*, 26 October 1934, p. 25.
42. *JC*, 3 April 1936, p. 42.
43. *JC*, 17 June 1938, p. 23.
44. *JC*, 16 October 1936, p. 20.
45. *Co-operative News*, 7 March 1936, p. 12.
46. LMA ACC/4175/01/01/002, minutes of the Council of the Federation of Women Zionists, 4 November 1936.
47. Cecil Bloom, 'The British Labour Party and Palestine', *passim*.
48. *Woman's Outlook*, 3 June 1939, pp. 154–5, article by Rose Simpson on the protest against the Military Training Bill.
49. *Co-operative News*, 7 November 1936, p. 12.
50. *Woman's Outlook*, 24 June 1939, p. 274.
51. The same, 27 May 1939, p. 110.
52. Helen Jones, 'National, Community and Personal Priorities: British Women's Responses to Refugees from the Nazis, from the Mid-1930s to Early 1940s', *Women's History Review* 21.1 (2012), p. 124.
53. This was also known as the Women's British-Soviet Committee: M&S R/1/3, biographical notes on Mrs Sieff, 1949; M&S R/1/1/1 contains correspondence with and concerning the British Red Cross Society and the British-Soviet Committee, including correspondence with Edwina Mountbatten on the appeal for medical aid to the Soviets in 1943; Lee, *My Life*, p. 146.
54. The Women's Library (henceforth TWL) 5WPP/A1, Minutes of the Women's Publicity Planning Association 12 December 1939.
55. TWL 5/WPP/A2, Minutes of the Women's Publicity Planning Association 5 and 25 April 1940.
56. The same, 20 June 1940.

57. The same, 15 and 25 April, 3 May and 20 June 1940. See also obituary of Rebecca Sieff by M.I.C.A. [Corbett Ashby] in *International Women's News* 61.3 (1966), p. 22.
58. The same, 25 April and 28 June 1940.
59. An excellent summary of the history of the WPPA can be found in the TWL@LSE catalogue, under the code NA1264. Women for Westminster is similarly covered under NA1139.
60. Lee, *My Life*, pp. 143–5.
61. Laura Beers, '"Women for Westminster", Feminism, and the Limits of Non-partisan Associational Culture', in Julie Gottlieb and Richard Toye, eds, *The Aftermath of Suffrage: Women, Gender and Politics in Britain, 1918–1945* (Basingstoke and New York, Palgrave, 2013).
62. R.D. Sieff, 'Should the Women's Movement be Re-created?', *International Women's News* 35.9 (1941), pp. 167–8.
63. TWL 5WPP/A/3, letter of Norah Jeans to Rebecca Sieff, 22 June 1940.
64. TWL 5WPP/C/1, letter of Dorothy Evans to Rebecca Sieff, 29 December 1943.
65. Obituary of Rebecca Sieff by Corbett Ashby, *International Women's News* 61.3 (1966), p. 22.

CHAPTER 10

Refuge and Asylum

British society in the 1930s was no stranger to the concepts of refuge and asylum. It is true that a Victorian liberal tradition of hospitality to Continental radicals had given way by 1905 to a countervailing fear of 'alien' (for which read, largely, Jewish) immigration. Nevertheless, within very recent memory was the reception afforded to no fewer than 250,000 refugees from Belgium on the outbreak of World War I.[1] The social and organisational history of this episode offers striking parallels with events following the rise of Hitler; and a study of precedents can be instructive in considering the narrative of German and Austrian Jews' attempts to flee their homelands.

The names of a few of the organisations that helped Belgian refugees reflect two important themes in this history: the role of women and the salience of social class. The Lady Lugard Hospitality Committee for the Relief of Better-Class Belgian Refugees, the Duchess of Somerset's Homes for Better Class Belgian Refugees and the Exiled Gentlewomen's Outfitting Association indicate the wholly unembarrassed consciousness of class distinction which had not vanished, but was at least somewhat veiled by the time World War II broke out.[2] It is true that a less rarefied female social stratum was evident in the many local hospitality committees formed from 1914 by members of the National Council of Women, the National Union of Women's Suffrage Societies and the women's sections of political parties, political campaigning having of course been suspended for the duration. The War Refugees Committee was a government-sponsored voluntary organisation, and many others were established with distinguished male figureheads far outnumbering the women on their executive committees but, as has been wisely observed, 'the ratios were reversed on the general committees which did the real work. ... the bulk of the work was taken up with household management: running hostels, catering, and teaching refugees how to shop in an alien system'.[3]

Different organisations—by one estimate as many as 2500—handled local arrangements.[4] There were committees making arrangements for urban and for agricultural labourers; rail workers offered hospitality to rail workers, and firemen to firemen; Catholic communities agitated for Belgian children not to be constrained to receive a secular or Protestant schooling; the National Vigilance Association, and soon a female police force, patrolled stations to protect unaccompanied women from white slavers; a maternity home was set up for pregnant arrivals. Under the initiative of Otto Schiff, the Council of the Jews' Temporary Shelter in London expanded to form a Jewish War Refugees' Committee, subsidised by government, whose 'better-class' clientele were taken under the wing of the Union of Jewish Women; working-class Jews also set up a Jewish Workers' War Emergency Relief Fund.[5] However, many women in the Anglo-Jewish community worked with their non-Jewish neighbours and colleagues as they had before the war. The Rothschild, Franklin and Samuel families, among others, were well represented.[6] Overall responsibility rested with Herbert Samuel as President of the Local Government Board, with Cecil Chesterton's *New Witness* characteristically complaining that 'To give Jews the control of our honoured Belgian guests is an outrage'.[7]

The epithet 'honoured' was an unstable one. Even in August 1914 the Home Secretary, Reginald McKenna, thought that too many refugees 'might after a time become a considerable source of embarrassment', and security considerations dictated that no foreigner was allowed to settle in certain locations. While few in office believed that the war would be over by Christmas, government was clear that the refugees must be repatriated at the first opportunity. There was a popular belief that refugees were receiving higher rates of relief than British soldiers' families; Belgian men were not at first conscripted into the armed forces; and cities experiencing housing shortages thought the incomers to blame.[8] It cannot have helped that the names of many Flemings, like those of East European Jews and Scandinavian settlers, looked and sounded German. Anti-Belgian riots broke out at Fulham in May 1916 and in County Durham later that year. Most Belgians were despatched home, willing or not, in 1919.[9]

A second episode which foreshadowed the help given to Jewish refugees from Nazism related to the contemporaneous emergency in Spain. In May 1937, 4000 children were evacuated from Spain to Britain. Usually referred to as 'the Basque children', their age conferred on them a status outside politics in a crisis which became a source of deep ideological contention in Britain, as elsewhere in the West. In a striking and paradoxical demonstration of the respect accorded to the figure of 'the child', the British government, which refused to send any form of military aid to the legal Republic of Spain, permitted Royal Navy destroyers to escort civilian evacuation ships through international waters.[10] Similarly, members of the British Labour and Communist parties, bitterly divided on other matters, were able to cooperate over provision for the children.[11]

In November 1936 a National Joint Committee for Spanish Relief, led by Katherine Duchess of Atholl, and including the MPs Eleanor Rathbone and Ellen Wilkinson, had been established to c-ordinate the efforts of a number of different organisations. Atholl, Rathbone, Wilkinson and Rachel Crowdy[12] visited Madrid in April 1937, shortly before the bombardment of Guernica confronted the Western world with the newest form of wartime atrocity against European civilians. Soon afterwards the former MP Leah Manning was in Bilbao making arrangements to evacuate children from the region, and the Basque Children's Committee was established. Its purpose was to raise funds and provide accommodation in Britain for Spanish children whose homes and neighbourhoods already were, or were in danger of being, reduced to total devastation.[13]

The British government made it clear that the children's stay was to be of short duration. The first repatriations began as early as November 1937.[14] Government also insisted that financial as well as administrative responsibility for the maintenance, welfare and eventual repatriation of the children rested entirely with the Basque Children's Committee. Organisations on the political left were conspicuous in their support: the Trades Union Congress raised nearly £9000 within a month, local groups of the Women's Co-operative Guild rallied to the cause, and Oxford car workers and Welsh mining villages were famously hospitable.[15] The Peace Pledge Union sponsored a 'colony' of children for two years, and its members also took children into their own homes.[16] There were many other local initiatives, as during World War I, and as before, the Catholic hierarchy was concerned about the children's education and attendance at church. Although almost a third of the Basque children are thought to have been supported by the Catholic laity, the hierarchy was destined to be disappointed by some young Spanish Republicans' indifference or even hostility to the faith.[17]

Many of the local initiatives arose more from humanitarian than political considerations, such as those of the Salvation Army, Cambridge University and the appeal launched by the Conservative Lord Mayor of Birmingham and organised with the help of the Cadbury family. Unfortunately, donations often dried up within a short period, or were insufficient to fund the necessary provision. As 'colonies' and hostels closed down, many children were moved from pillar to post. The agreed sum of 10 shillings per week per child was in itself barely sufficient to cover board, lodging, medical care and education.[18] Physical and emotional welfare were often inadequate, despite voluntary workers' best intentions.[19] As Adrian Bell, who interviewed many of the children in later life, rightly states, 'This was the largest single contingent of child evacuees ever to enter this country'. They were soon to be followed by a still larger contingent from Germany and Austria. In one telling recollection, a Basque interviewee admitted to Bell that, freezing and almost starved in their Margate hostel, 'We used to steal from another big, nearby house, full of East European Jewish refugees. They were very well organised and provided for'.[20] Despite their material and emotional hardships, some children were, nevertheless, the targets of resentful comments of the type experienced by the Belgian refugees: complaints were expressed that Basque children were receiving privileges denied to native children in areas of unemployment.[21]

Some of the Basque children were fortunate enough to be fostered on a permanent basis. George and Barbara Cadbury became the legal guardians of Helvecia, Elvio and Delia Hidalgo, sent them to a Quaker boarding school, and looked after them during the school holidays.[22] Arthur and Mabel Exell, working-class Communists in Oxford, recalled 'It wasn't easy to look after them; we were on the dole, a lot of us, and we never got any money for looking after them'. They took in 'a smashing lad … we grew to love him' who asked to be called Chatto. A politically sophisticated teenager, he told them that he dreaded what would befall him and other Republicans if Franco were not defeated. As soon as Franco's victory ended the civil war, the British government prepared for the return of all the Basque children: 'I can remember when we said goodbye to him.' Shortly afterwards, a friend reported: 'Chatto threw himself out of the train at Waterloo and got killed'.[23]

These episodes furnish essential background to a survey of the movement to give asylum in Britain to refugees from Nazism between 1933 and 1939. Demonstrably, the British government's response to proposals of asylum on a large scale was to insist that immigration be on a strictly temporary basis, and state financial support limited, or non-existent. The Basque Children's Committees discovered, literally to their cost, that the enormous reserves of money, expertise and labour required of the voluntary sector would often be found wanting. Government officials were aware, as early as 1916, that in times of stress and hardship the 'native' population could turn violently against newcomers of any origin—in that first instance white, Christian families from Belgium. Those involved in the Herculean task of rescuing and supporting Jewish refugees in the 1930s, and many of their historians, have seen the obstacles placed in their path as evidence of antisemitism in high places, and indeed within British society at large. However, the fear of uncontrollable anti-immigrant feeling was not necessarily or wholly based on prejudice against Jews; neither was the insistence that very large sums be furnished as guarantees for each individual refugee, with none forthcoming from government.

Jewish refugees were, however, situated differently from Belgians because it was clear that they could not be repatriated. In the case of the Basque children, there appears to have been no official acknowledgement that the refusal of leave to remain, although consonant with previous policy, could be tantamount to a death sentence; but there was a clear understanding that one could not speak of returning Jewish refugees to Germany. However, while re-emigration was required of the Jews by the government, no provision was made for it. The supposed consistency and continuity of policy on refuge and asylum in Britain was exacerbated, if not indeed contradicted, by official reluctance to admit many more Jewish migrants to Palestine, and by the absence of any considered programme of settlement in other parts of the British Empire. While the inadequacies of the British response may be deplored, the lamentable failure of other potential host countries, most signally the USA, to offer hospitality on a scale proportionate to that provided by Britain, or to agree on an international approach to the issue, may prompt a measure of appreciation for what was actually achieved before the outbreak of World War II.[24]

* * * * *

It is estimated that some 60,000 souls arrived in Britain between the spring of 1933 and the summer of 1939.[25] In keeping with Britain's eclectic voluntarist tradition, a plethora of bodies attempted to provide for their needs. None received any governmental support, and all had to find their own funds and guarantee the financial maintenance of incomers. Predictably, different communities provided for their own. However, in contrast to previous episodes, many asylum seekers fell into new social categories, created by Nazi ideology. Quakers, for example, had not suffered political persecution in the West for centuries. The world had, indeed, grown used to seeing them among the first to offer relief to distressed and displaced populations. Now, as declared pacifists, German Quakers were public enemies of the Nazi state. The Society of Friends had to raise funds to support their counterparts in Germany who were dismissed from employment or hounded to the point of mental breakdown. For Anglo-Jewry, collective persecution of coreligionists overseas was of course no novelty—though the extent of physical assault and humiliation within a modern Western polity like Germany was a shock beyond previous experience. The establishment in March 1933 of the Jewish Refugee Committee (from 1938 known as the German Jewish Aid Committee) led in May to the founding of a Central British Fund for German Jewry, providing overall funding and advice to local Jewish initiatives; in April the Society of Friends formed their own Germany Emergency Committee.[26]

An entirely new category of non-citizens was next created by the Nuremberg Laws of September 1935, which imposed the same disabilities on individuals with Jewish grandparents as were already suffered by those in wholly Jewish families, and banned sexual relations between Jews and non-Jews. The plight of 'Non-Aryan Christians' (or 'Hebrew Christians', in old missionary parlance)—who were bewildered individuals, couples and families with no sense of Jewish identity—did not at first come home to fellow Christians in Britain, and they were in danger of falling between the cracks of existing philanthropic provision. Ultimately George Bell, Bishop of Chichester, became their champion, forming the Church of England Committee for Non-Aryan Christians in 1937.[27] By the end of 1938, again on Bell's initiative, a non-denominational committee coordinated the ongoing work of Anglican, nonconformist and Catholic groups.[28] The numbers in need of succour rose further after Germany's *Anschluss* with Austria in May 1938, and the partition of Czechoslovakia after the Munich agreement of September that year.

The division of labour between Jewish and Christian committees was of necessity pragmatic and porous, and collaborative networks emerged from an early stage. As soon as the Friends' Germany Emergency Committee (GEC) was established, it liaised with Jewish refugee workers, whether through the newer relief groups, the Zionist movement, the Board of Deputies of British

Jews, the Anglo-Jewish Association, ORT-OZ (which provided technical training for young Jewish people in Europe and Palestine), or individual contacts such as Rabbi Israel Mattuck of the Liberal Synagogue and Ethel Behrens of the Jewish Peace Society. Discussions took place concerning the creation of schools for Quaker children exiled in the Netherlands which might also admit Jewish children, and putative 'settlements' of refugees in France and Spain; there was a revival of an early Zionist speculation that Jews might be allocated territory in southern Africa by the British or Portuguese colonial authorities.[29] The committee allocated money to Jewish causes and publicly proclaimed, that 'it is unjust and unfair to leave the whole burden upon the Jewish community'.[30] In turn it received practical assistance from its Jewish opposite number, for example by a loan of equipment from the Gestetner Company; more substantially, as the crisis worsened, the GEC admitted that 'with regard to emigration, finding posts for refugees in this country, and training people for either purpose, the old-established and experienced sub-Committees of the German-Jewish Aid Committee give the G.E.C. workers much-needed advice'.[31]

While some Nazi categories made a division of labour between the organisations fairly straightforward, the proscription of marriages between Jews and Gentiles put both sides in a dilemma. A rather surprising exchange—from the point of view of Jewish religious law—took place in February 1939 between Joan Fischl of the Germany Emergency Committee and Ruth Fellner of the German-Jewish Aid Committee. Who would take responsibility for families where the spouses were of different religious origins? The former wrote to confirm her understanding that the Friends should take on the casework where the husband was a Christian and the wife Jewish; the latter agreed that her organisation would take care of 'cases of mixed marriages when the husband or head of the family is of Jewish faith, and all other cases will be referred to your Committee'.[32] This decision ran directly counter to Jewish *halacha*, which defined as Jewish any child of a Jewish mother, with the father's faith and origin remaining immaterial. That *halacha* was thus trumped by patriarchy seems not to have attracted attention or caused any controversy in this instance, although orthodox objections, as will be seen, were raised by many of the arrangements made for Jewish children as the war approached.

* * * * *

As might be expected from the history of previous episodes—and inferred from the above exchange—women from Jewish and Christian communities played key roles in organisations for the relief of refugees from Nazism. While campaigners such as Dorothy Buxton and Eleanor Rathbone were constantly in the public eye, behind the scenes literally hundreds more women were heavily involved in the practical administration and, ultimately, strategy of many schemes, and no listing can do justice to the number of individuals to whom honour is due.[33] The National Council of Women (NCW) took early cognisance of the issue. Like the Quakers, in 1933 the NCW had had the shock of seeing its German colleagues fall foul of their own government. On refusing to accept Nazi control and exclude its Jewish membership, the Bund Deutscher Frauenvereine disbanded, and German participation in the International Council of Women (ICW) came to an end.[34] In September 1933 the congress of the ICW resolved to support the International Committee for securing employment for refugee professional workers, and shortly afterwards the NCW appealed to branches and individual members to offer their assistance to the British section of this Committee. They were to do so via an umbrella organisation which appears to have been the first of many attempts to coordinate relief efforts: the German Refugees Assistance Fund (Academic and Professional) comprised the Academic Assistance Council (later better known as the Society for the Protection of Science and Learning); the International Student Service; the Friends' Germany Emergency Committee and the Save the Children Fund Germany Appeal Committee.[35]

After 1935, with the numbers of refugees increasing rapidly, NCW members continued to collaborate with many organisations—with the Society of Friends in Manchester, for example, and with the British Federation of University Women in Birmingham—and their local branches, with affiliates such as the Women's Citizens' Association, often formed the core of the refugee committees springing up all over Britain.[36] Branches 'adopted' individual refugees, fundraised for the training of older children, set up clothing depots, found and furnished houses to serve as hostels and organised entertainments for the new residents.[37] Interfaith refugee initiatives were to be found in large centres of population such as Birmingham, Manchester and Bristol,[38] but these were, understandably, less in evidence in districts without Jewish communities. NCW members and their associates were organising and working on behalf of men, women and children who could in no obvious sense be described as 'their own'. The resolution passed at the Executive meeting of November 1938, in the presence of Netta Franklin, that the NCW 'desires to place on record its appreciation of the valuable service rendered by its Jewish members throughout its history and wishes to express its profound sympathy in the sorrows which have recently beset their race'[39] was more than a form of words; it was bolstered by actions which deserve to be acknowledged in perpetuity.

However, the NCW was not always able to help incomers in the way they, and the ICW, had originally intended. As a predominantly middle- and upper-class organisation, it had been sympathetic to the goal of securing employment appropriate to the educational level of professional women exiles. Increasingly, however, this goal had to be abandoned. Government policy was to offer visas only where a shortage of labour had been identified; many professional bodies in Britain, such as those for doctors and dentists, declared a 'closed shop'.[40] However, one area of female employment was deemed capable of expansion, and this was in the area of domestic service. Here, it might be said that an element at least of self- or class-interest came into play for the ladies of the NCW.

The seemingly limitless demand for domestic servants in interwar Britain can seem startling to anyone who has absorbed the popular historiography of World War I, which suggests that women's lives were subsequently transformed by extended opportunities in manufacturing work and other new employments. A very different picture emerges from the 1931 census, which shows over 2 million women employed in domestic service—much the same figure listed in the census of 1911, and still the single largest occupational sector for women in employment. While it is true that domestic staff were for some employers a marker of bourgeois social status and display, their functions were for the most part severely practical. Housing in interwar Britain was rarely designed around the needs of housewives: if any of today's younger readers were, for example, dependent on solid fuel to keep their families clean, warm and fed, they would soon, if they could afford it, be looking for extra pairs of hands. The NCW provided an interesting and quasi-eugenic slant on the issue, resolving in October 1937 that: 'The National Council of Women, being of opinion that the difficulty of obtaining domestic help tends to restrict families to an extent dangerous to the State, urges the Home Secretary to grant permits freely to approved young women of other nationalities' who wished to migrate in order to take up this occupation, adding that their residence permits should be renewable if they remained in domestic service.[41]

In 1935, over 4000 female immigrants came to take up domestic service posts in Britain; in 1936, the total was 8449; in 1937, it was some

14,000. A year later another 7000 arrived, and under pressure from the NCW and Jewish groups, regulations were relaxed to the extent of lowering the age of visa applicants from 18 to 16, allowing married couples to enter as domestics, and admitting the possibility of their seeking other employment after two or three years. In the last year of peace domestic servants were allowed to enter without guaranteed posts, and up until the outbreak of war were arriving at the rate of 400 a week.[42] There is no evidence to suggest that—following the logic of the NCW resolution—their presence enabled housewives to boost the British birth rate. It is indeed unlikely that this would have been the outcome even if war had not been declared in September 1939.

Many women refugees' memoirs recall the conditions placed on their entry with, at best, chagrin. As Home Office regulations favoured asylum applications from the well-to-do (or at least the well connected), these had themselves often come from comfortable homes with live-in servants; and promising professional careers in Germany and Austria were nipped in the bud in Britain.[43] Not all employers were considerate or kind, though many had the best intentions. One was full of praise for the cooking and housework of a refugee domestic, formerly a senior manager in a company: 'She only seems awkward serving at the table when we have guests.'[44] At least one such employee seems to have cracked under the strain: a former philosophy lecturer working as a parlourmaid in Park Lane overheard a luncheon guest opine that 'life is solitary, poor, nasty, brutish and short, as Pascal remarked', and allegedly 'plonked the man's soup in front of him saying "Not Pascal: Hobbes". As a result she lost her job and we gained an excellent custodian of records'.[45] The outbreak of war brought confusion, upheavals, dismissals and sometimes internment in its wake.[46] The fact remains that the lives of some 20,000 women were saved by the self-interest of the female middle classes—and by the British government's noteworthy sensitivity to their demands.

* * * * *

The best-remembered collaboration between Christians and Jews over refugee relief, in which women activists played key roles, concerns the rescue of children from the Nazi regime. The earliest suggestion of a focus on the child victims of Nazism appears to have come from Helen Bentwich née Franklin, a niece (by marriage) of both Netta Franklin and Herbert Samuel. Her husband Norman Bentwich, who had been the first Attorney-General of Mandate Palestine while her uncle was its first High

Commissioner, was from 1933 to 1935 Director of the League of Nations High Commission for Refugees from Germany. Vera Fast's research in the archive of Bishop Bell reveals that in the autumn of 1933 Helen brought the likely fate of 'non-Aryan' Christians to the Bishop's attention, and proposed that the well-established Save the Children Fund be encouraged to assist the children of such families. She added that her name should not be mentioned in any appeal for funds since 'I am both Jewish and a known Socialist and Pacifist'.[47] After the Nuremberg Laws of 1935 bore out her predictions, Gladys Skelton and Francis Bendit established a subcommittee of Save the Children, known as the Inter-Aid Committee for Children from Germany. It was chaired by Wyndham Deedes, who had formed close ties with the Bentwiches while serving in the Palestine administration; there may have been a further Bentwich connection in that Gladys Skelton had been a Girton contemporary of Norman Bentwich's sister Rosalind, who died in 1922.[48]

By the end of 1938, Inter-Aid had helped 471 children to be placed in schools in England. Jewish and 'non-Aryan' Christian children were helped in almost equal numbers, and much of the funding came from the Jewish community, including Rebecca Sieff's Women's Appeal Committee.[49] However, it had become clear, following Germany's *Anschluss* with Austria and occupation of the Sudetenland, that many more Jews and 'non-Aryans' would be seeking to escape from these and other centres of Jewish population in eastern Europe. The British government sought to limit the admission of adult refugees, claiming that they would stir up home-grown antisemitism and place unsustainable pressure on an already depressed economy;[50] but, as sympathisers with Republican Spain had found, there was rather less prejudice against children. In November 1938 representatives of Inter-Aid, the Jewish Refugee Committee and the Germany Emergency Committee, led by Herbert Samuel, met with the Home Secretary and gained official sanction for an unspecified number of unaccompanied children under the age of eighteen to be admitted 'for educational purposes', and at no expense to the taxpayer. No distinction was to be made between partly and wholly Jewish children. Inter-Aid merged the following year with the Movement for the Care of Children from Germany, which became known as the Refugee Children's Movement (RCM), and is remembered now as the Kindertransport.[51]

In December 1938 the Home Office simplified its entrance procedures for children, and a vastly expanded and accelerated programme of enlisting foster parents, organising hostels and arranging station and quayside receptions took place on the basis of the earlier work for refugees. Between then and August 1939, around a thousand children entered Britain every month—a total of some 7700: the previous monthly average had been thirteen. Twelve regional and sixty-five area committees had been established by the outbreak of war.[52] Dorothy Hardisty, a former civil servant with years of experience in the Department of Labour, headed the RCM's operations at Bloomsbury House, where almost all refugee committees were based after January 1939; among the Jewish colleagues with whom she worked closely were Rebecca Sieff's sister Elaine Laski (later Elaine Blond) and Eva Isaacs, Marchioness of Reading. Eight of the twelve regional committees were headed by women, all committees were heavily dependent on women's voluntary effort, and many, like the central RCM, were joint Jewish and Christian collaborations. As Sybil Oldfield has pointed out, the work was 'often based on existing networks of Jewish and Quaker women already alerted to the refugee problem'.[53]

Where and how the children should be cared for presented complex problems. The government's wish to disperse the children, rather than to enlarge existing areas of Jewish residence by settling them there, often placed children beyond the reach of Jewish congregations and interfaith cooperation.[54] Chief Rabbi Joseph Hertz set up his own Emergency Council to negotiate directly with the Home Office, and with his son-in-law Rabbi Solomon Schonfeld worked for the admission of orthodox children and yeshiva (religious seminary) students. Their determination that Jewish children should not be lodged with non-Jewish families was undermined by the inability of orthodox families in Britain to offer enough placements.[55] The policy of dispersing the children throughout the country in itself limited these placements, and it is sometimes forgotten that the Anglo-Jewish community was not uniformly wealthy: an undertaking to pay £50 as a preliminary guarantee, and to maintain a child up to the age of 18, was beyond the capacity of many households.[56] Dorothy Hardisty and her local organisers, such as Greta Burkill in Cambridge, often felt harassed and exasperated by Orthodoxy's complaints; it should be noted that they also had to contend with the strictures of the Roman Catholic hierarchy when Catholic children were placed in Protestant homes.[57]

Many Jews were glad to sanction generous offers of hospitality from non-Jewish families, particularly in view of the assimilated, secular way of life which some of the children had known in Germany and Austria.[58] Few Jewish activists would have echoed the Chief Rabbi's statement—in a letter which he may later have wished unwritten—that 'there are things I fear worse than pogroms'.[59] There were, indeed, non-Jewish families who took pains to respect their foster-childrens' distinct religious needs; however, it is also true that some conversionists saw the children as an opportunity, and that Christians did not necessarily sympathise with the Jews' dread of a religious and cultural extermination compounding a physical one. The Reverend Gray cannot have been alone in thinking 'When all repression ceases and education is really offered to them all will not Judaism certainly die?'[60] Arguably, the present age is more sensitive to cultural difference and to the individual needs of the child than was the case in the 1930s; whether the present age could, on the basis of an almost entirely voluntary female labour force, find decent and often loving accommodation for over 7000 foreign children in less than a year is a moot point.

Religious issues were not the only factors complicating the arrangements made for the young immigrants. Zionism could divide opinions within the same family, let alone the same committee. Elaine Laski did not share her sister Rebecca Sieff's commitment to a Jewish state. Rebecca wanted teenage refugees to be lodged in hostels, to develop a sense of community while receiving appropriate training for life in Palestine; Elaine favoured the system of individual foster homes.[61] Unexpectedly, it also proved particularly difficult to find individual homes for adolescent boys, who were therefore more liable to end up in an institutional form of care.[62] The outbreak of war put an end, for the duration, to any plans for re-emigration to Palestine. However, the perceived need to evacuate schoolchildren from the large cities liable to bombing raids subjected many child and adolescent refugees to further displacement. The deep emotional traumas of the 'Kinder' are revealed in their published memoirs, and not even the kindest and most stable foster care could have compensated for indefinite separation from parents and continuing uncertainty about the future.

* * * * *

Some of the bonds forged between Jewish and Christian organisations in previous decades proved unequal to the pressures of the 1930s. The pre-1914 links between the Travellers' Aid Society and the Jewish Association for the Protection of Girls, Women and Children (JAPGWC)[63] might have been expected to produce a co-operative response of great value as refugee girls and women arrived to take up, or seek out, posts in domestic service. However, these links had become weaker in the 1920s and early 1930s. Partly in consequence of legislation to restrict immigration to Britain and the United States, the number of Jewish and other female migrants from

Eastern Europe diminished; prison, police-court and home-visiting work replaced attendance at docks and stations. JAPGWC looked increasingly to work with the new League of Nations to secure the safety and rights of female travellers. Fundraising and administration focused largely on the maintenance of schools and residential homes—for unmarried mothers, vulnerable youngsters and 'Respectable Working Girls'.[64] Jewish representatives continued to be appointed to the Travellers' Aid Society, but do not seem to have reported back on any of their meetings.[65] It is possible, also, that the Association may have had difficulty in recruiting younger members as older activists passed away. It was not in sympathy with the changed postwar social climate: by 1936 the Case Committee was deploring the trend for a generation of economically independent girls and women in Britain to disregard the wishes of their parents or husbands, and even to leave the parental or marital home.[66]

Despite the rather pious declaration in the Jewish Association's Report for 1935–1936, that 'Less than ever today can we excuse any indifference to situations involving moral danger where our sisters in faith are concerned', the Association did not throw itself wholeheartedly into the cause. The same Report thanked colleagues working for the Jews' Temporary Shelter (JTS) for sharing the expense of repatriating several girls and women who had arrived as penniless 'holiday-makers' or in search of domestic employment, and for cooperating in steps to discourage further arrivals. The Case Committee of the Association took a remarkably unsympathetic tone, decrying the lack of 'thought being given to the difficulties which must inevitably arise when—to quote an example—a girl takes a situation as a cook, for which her only qualification is an architect's diploma'.[67] Even though the Secretary 'thought that this was an opportunity, in view of the great demand for domestics, to re-open the employment register which used to be kept at the office for such foreign girls', the Jewish Association was reluctant to take on additional responsibilities;[68] and it seems to have left to the German-Jewish Aid Committee and the JTS the traditional function of meeting Jewish travellers off the boat train to Victoria and Charing Cross, often very late at night, and sending them on to a safe destination in London.

It was the Travellers' Aid Society, merged since autumn 1938 with the National Vigilance Association, which, with increasing irritation, was bridging the gap. By early 1939, tempers were frayed on both sides. At the end of February, a Travellers'/Vigilance 'station worker', one S. Peters, reported a JTS representative as saying 'it was useless to send anyone to the shelter as they were full up:—"You must put them up in your own Hostels, you have plenty round here"—To this I answered that first, none of the Hostels would have sufficient room ... and secondly none of "Our" Hostels had the funds necessary to provide for Jewish Refugees, it is all they can do to provide for our own girls'.[69] It might have helped if he had explained the pressures on the JTS at this time: the minutes of its House Committee reveal that 'a good many of the refugees and the bulk of the domestics had to be cleared from its Institution in consequence of having been approached by the Committee for the Care of Refugee Children to accommodate 1500 children due to arrive in parties three times weekly at the rate of 60 in each party, who would stay in the Shelter for a day or two, until they were dispatched to their various destinations'. Dormitories were kept empty, but in the end, only forty children arrived.[70] The reference to 'domestics' was probably to Shelter staff; however, it was also the case that young women who disliked their domestic situations were leaving them and returning unexpectedly to the Shelter. Their needs, together with those of the newer arrivals, required the Secretary 'to turn several sitting rooms into temporary dormitories'. By July the JTS was applying to the local health authority for permission to convert more living space into dormitories, and to instal 'double decker beds'.[71]

Records indicate that JTS volunteers were by April turning out to meet their late-night arrivals, but there remained areas where irritation and antipathy could surface. In many cases, the desperate Jewish refugees coming off the boat train did not look the part. A frightened child, a sobbing old woman, were visibly wretched individuals. But it was, it appears, difficult for some voluntary workers to sympathise with an adult who, having managed to bring some money out with her, and having no idea where her next penny was coming from, was probably hoping to make a good impression on her new hosts by looking carefully after the well-made clothes she stood up in. While the first Travellers'/Vigilance worker quoted had correctly observed that many refugees were penniless, and considered this a reproach to the Jewish community whose representatives had not come to help them, another, Kathleen Kelly, took a quite different view. She reported that 'the Jewish people do not like to be asked to pay for accommodation. ... they invariably inform myself or my colleague that they have no money, and we find it difficult to even get them to pay the porters who get their heavy luggage from the Customs, and they also dislike having to pay storage on their baggage'. Her response three months later, to the arrival of 275 refugees who had sailed all the way to Cuba only to be denied entry there, was that 'all these people were extremely well dressed, and brought beautiful luggage with them, and they all looked well'.[72]

The refugees themselves had great difficulty adjusting to their new status. They were unfamiliar with their new role as victim and supplicant. Many an educated immigrant woman, not unreasonably, considered herself entitled to the respect of her middle-class counterparts. However, if a Jewish charity showed itself unable to sympathise with the architect required to shed her identity and become a domestic servant, it is unsurprising that others could display indifference, or even the hostility which arises when the philanthropist, too, is confused as to her role. Kathleen Kelly also reported that 'some of the hostels do not want to take in Jewish girls or women, because I understand they cause too much trouble and want everything for nothing'.[73] What the JTS heard was that six women whom they had sent to Cecil Chesterton House 'complained that they had to share the dormitories there with women whom they considered of ill repute, and they seemed to have been suffering from skin diseases which looked like Eczema. They returned to the Shelter the same night'.[74] Perhaps the children and adolescents, young enough to adapt to the new roles required of them, to become English or proto-Israeli, to share sleeping space, to take up domestic service or agricultural labour and gradually to allow an imagined future to displace a remembered past, were, despite their personal tragedies, the more fortunate of the refugees.

In one matter Travellers' Aid/National Vigilance and JAPGWC reached agreement, and that was in finding the attempted coordination of refugee relief and resettlement activities at Bloomsbury House a near-total failure. In June 1939, Solomon Cohen, the JAPGWC Secretary, wrote to his opposite number, Frederick Sempkins, that girls whom the Shelter could not accommodate were sent to Bloomsbury House, but that he had 'no knowledge at all as to what Bloomsbury House does with them. I have not been able to get any satisfaction, and in fact I have not been going near Bloomsbury House'. Shortly afterwards, Sempkins found that the Domestic Bureau at Bloomsbury House had no knowledge of his organisation's work on behalf of refugees, but having established what looked like a useful point of contact, he soon despaired: 'This is at present a quite impossible place: it takes hours to find anybody you want to see and when you find them they are not able to help you'.[75] The Jewish Association's Report for 1939–1940 stated that the numbers of refugees 'have increased beyond all possibility of satisfactory handling'.[76] That the arrival of 400 women a week and 1000 children a month should have strained the organisational resources of the voluntary sector as Britain began to prepare for war can come as little surprise. It is perhaps too easy for critics of this country's reception of refugees to attribute its failings to prejudice and intentional unkindness, and to exaggerate the organisational capacity of the state and civil society as Britain prepared for military mobilisation and the evacuation of urban civilians.

Scope for misunderstandings, and scope for the expression of ambivalent emotions, abounded throughout this crisis. Humanitarians have human faults and failings; the behaviour of victims does not always seem lovable or comprehensible; good intentions do not necessarily translate into good organisation. Chaos there may have been, but refugees do not seem to have starved, or to have ended up on the streets. There can be no definitive history, and certainly no definitive moral judgement of Britain's reception of refugees from Nazism, which varied from city to city and village to village, but it is important to remember Helen Jones's statement that Britain 'seems to be the only country where non-Jews organised support locally for refugees';[77] and one thing that can be said with certainty is that without the voluntary effort of British women of all faiths, relief and rescue would have been words on paper only. Cooperation across the communities could not always be harmonious; but people could stay up till all hours, working together for a good cause, without exactly liking each other. 'Living with difference' was not uppermost in these volunteers' minds; it was, nevertheless, a reality.

Few contemporaries would have agreed that these activities diluted and anglicised the Jewish community.[78] Nor is there a clearly discernible pattern in Jewish-Christian collaborations. Helen Jones has suggested that there was close collaboration at the national level in the 1930s, tending towards more separate work at the local level by 1939, after which resources were pooled.[79] However, relief efforts were so dispersed and varied that it is hard to construct a strong chronology for their history. What is clear is that all sectors of society were more closely integrated with the state in the situation of total war after 1939, but communal identities were not effaced. Education and integration into the host society had, after all, been part of the Jewish immigrant experience for at least two decades. The Jewish women active in relief and rescue were thoroughly accustomed to managing their dual membership of secular civil society and Anglo-Jewry; the steep learning curve of the wartime experience was no more challenging for them than for their non-Jewish peers. It is true that some children were indeed lost to Jewish religion and culture through evacuation and dispersal, but overall communal cohesion remained extremely strong. Arguably, it would have remained so even without the reinforcement of the concept of Jewish identity through the creation of a Jewish state in Palestine in 1948.

Notes

1. Tony Kushner, 'Local Heroes: Belgian Refugees in Britain during the First World War', *Immigrants and Minorities* 18.1 (1999), p. 2, points out that this was the largest refugee movement in British history. Peter Cahalan, *Belgian Refugee Relief in England during the Great War* (New York and London, Garland, 1982) p. 508, remarks that this was 'the first clear case of an influx of refugees on a large scale since the French emigrés during the Revolutionary era'.
2. In 1918 the Union of Jewish Women (henceforth UJW) reported of its war work that it had 'kept in touch with some of the better class Belgian Refugees': 15th *Annual Report*, p. 11. In 1933, referring to its Loan Fund, 'It was unanimously agreed that the word "gentlewoman" should be omitted from the letter & "educated girls & women" substituted': University of Southampton Library (henceforth USL) MS 129 AJ 26/B/7, UJW Executive Minutes p. 394, 9 May 1933.
3. Cahalan, *Belgian Refugee Relief*, pp. 176–7.
4. Kushner, 'Local Heroes', p. 6.
5. Cahalan, *Belgian Refugee Relief*, pp. 144, 146–8, 348.
6. Helen Bentwich, *If I Forget Thee: Some Chapters of Autobiography, 1912–1920* (London, Elek, 1973), pp. 10–11; Cahalan, *Belgian Refugee Relief*, pp. 36, 49; Katherine Storr, *Excluded from the Record: Women, Refugees and Relief 1914–1929* (Bern, Oxford, Peter Lang, 2010), p. 39.
7. Bernard Wasserstein, *Herbert Samuel: a Political Life* (Oxford, Clarendon Press, 1992), pp. 170–1.
8. Kushner, 'Local Heroes', pp. 12, 16–17.
9. Tabili, *Global Migrants, Local Culture: Natives and Newcomers in Provincial England, 1841–1939* (Basingstoke, Palgrave Macmillan, 2011), pp. 194–5; Kushner, 'Local Heroes', pp. 16–17, 21, 24.
10. Adrian Bell, *Only for Three Months: the Basque Children in Exile* (Norwich, Mousehold Press, 1996), p. 28; Kevin Myers, 'The Ambiguities of Aid and Agency: Representing Refugee Children in England, 1937–8', *Cultural and Social History* 6.1 (2000).
11. Tom Buchanan, *The Spanish Civil War and the British Labour Movement* (Cambridge, Cambridge University Press, 1991), makes the point that rank-and-file trade unionists and Labour Party members took the initia-

tive, with Labour leadership remaining apprehensive of Communist Party infiltration.
12. Bell, *Only for Three Months*, p. 7; Storr, *Excluded from the Record*, p. 295. From 1919 to 1931 Rachel Crowdy was Head of the Social Questions and Opium Traffic Section of the League of Nations. Subsequent to the restructuring which re-assigned these functions, no other woman achieved this level of seniority at the League.
13. Bell, *Only for Three Months*, p. 8; Susan Pedersen, *Eleanor Rathbone and the Politics of Conscience* (London, New Haven, Yale University Press, 2004), pp. 286–7.
14. Bell, *Only for Three Months*, p. 9.
15. The same, pp. 64, 84, 91; Myers, 'The Ambiguities of Aid and Agency', p. 40; Arthur Exell, 'Morris Motors in the 1930s: Part II', *History Workshop Journal* 7 (1979), p. 64.
16. Bell, *Only for Three Months*, pp. 84–5.
17. The same, p. 121; Myers, 'The Ambiguities of Aid and Agency', pp. 32, 39.
18. Bell, *Only for Three Months*, pp. 72–5; Myers, 'The Ambiguities of Aid and Agency', pp. 36–7.
19. Tom Buchanan, 'The Role of the British Labour Movement in the Origins and Work of the Basque Children's Committee, 1937-9', *European History Quarterly* 18.2 (1988), p. 160.
20. Bell, *Only Three Months*, pp. 62, 79.
21. Tom Buchanan, 'The Role of the British Labour Movement', p. 166.
22. *Guardian*, 'Other Lives', 2 August 2014.
23. Exell, 'Morris Motors in the 1930s: Part II', pp. 64–5.
24. Richard Breitman and Alan M. Kraut, *American Refugee Policy and European Jewry, 1933–45* (Bloomington, Indiana University Press, 1987) p. 9, estimate that between 1933 and 1944, just over 120,000 refugees were admitted from Germany and Austria, with possibly another 130,000 other Jewish refugees leaving from other countries; Frank W. Brecher, *Reluctant Ally: United States Foreign Policy toward the Jews from Wilson to Roosevelt* (New York, Greenwood Press, 1991) p. 137 reference 21, estimates that over 150,000 Jewish refugees entered the USA between 1938 and 1940, and about 210,000 during the entire Hitlerian period.
25. Todd Endelman, *The Jews of Britain 1656 to 2000* (Berkeley and Los Angeles, University of California Press, 2002), p. 215; Pamela Shatzkes, *Holocaust and Rescue: Impotent or Indifferent? Anglo-Jewry 1938–1945* (London, Vallentine Mitchell, 2002), pp. 80–1. These are approximate net figures which take account of re-emigration.
26. Shatzkes, *Holocaust and Rescue*, p. 26; Central British Fund for Jewish Relief and Rehabilitation, *Report for 1933–43*, p. 3 Lawrence Darton, *An Account of the Work of the Friends Committee for Refugees and Aliens, First*

Known as the Germany Emergency Committee of the Society of Friends, 1933–50 (FRCA, duplicated text, 1954), pp. 2–3.
27. British Library (henceforth BL) Add Ms 51154 B, Cecil of Chelwood Papers, f. 97, Bell to Cecil 23 October 1937; Andrew Chandler, 'George Bell and the Internment Crisis of 1940' in Andrew Chandler, ed. *The Church and Humanity: the Life and Work of George Bell, 1883–1958* (Farnham, Ashgate, 2012), p. 78; Andrew Chandler, 'A Question of Fundamental Principles: the Church of England and the Jews of Germany 1933–1937', *Leo Baeck Institute Yearbook* 38 (New York, Leo Baeck Institute, 1993), pp. 238–9, 252.
28. Andrew Chandler, 'The Church of England and the Jews of Germany and Austria in 1938', *Leo Baeck Institute Yearbook* 40 (New York, Leo Baeck Institute, 1995), p. 238.
29. Friends House Library (henceforth FHL), FCRA/1, minutes of the Germany Emergency Committee, ff. 1–2 [n.d.: 7 April?] 1933; f. 18, 19 April 1933; ff. 39–40, 24 May 1933; f. 47, 14 June 1933; ff. 76–8, 84–5, draft and copy correspondence regarding ORT, and the possibility of an Angola settlement, 3 October and 9 September 1933; ff. 140–189, discussion regarding schooling, February–October 1934.
30. FHL FCRA/18/1, German Refugee Assistance Fund leaflet, n.d. [1933-5].
31. FHL FCRA/3, minutes of the Germany Emergency Committee, p. 3, 14 February 1939; FCRA/2, f. 141, 1 December 1938.
32. FHL FCRA/25/4, Joan Fischl to German-Jewish Aid Committee, 8 February 1939; Ruth Fellner to Joan Fischl, 9 February 1939.
33. See e.g. Veronica Gillespie, 'Working with the "*Kindertransports*"' in Sybil Oldfield, ed., *This Working-Day World: Women's Lives and Culture(s) in Britain 1914–1945* (London, Taylor & Francis, 1994); Sybil Oldfield, *Women Humanitarians: a Biographical Dictionary of British Women Active between 1900 and 1950* (London, Continuum, 2001); Sybil Oldfield, '"It is usually She": the Role of British Women in the Rescue and Care of the Kindertransport' *Shofar: An Interdisciplinary Journal of Jewish Studies* 23.1 (2004); Susan Cohen, *Rescue the Perishing: Eleanor Rathbone and the Refugees* (London, Vallentine Mitchell, 2010).
34. *Women in Council*, May 1933, p. 166; September 1933, p. 219; Ute Frevert, *Women in German History: from Bourgeois Emancipation to Sexual Liberation* (Oxford, Berg Publishers, 1989), p. 212.
35. *Women in Council*, January 1934, p. 5. In 1933 the British Federation of University Women (BFUW) began providing grants for German and Austrian academic exiles to continue in their professional work; the BFUW did not set up its own refugee committee until 1938. See Helen Jones, 'National, Community and Personal Priorities: British Women's Responses

to Refugees From the Nazis, From the Mid-1930s to Early 1940s', *Women's History Review* 21.1 (2012), p. 125; *Women in Council*, November 1938, pp. 126–7.
36. Bill Williams, *"Jews and other Foreigners": Manchester and the Rescue of the Victims of European Fascism, 1933–1940* (Manchester, Manchester University Press, 2011), p. 180; *Women in Council*, November 1938, p. 127.
37. *Women in Council*, April 1939, pp. 42–3; The Women's Library (henceforth TWL) 5NWC/2/C/01/3, General Committee minutes of the Coulsdon and Purley branch of the Women's Citizens' Association, 27 June and 29 November 1939, 2 January and 15 May 1940.
38. Zoe Josephs, *Survivors: Jewish Refugees in Birmingham 1933–1945* (Oldbury, Meridian, 1988), pp. 46, 77, 174; Williams, *"Jews and other Foreigners"* pp. 147–8; *Hilda Cashmore 1876–1943* (Gloucester, printed for private circulation by John Bellows, 1944), p. 44.
39. London Metropolitan Archives (henceforth LMA) ACC/3613/01/012, Minutes of the Executive of the NCW, 18 November 1938, pp. 103–04.
40. Paul Weindling, 'The Contribution of Central European Jews to Medical Science and Practice in Britain, the 1930s–1950s', in W.E. Mosse, ed., *Second Chance: Two Centuries of German-speaking Jews in the United Kingdom* (Tübingen, J.C.B. Mohr, 1991), pp. 246–7; the same, 'From Refugee Assistance to Freedom of Learning: the Strategic Vision of A.V. Hill, 1933–1964' in Shula Marks, Paul Weindling and Laura Wintour, eds, *In Defence of Learning: the Plight, Persecution and Placement of Academic Refugees, 1933–1980s* (Oxford, Oxford University Press, 2011), pp. 68–9.
41. LMA/ACC/3613/002 NCW Conference Programme for 1937.
42. Tony Kushner, 'An Alien Occupation—Jewish Refugees and Domestic Service in Britain, 1933–1948', in Werner Eugen Mosse, ed., *Second Chance*, pp. 554–9, 562–3.
43. Annie Altschul, who died in 2001, was one exile who overcame this disadvantage to the great benefit of her adopted country: forced to break off her mathematical studies in Vienna to work as a nanny in London, she entered hospital to train as a nurse and ended her career as a highly distinguished pioneer of psychiatric nursing. Among other obituaries, see the *Guardian*, 8 January 2002; see also, the 1995 interview of Professor Altschul by Dr Anne-Marie Rafferty in the archives of the Royal College of Nursing.
44. *Woman's Outlook*, 4 March 1939, pp. 630–1.
45. Gillespie, 'Working with the *"Kindertransports"*', p. 127.
46. Kushner, 'An Alien Occupation', pp. 572–3.
47. Vera K. Fast, *The Children's Exodus: a History of the Kindertransport* (London, I.B. Tauris, 2011), p. 122. Helen Bentwich was a parliamentary

candidate for the Labour Party in the 1930s and the Chair of London County Council in the mid-1950s.
48. Gladys Skelton née Williams *afterw*. Bendit was born in Australia in 1885, received most of her education in England, and worked in a variety of educational institutions before becoming Joint Hon. Sec. of the Inter-Aid Committee. She wrote under the pseudonym 'John Presland'. *Girton College Register 1869–1946* (Cambridge, privately printed, 1948), p. 158.
49. Mary Ford, 'The Arrival of Jewish Refugee Children in England 1938-9', *Journal of Immigrants and Minorities* 2 (July 1983), p. 137. An estimated 45 % of these children were 'non-Aryan Christians'. LMA ACC/2793/01/13/01, Council for German Jewry, *Report for 1936*, p. 10.
50. Geoffrey Alderman, *British Jewry since Emancipation* (Buckingham, University of Buckingham Press, 2014), p. 276, quotes the Home Secretary, Sir Samuel Hoare in April 1938: 'If a flood of the wrong type of immigrants were allowed in there might be serious danger of anti-semitic feeling being aroused in this country'.
51. Darton, *An Account of the Work of the Friends*, p. 50 and n.1; Ronald Stent, 'Jewish Refugee Organisations' in Mosse, *Second Chance*, p. 590; Fast, *Children's Exodus*, pp. 18–19.
52. Ford, 'The Arrival of Jewish Refugee Children', pp. 138–9, 149. Fast, *Children's Exodus*, pp. 20, 188. Fast, p. 188 estimates a total of 9354 of child migrants from RCM records.
53. Oldfield, '"It is usually She"', pp. 57–8, 62–3, 65–6.
54. Louise London, 'Jewish Refugees, Anglo-Jewry and British Government Policy 1930–40' in David Cesarani, ed., *The Making of Modern Anglo-Jewry* (Oxford, Blackwell, 1990), p. 187.
55. Ford, 'The Arrival of Jewish Refugee Children', pp. 140–1, 143. See also Derek Taylor, *Solomon Schonfeld: a Purpose in Life* (London, Vallentine Mitchell, 2009).
56. Fast, *Children's Exodus*, p. 21.
57. Oldfield, '"It is usually She"', p. 68; Fast, *Children's Exodus*, p. 226 note 76.
58. The Liberal Rabbi Leslie Mattuck wrote to Sir Robert Waley Cohen in March 1939: "I and those working with me cannot accept … the idea that Jewish children should not be placed in non-Jewish homes': Ford, 'The Arrival of Jewish Refugee Children', pp. 147, 151 note 50.
59. Lambeth Palace Library Ms William Temple 16, Hertz to Temple 23.6.1942. He was writing to the Archbishop of Canterbury in the context of the formation of the Council of Christians and Jews: see Chap. 8.
60. USL MS 60 17/8, Gray to Parkes, 6 Apr [1930?]. See also Chap. 8 for the context of this remark.

61. Oldfield, '"It is usually She"', p. 64.
62. Ford, 'The Arrival of Jewish Refugee Children', p. 141.
63. See Chap 3. The word 'children' was added to the Association's title in 1932.
64. JAPGWC *Annual Report* for 1925, pp. 13–14, 15–16, 20. See also *Annual Reports* for 1925–1939, *passim*.
65. *Annual Reports* for 1925–1939, *passim* ; USL MS 173 2/4/4, JAPGW General Purposes Committee, Minutes 7 February, 20 December 1934; 4 March 1936; 18 February, 24 November 1937.
66. JAPGWC Annual Report for 1935–6, p. 17.
67. JAPGWC Annual Report for 1935–6, pp. 20, 50.
68. USL MS 173 2/4/4, JAPGW General Purposes Committee, Minutes 17 June 1937, 15 November 1938.
69. TWL 4NVA/4/17, file, 'Notes Concerning the Help to Refugees at Stations', paper by S. Peters, 1 March 1939.
70. LMA ACC/4184/01/01/002, Jews' Temporary Shelter House Committee minutes, 6 February 1939.
71. The same, 10 January, 8 March, 3 July 1939.
72. TWL 4NVA/4/17, file, 'Notes Concerning the Help to Refugees at Stations', reports of Kathleen Kelly, 2 March, 22 June 1939. Compare this with the Annual Report of the Jews' Temporary Shelter for 1938–9, p. 11, appeal for gifts of clothing as 'Many of the refugees and emigrants arrive at the Shelter very poorly clad and present a pathetic sight'.
73. The same, report 2 March 1939.
74. LMA ACC/4184/01/01/002, Jews' Temporary Shelter House Committee minutes, 5 June 1939.
75. TWL 4NVA/4/17, file, Letters sent to Woburn House and Bloomsbury House and Mr Cohen: Letter of Cohen to Sempkins, 9 June 1939; Sempkins to Carpenter, 12 July 1939.
76. JAPGWC *Annual Report* for 1939–40, p. 13.
77. Jones, 'National, Community and Personal Priorities', p. 124.
78. London, 'Jewish Refugees', pp. 189–90.
79. Jones, 'National, Community and Personal Priorities', pp. 134–5.

CHAPTER 11

Conclusions

Gendering the topic of Christian and Jewish relations allows us to view many other inquiries in a fresh perspective. It becomes possible to reassess the relationship between voluntary, philanthropic and political agency, and to rethink the significance of religious identities, individual and communal, in all these spheres. The process by which Victorian women's charitable work propelled many of them into demands for social and legislative change is well known, as is the religious and spiritual content of much suffragist rhetoric and commitment. However, neither phenomenon would lead one to infer that the suffrage movement would pioneer interfaith cooperation before 1914, nor that Jewish women would be at the forefront of interfaith initiatives between the world wars. The *longue durée* of religious engagement in the twentieth century and the very broad spectrum of activities which can be subsumed (and too often have been dismissed) under the heading of philanthropy, should underpin any research into women's internationalism, social and educational innovation, and relief efforts for refugees in this period. Moreover, while activities in these areas were by no means confined to the female half of the population, it needs to be acknowledged how often men were the followers, rather than the leaders of such initiatives.

Inevitably, gendering this topic throws a radically different light on the history of Anglo-Jewry. The historiography of Jewish women may have been held back by an unconscious reluctance to contest the structures of an existing narrative. Certainly much scholarship has underplayed the extent to which Jewish women challenged their male-dominated communal institutions in the early decades of the twentieth century. The age-old official line—that woman's role in preserving Shabbat and kashrut within the home is not only sacred but equal in merit and importance with a man's public participation in the prayers and affairs of the synagogue—has more recently been buttressed by research suggesting that with the upheavals of migration, domestic religious practice actually had more significance than it had enjoyed while Jewish communities remained within Eastern Europe.[1] Leaving aside the fact that we have no real way of knowing that it was *more* important than before—whoever asked this question of their mother or grandmother?—this 'separate spheres' analysis has created an impression of stasis which is in itself ahistorical. Adhering to this complementary history of female religious practice leaves the male narrative—most particularly that of male–female relations—securely in place. It rules out any discussion of the reasons why women agitated for change, and why even the most moderate of their demands were refused.

As can be seen from their participation in the suffrage movement and the evidence of their involvement in contemporary social-work initiatives, Jewish women could experience a far greater degree of autonomy and equality outside the Anglo-Jewish community than within it. The paradigm of religious complementarity has diminished the multi-dimensional nature of female agency and obscured the gender dynamics of Anglo-Jewry. These women defined themselves, and carved out their paths of action, in response to the challenges of living in a modernising non-Jewish world, and also in reaction against the roles ascribed to them by Anglo-Jewish men. The occlusion of their dual identities, sometimes amounting to a conscious erasure, has also left the way clear for a socialist and feminist critique of their interventions which now merits modification. Historians have invoked the concepts of 'social control' and social condescension to characterise and condemn welfare work which at the time met with Jewish male condemnation as the exercise of a pernicious 'suffragette' influence.[2] The paradigm of 'social control', if it is not to be entirely abandoned, has to be expanded: the question 'who was trying to exercise social control over whom?' has more than one answer.

The near-total absence of the Jewish League for Woman Suffrage from the historical record has had the effect of obscuring the continuing influence of pre-1914 feminism and suffragism on Jewish women's continuing efforts to improve their communal status, as well as their important contribution to the Zionist movement in Britain. This is a significant element in the wider story of the post-suffrage movement in Britain. The decision of Rebecca Sieff, the leading figure of the Federation of Women Zionists, to settle in the new state of Israel for the last decades of her life has disrupted the linked histories of Jewish and non-Jewish feminism in Britain, which would otherwise be better known, and within which Sieff's role would be justly celebrated. It is difficult to shift the popular misunderstanding of the campaign for the female vote: its success, together with the upheavals of World War I, is widely seen to have brought about an era of gender equality. Ignorance of the obstacles remaining in the path of the interwar 'post-suffragists' is one of the reasons this goal of equality remains to be achieved. Similarly, it is in part because the relatively privileged Jewish women studied here have been largely hidden from the history of communal and national progressive movement that some of their communal battles remain to be fought over and over again.

Multiculturalism in present-day Britain is largely outside the remit of this book, but the issues of social control and autonomy which it raises are not confined to Anglo-Jewish history. The gender dynamics of Anglo-Jewry find their echo in many immigrant and minority communities. A number of talented women from South Asian families have achieved social and political prominence in this country with the warm encouragement of those families; a larger number of young women who have attempted to forge their own path into the host society have met a terrible fate at the hands of male relatives. It may even be the case that the best interpretation of the motives of teenage girls fleeing London for the camps of the so-called Islamic State may lie, tragically and perversely, with their desire to escape a future in which their lives will be, however lovingly, rigidly controlled, and to assert some form of autonomy in the face of a patriarchal domesticity.

A particular focus on relations between women can throw new light on antisemitism, without altering the fact that it will always be a contentious and perplexing issue. I have no desire to suggest that women are necessarily nicer than, or morally superior to men. There is no disputing the fact that British fascism had its active female supporters. However, the rivalry and competition underlying some tensions between communities can be differently configured for women and men. It is clear from these studies that many Jewish women enjoyed relationships with their non-Jewish counterparts which were based on shared social values, and were not tainted by either mutual or one-sided suspicion or jealousy.

Nevertheless, in this as in any inquiry, there must always be a subjective element in the exploration of words and their relation to actions. All texts should be treated with care, and quotations should not be too selective. Quoting from Rosalind Franklin's biographer Brenda Maddox, Antony Julius recounts that in the late 1930s, 'a new friend of the then undergraduate Rosalind Franklin was warned off by another undergraduate, "I don't know what you see in Ros—you know she is a Jew, don't you?"' without adding Maddox's very next sentence, which offers the other side of the story: 'Peggy [the new friend] was staggered because she had no personal knowledge of antisemitism'.[3]

Another occupational hazard for historians exists in our ability to find a valid quotation to suit almost any argument. Julius, discussing 'social distance', cites Lady Halifax, who considered some of the conventions of the Indian viceroyalty when the position was held by Rufus Isaacs, Marquess of Reading, to have verged on vulgarity.[4] By contrast I would cite Iris Butler, a young woman in India at that time, who gratefully remembered the kindness shown her by Lady Reading, and offered a more generous, if nonetheless nuanced view: Rufus and Alice Isaacs 'were free of the normal prejudices of the English ruling caste. ... Lady Reading's ancestral voices were very ancient and subtly different from most of her predecessors', enabling her 'to keep in step with the quick emotional reactions of Eastern people'.[5] Iris Butler acknowledged difference, but did not translate it into distance, and in this she resembled many of her peers in her own and earlier generations.

The present study subscribes to the view that 'drawing a balance sheet of Jewish-Gentile relations is always difficult and also a dangerous pursuit. Generalizing even about an area or a town is hard enough, given the diversity of human responses. Applying this on a national scale becomes near impossible'.[6] This statement is quoted from Anthony Julius's recent work on antisemitism in England, whose 800 pages recount a very different history from that recorded here. Without wishing to paint a rosy picture, or one at variance with common sense about human behaviour at an individual or collective level, I have asserted—or reinstated—a history of a country in which prejudice and exclusivity were not universal, and did not mutate into vicious behaviour. On the contrary: genuine efforts at understanding and generous gifts of time and labour were made by Christian to Jewish women throughout the period in question, and my chapter on refugee relief in Britain barely does justice to the geographical extent and social commitment of thousands of its female citizens. It is possible to surmise that Britain's island status, which largely protected it from Nazi invasion and occupation, has also protected latent British antisemitism from the exposure and salience to which a different wartime history could have given rise. But just as one cannot deny the existence of the chameleons of the Galapagos because they could not exist anywhere else on earth, the evolution of a human island species must also be accepted for what it is.

Throughout this book there has been little emphasis on philosemitism as a category of analysis. I have preferred instead to stress a prevailing culture of decency, interwoven with the ambiguities which bedevil all private and public relationships. Except among the monomaniacal, attitudes to the Other are rarely fixed and homogenous: anti- and philosemitism are attitudes which are available to groups and individuals in partial, complex, nuanced and untidy ways. If the same also holds true for relations between the different denominations of Islam and the Western communities (broadly speaking), this opens up ways of thinking about the possibilities for future communal coexistence in Europe. A gendered history of cross-communal collaboration and interfaith communication before World War II may offer at least some helpful lessons for those dealing with comparable issues in today's multicultural Britain. The issue can hardly be consigned to the groves of academe.

However, one condition for the kind of voluntary associational collaboration I have described will undoubtedly be lacking. Now and for the foreseeable future, large numbers of mature and educated women will not be found to give up hours of the working week for little or no pay. Women in the West today expect salaried employment, and the organisations of the voluntary sector do not stand outside this trend; indeed, many charities now employ full-time Chief Executives and other staff for salaries which prospective donors may consider excessive. Sustained work, for non-profitmaking goals, is certainly called for in the interfaith sphere; but the pool of labour to undertake it may not be found. Moreover, at the time of writing, such initiatives are often suspected of being covertly political or sectarian.[7]

In a development reminiscent of the difficulties encountered by the Society of Jews and Christians, some of the most generous cross-communal initiatives currently originate with liberal British Muslims, including some converts. However, institutions such as the Quilliam Foundation are not representative of the bulk of congregations. It is likely that, as with the formation of the Council of Christians and Jews, interfaith understanding between Muslims, Christians and Jews will only gain a firm foothold when it is embraced by the senior and most representative clerics of all denominations—and when all faiths embrace a common cause, or experience a common danger. It is also likely that only Christianity will offer participation in the process to senior women clergy, and that this in turn may be a stumbling block (as was not the case in the more patriarchal 1940s) to the friendship and understanding which are so profoundly needed. Despite these caveats, there remains a historical fund of social and moral capital in this country on which its citizens can still draw; a culture of wishing for neighbourliness and understanding. While these are not yet extinguished, neither is hope.

Notes

1. Rickie Burman, 'Women in Jewish Religious Life: Manchester 1880–1930' in James Obelkevich, Lyndal Roper and Raphael Samuel, eds, *Disciplines of Faith: Studies in Religion, Politics and Patriarchy* (London, Routledge & Kegan Paul, 1987) p. 51.
2. See, e.g. *Jewish Chronicle*, 18 July 2014, p. 12; 7 November 2014, pp. 11, 45.
3. Anthony Julius, *Trials of the Diaspora: a History of Anti-Semitism in England* (Oxford, Oxford University Press, 2010), p. 372; Brenda Maddox, *Rosalind Franklin, the Dark Lady of DNA* (New York, HarperCollins, 2002), p. 49.
4. Julius, *Trials*, p. 384.
5. Iris Butler, *The Viceroy's Wife: Letters of Alice, Countess of Reading, From India, 1921–25* (London, Hodder & Stoughton, 1969), pp. 14, 23.
6. Julius, *Trials*, p. 236. A recent study making considerable use of oral testimony demonstrates the difficulty of drawing up a balance sheet for a single city: Avram Taylor, '"Are you a Billy, or a Dan, or an old tin can?" Street Violence and Relations between Catholics, Jews and Protestants in the Gorbals during the inter-war years', *Urban History* 41.1 (2014).
7. The cross-communal organisation known at the time of writing as 'London Citizens' is considered by some to be too political, e.g. in its demands to introduce the 'living', as opposed to the 'minimum' wage; others fear that its Muslim affiliates may have connections to extremist elements.

CHAPTER 12

Coda: Rachel Bernstein Goes to Surrey Lane

My mother was born in London in 1910, the sixth and youngest child of parents who migrated from the Vilna region in the 1890s. Her grandparents were country people; her father's journey was prompted, not by pogroms, but by the poverty visited on nine siblings after their father, a blacksmith and woodcutter, died under a falling tree. Rachel Bernstein grew up in a materially poor household. Home was a terraced dwelling with an outdoor privy, but without a room in which to have a bath or shower; the nearest public baths were visited on the eve of every Sabbath. Despite these limitations, my mother's mother kept a spotlessly clean house in which no cobweb was ever to be seen, and where the laws of kashrut were scrupulously observed. My mother's mother could neither read nor write, and my grandfather's studies were (when time permitted) devoted to the Bible and the Talmud. But—and no matter how clichéd this sounds, it is no more than the truth—they valued the education this new world had to offer their children. When my uncle's schoolteacher visited the house to plead for the boy to be allowed to proceed to degree-level studies at the Regent Street Polytechnic, he was—figuratively—knocking at an open door. When, in 1924, my mother passed the exams which qualified her for a public scholarship, thus permitting her to progress beyond elementary school (the vast majority of British children were then educated only to the age of 14), off she went to Surrey Lane Central School for Girls.

© The Author(s) 2017
A. Summers, *Christian and Jewish Women in Britain, 1880–1940*,
Palgrave Critical Studies of Antisemitism and Racism,
DOI 10.1007/978-3-319-42150-6_12

The two years she spent there were almost certainly the most important in my own life. My mother recalled that she was the only Jewish girl at the school—living in South London, she was part of a tiny community. However, Jewish names do occur in the minute book of the school managers between 1924 and 1926;[1] either her recollection was at fault, or she was remembering being the only strictly orthodox pupil. On her first day, in fear and trembling, she asked her new headmistress if she might be excused morning prayers. 'Certainly', was the reply: but Rachel must not come to school later than the other girls, she must come into the hall in time for the post-prayer announcements, and she must not be idle in the interim. She should learn a poem by heart every morning, and the headmistress would hear her recite it at the end of every day. Rachel remembered most of those hundreds of poems well into her nineties. When I was seven years old, she opened one of her old school anthologies, and asked me to read from it. "Why are you using that sing-song voice?" she demanded. "The poems mean something. Read them for their meaning". At one remove, I had heard the voice of that extraordinary teacher.

Helen Elizabeth Lacy was a Fabian Socialist, and an early member of the London Shakespeare League. The post-prayer announcements were in fact readings from George Bernard Shaw and Robert Lynd and other contributors to the *New Statesman*, and one-woman performances of scenes from Shakespeare. These were followed up by group visits to performances staged at the Old Vic Theatre, also in South London. Rachel was a good student, and I suspect that Miss Lacy found every opportunity she could to award her prizes—for literature, for geography, for conduct— which would build up her library for later life. All Shakespeare's works, of course, in the Everyman volumes; the poetry of William Blake, Robert Browning, William Morris and Robert Bridges; these I observed on our bookshelves as constant companions to the Brixton Synagogue Hebrew and Religion Class prizes of Maurice Liber's *Rashi* and the Revd Morris Joseph's *Judaism as Creed and Life*.

Miss Lacy's own religious leanings are difficult to discern, and may well have been non-existent. School prayers and religious instruction were compulsory in state-supported education, but at Surrey Lane they may have been adhered to more in form than in spirit. At one point a lively correspondence erupted between Miss Lacy and the school managers over the prospect of girls 'being withdrawn from school for the purpose of attending Sunday School Outings … she hoped that those who attend such outings will not contribute to any presentation that might be made to her ...'.² The tone of her letters is tinged with an almost aristocratic disdain—my mother thought that Miss Lacy's family were Norfolk gentry whose emblem was the 'Lacy Knot'—and her disregard for many of the social norms imposed on state schoolteachers (or self-imposed, for fear of dismissal) was indeed remarkable. I used to disbelieve my mother when she told me that her headmistress lived in a *ménage à trois* with a former chorus girl and an unfrocked clergyman, but this was pretty accurate. The Revd Stewart Headlam was a founder of the Church and Stage Guild, and a dancer named Martha Lugg Wooldridge, known to my mother, remained permanently under his wing. He too was a Fabian and a founder of the London Shakespeare League, whose political radicalism had led to his losing his licence to serve as a priest in the Church of England. In 1887, he had conducted the funerals for the victims of 'Bloody Sunday', a demonstration in Trafalgar Square combining protests against unemployment and coercion in Ireland, which had been so violently suppressed by the Metropolitan Police that two men died of their injuries.³

Nor did I at first believe the story that Rachel had attended Stewart Headlam's own funeral in November 1924. She described what sounded like a very High Church affair: lots of candles and a coffin heaped up with dark red roses. 'How could you have been in church? Zeide [my grandfather] would never have allowed it'. 'Zeide didn't know'. Headlam's biographer specifically mentions those roses.⁴ Zeide assuredly did not know; nor may he have been aware that Rachel borrowed a costume from a school friend so that she could join in swimming lessons, or that she was the star athlete of the school, running and jumping in the knee-length divided skirts which he prohibited as shockingly immodest. One year, when she carried off all the medals in an inter-schools meeting, Rachel's subterfuges were mentioned by a Surrey Lane teacher to a rival colleague. By coincidence, in subsequent years these inter-school competitions were held on a Saturday. Rachel's transgressions could not extend as far as breaking the Sabbath. She left Surrey Lane at sixteen, but seems to have maintained contact with a Miss A.M. Grice, perhaps her English teacher, who gave her a book for her birthday in 1927. She claimed never to have had career ambitions, and was employed in office work and then with a beautician; as the youngest child, still unmarried, she was frequently taken out of work to look after her parents as they became frail. When she met and married my father, love of literature was a very strong bond: and every wedding anniversary was marked by my father's gift of a bouquet of roses, with a line of verse attached: 'how beautiful, how red those roses were'.

Anecdotes about individual lives, consciously or not, inform subjective bias in academic writing. It is not possible for me to denounce as institutionally antisemitic a society which produced teachers so considerate of the development of my parents, and respectful of their religious differences. They did not assume that Shakespeare and Browning were irrelevant to, or wasted on, the children of immigrant and illiterate parents; and what they invested in my parents allowed me in turn to pick up where my parents left off. The Anglo-Jewish establishment's ambition to create law-abiding citizens, who would absorb along the way the cultural riches denied to the residents of ghettos and *staedtls*, seems to me wholly rational and commendable, as does the desire to contribute to the good of the gentile world and to raise the honour in which the Jewish community would be held. Moreover, as my grandparents' own choices evince, such ambitions were not necessarily confined to notables, and should not be seen simply as their imposition upon the immigrant poor. Those historians scornful of the Anglo-Jewish establishment's project do not offer an alternative social model for a religious minority, and need to reflect on the unremitting need to build and repair bridges between neighbouring communities, and to find spaces where civic values and social and artistic enjoyments can be shared.

My first book was dedicated to my parents, but this one is dedicated with almost equal gratitude to Helen Elizabeth Lacy and to my own teacher, Elaine Kaye.

Notes

1. London Metropolitan Archives A2A, Battersea Group (Battersea Central School for Boys, Surrey Lane South and Battersea Central School for Girls, Surrey Lane South): Minutes of Managers, entries for 8 October 1925 and 3 December 1926, pp. 69, 118.
2. The same, 22 October1924, pp. 30, 36.
3. There is much more to be said about the life of this extraordinary man. See F.G. Bettany, *Stewart Headlam: a Biography* (London, John Murray, 1926); John Richard Orens, *Stewart Headlam's Radical Anglicanism: the Mass, the Masses and the Music Hall* (Urbana, University of Illinois Press, 2003).
4. Bettany, *Stewart Headlam*, p. 241: 'A cross of crimson roses was placed on the coffin … The funeral service was held at All Souls', St. Margaret's on Thames'. Orens, *Stewart Headlam's Radical Anglicanism*, pp. 28 and 41 ref. 4, points out that Headlam and his wife Beatrice had separated around 1885 because she was lesbian. Orens describes 'Pattie' Wooldridge as his 'housekeeper' (p. 152).

Bibliography

Archival Sources

Armitt Gallery, Ambleside
Charlotte Mason Archive

Atria (formerly *Aletta,* formerly IIAV), Amsterdam:
Fawcett-Auerbach Letters Folder 10

Bibliothèque Publique et Universitaire de Neuchâtel
Fonds Felix Bovet Ms 2098/86

Bishopsgate Institute, London
Archives of the Co-operative Movement and the Women's Co-operative Guild

Bodleian Library, Oxford
MS Dep. CMJ 68/14 [the Church Mission to the Jews]

British Library

Lady Battersea Papers
Cecil of Chelwood Papers

Central Zionist Archive, Jerusalem

Archives of Israel Zangwill

Friends House Library, London

Minutes of the Germany Emergency Committee
Papers of the German Refugee Assistance Fund

International Institute for Social History, Amsterdam

Sylvia Pankhurst Papers

Lambeth Palace Library

William Temple Papers

London Metropolitan Archives

ACC/3529, Correspondence of Lily Montagu
Microfilm X041/055, Lily Montagu Archive
ACC/3613/01, records of the National Union of Women Workers, subsequently the National Council of Women
ACC/3686, records of the Society of Jews and Christians
ACC/3121/E1/54, Jewish Peace Society Archive
ACC/4175, records of the Federation of Women Zionists
ACC/2793, Council for German Jewry
ACC/4184, Jews' Temporary Shelter

London School of Economics, Archives:

Coll Misc 0512, Letters of Octavia Hill to Henrietta and Samuel Barnett
MS WIC D2, Clubs' Industrial Association

Manchester County Record Office:

M 182/5/2, minutes of the Jewish Ladies' Visiting Association.

Montagu Centre, West Central Liberal Synagogue, London:

Reports and news cuttings relating to Lily Montagu and Liberal Judaism

Musee d'Art et d'Histoire du Judaisme, Paris:

Correspondence at http://dreyfus.mahj.org/consultation/index.php

Rothschild Archive:

000/84; Letters of Charlotte de Rothschild to her son Leopold, online transcriptions at http://www.rothschildarchive.org/RESEARCH

The National Archives

PRO 30/69, Papers of James Ramsay MacDonald and Margaret Gladstone MacDonald

TNA webpage, 'Security and Intelligence History, Your Guide to Resources', Reference: KV 2/1983

The Women's Library@LSE

4TAS, records of the Travellers' Aid Society
4NVA, records of the National Vigilance Association
7HFD, archive of Hugh Franklin and Elsie Duval
2LSW, records of the London Society for Woman Suffrage
5NWC, records of the Women's Citizens' Association
5WPP, records of the Women's Publicity Planning Association
Microfiche 9/01/0965
Recorded interviews, series 8SUF/B

Tower Hamlets Archives:

Edith Ramsay papers

UNIVERSITY OF LEEDS

Marks and Spencer Company Archives

UNIVERSITY OF SOUTHAMPTON LIBRARY:

MS 60, Papers of the Revd James Parkes
MS 122, records of the West End Jewish Literary Society
MS 129 AJ 26, archive of the Union of Jewish Women
MS 173, archives of the Jewish Board of Guardians; the Jewish Association for the Protection of Girls, Women and Children
MS 363, A3006, 3/2/3, Waley Cohen Correspondence

PRINTED PRIMARY SOURCES

UK Census for 1881, 1891 and 1901
Central British Fund for Jewish Relief and Rehabilitation, *Report* for 1933–43
The Church League for Women's Suffrage, *Bulletin*
Co-operative News
Council for German Jewry, *Report*, 1938
Daily Chronicle
The Free Church Suffrage Times
Girton College Register 1869–1946
The International Women's News
Jewish Association for the Protection of Girls, Women and Children, *Annual Reports*
Jewish Chronicle
Jewish Ladies' Visiting Association, *Annual Reports.*
The Jewish Literary Annual
The Jewish Bulletin
Jewish Religious Union Bulletin
The Jewish Review
Jews' Temporary Shelter, *Annual Reports*
Manchester City News
Manchester Evening Mail
Manchester Guardian (subsequently *Guardian*)
Manchester and Salford Ladies' Public Health Society (also known as: Manchester and Salford Ladies' Sanitary Association; Ladies Health Society; Ladies' Sanitary Reform Association), *Annual Reports.*
National Union of Women Workers (later the National Council of Women), *Conference Reports*
Parents' Review
Peace News

Slater's Directory of Manchester (1888)
The Threefold Cord
The Times
The Woman's Signal
Travellers' Aid Society, *Annual Reports*
Union of Jewish Women, *Annual Reports*
Women's Industrial Council, *Annual Reports*
Women in Council
Women's Industrial News
Woman's Life
Woman's Outlook
Norman and Jeanne Mackenzie (eds,) *The Diary of Beatrice Webb* Vol. 2, (London, Virago, 1983)

SECONDARY SOURCES: BOOKS AND ARTICLES PUBLISHED UP TO 1940

Mary Sophia Allen and Julie Helen Heyneman, *Woman at the Crossroads* (London, Unicorn Press, 1934)
Mary Sophia Allen, *Lady in Blue* (London, Stanley Paul, 1936)
Frederick George Bettany, *Stewart Headlam: a Biography* (London, John Murray, 1926)
Vera Brittain, *Testament of Friendship* (London, Macmillan, 1940)
Blanche Athena Clough, *Memoir of Anne Jemima Clough* (London, Edward Arnold, 1897)
Angela Burdett Coutts, ed., *Woman's Mission* (London, S. Low, Marston & Co., 1893)
Mrs Nathaniel L. [Julia] Cohen, *The Children's Psalm-Book ... together with a Prayer-Book for home use in Jewish families* (London, G. Routledge and Sons, 1907)
COPEC *Commission Reports* II-IV, VIII, (London, Longmans Green, 1924)
George Dangerfield, *The Strange Death of Liberal England* (London, Constable, 1936)
Revd J. Tyssul Davis, *A League of Religions* (London, Lindsey Press, 1927)
E. Ethelmer (E C. Wolstenholme Elmy), 'Feminism', *Westminster Review* January 1898
Florence Farr, *Modern Woman: Her Intentions* (London, Frank Palmer, 1910)
Millicent Fawcett, *What I Remember* (London, T. Fisher Unwin, 1924)
Constance Flower, *Mehayil el Hayil, 'From Strength to Strength', Lessons for Jewish Children* (London, G. Bell & Sons, 1890)
——, as Lady Battersea, *Waifs and Strays* (London, A.L. Humphreys, 1921)
——, *Reminiscences* (London, Macmillan, 1922)

Geoffrey Franklin. Born May 11th 1890. Died September 11th 1930. [Memoirs and correspondence printed for private circulation] (Chiswick Press, 1933)

Maria Ogilvie Gordon, *Historical Sketch of the National Council of Women of Great Britain* (M.O. Gordon, 1937)

Lizzie Hands, *Some Legal Difficulties Which Beset the Jewess* (printed for private circulation, 1920)

Lucy Herbert, *Mrs Ramsay MacDonald* (London, Women Publishers, 1924)

In Memoriam Charlotte M. Mason (London, Parents' National Education Union, 1923)

Jennie Lee, *Tomorrow Is a New Day* (London, Cresset Press, 1939)

Clara Maria Susanna Lowe, *God's Answers: a Record of Miss Annie Macpherson's Work at the Home of Industry, Spitalfields, London, and in Canada* (London, J. Nisbet, 1882)

J. Ramsay MacDonald, *Margaret Ethel MacDonald, 1870–1911* (London and Lossiemouth, privately printed, 1911)

——, *Margaret Ethel MacDonald* (London, Hodder & Stoughton, 1912)

Charlotte Maria Mason, *Home Education* (London, Kegan Paul, 1886)

——, *Home Education* (London, Kegan Paul, 1905)

——, *Parents and Children* (London, Kegan Paul 1904)

——, 'Recollections of Miss Clough and her connexion with the P.N.E.U.', *Parents' Review* 8 (1897)

Lily [Lilian] Helen Montagu, *Naomi's Exodus* (London, T. Fisher Unwin, 1901)

——, *Broken Stalks* (London, R. Brimley Johnson, 1902)

——, *Samuel Montagu, First Baron Swaythling, Born Dec. 21, 1832, Died Jan. 12, 1911: a character sketch* (London [for private circulation only, 1912)

Estelle Sylvia Pankhurst, *The Suffragette Movement* (London, Virago, 1984) [originally published London, Longmans, 1931]

——, *The Home Front* (London, Hutchinson, 1932)

Bertha Pappenheim trans. Margery Bentwich, 'The Jewish Woman in Religious Life', *The Jewish Review* 3 (1912–1913)

Emmeline Pethick-Lawrence, *My Part in a Changing World* (London, Victor Gollancz, 1938)

Edith Picton-Turbervill, *Life is Good* (London, Frederick Muller, 1939)

Charles Russell and Harry Samuel Lewis, eds, *The Jew in London* (London, T. Fisher Unwin, 1900)

Evelyn Sharp, *Hertha Ayrton 1854–1923* (London, Edward Arnold, 1926)

Edward Shillito, *Christian Citizenship: the Story and Meaning of C.O.P.E.C* (London, Longmans, 1924)

Herbert Sidebotham, *England and Palestine: Essays towards the Restoration of a Jewish State* (London, Constable, 1918)

[Rachel Simon], *Records and Reflections Selected From Her Writings during Half a Century ... by Lady Simon* (London, Wertheimer & Lea, 1894)

Gertrude Spielmann, 'Woman's Place in the Synagogue', *The Jewish Review* 4 (1913–1914)
Mary H. Steer, *Opals from Sand: a Story of Early Days at the Bridge of Hope* (London, Morgan & Scott, 1912)
——, *The Bridge of Hope Mission: a Jubilee Thanksgiving* (London, Gillett Bros, 1929)
[Tonna] *Personal Recollections by Charlotte Elizabeth* [Charlotte Elizabeth Phelan, afterwards Tonna] (London, R.B. Seeley & W. Burnside, 1841)
William Purdie Treloar, *A Lord Mayor's Diary, 1906–7* (London, John Murray, 1920)
Rosa Waugh, *The Life of Benjamin Waugh* (London, T. Fisher Unwin, 1913)
The Woman's Who's Who 1934–35 (London, Shaw Publishing 1934)
[Wilkinson] *The Life of John Wilkinson the Jewish Missionary, by His Youngest Son Samuel Hinds Wilkinson* (London, Morgan & Scott, 1908)
G.M. Williams, *Mary Clifford* (Bristol, J.W. Arrowsmith, 1920)

Secondary Sources: Books Published after 1940

H. Pearl Adam, ed., *Women in Council* (London, Oxford University Press, 1945)
Geoffrey Alderman, *The Jewish Community in British Politics* (Oxford, Clarendon Press, 1983)
——, *British Jewry since Emancipation* (Buckingham, University of Buckingham Press, 2014)
Charlotte Baum, Paula E. Hyman and Sonya Michel, *The Jewish Woman in America* (New York, Dial Press, 1976)
Mary Beard, *The Invention of Jane Harrison* (London and Cambridge Mass., Harvard University Press, 2000)
Deirdre Beddoe, *Back to Home and Duty: Women between the Wars 1918–1939* (London, Pandora, 1989).
Adrian Bell, *Only for Three Months: the Basque Children in Exile* (Norwich, Mousehold Press, 1996)
Helen Bentwich, *If I forget Thee: some chapters Of autobiography, 1912–1920* (London, Elek, 1973)
Norman Bentwich, *Mandate Memories, 1918–1948* (London, Hogarth, 1965)
Chaim Bermant, *The Cousinhood: the Anglo-Jewish Gentry* (London, Eyre & Spottiswoode, 1971)
Pierre Birnbaum trans. Jane Marie Todd, *The Anti-Semitic Moment: a Tour of France in 1898* (New York, Hill and Wang, 1998)
Gerry Black, *J.F.S.: the History of the Jews' Free School, London since 1732* (London, Tymsder Publishing, 1998)
Lucy Bland, *Banishing the Beast: English Feminism and Sexual Morality, 1885–1914* (London, Penguin, 1995)

Elaine Blond with Barry Turner, *Marks of Distinction* (London, Vallentine Mitchell, 1988)
Margaret Bondfield, *A Life's Work* (London, Hutchinson, 1949)
Frank W. Brecher, *Reluctant Ally: United States Foreign Policy toward the Jews from Wilson to Roosevelt* (New York, Greenwood Press, 1991)
Richard Breitman and Alan M. Kraut, *American Refugee Policy and European Jewry, 1933–45* (Bloomington, Indiana University Press, 1987)
Edward J. Bristow, *Prostitution and prejudice: the Jewish fight against white slavery 1870–1939* (Oxford, Clarendon Press, 1982).
Vera Brittain, --, *Testament of Experience* (Bath, Cedric Chivers, 1971)
Tom Buchanan, *The Spanish Civil War and the British Labour Movement* (Cambridge, Cambridge University Press, 1991)
Iris Butler, *The Viceroy's Wife: Letters of Alice, Countess of Reading, from India, 1921–25* (London, Hodder & Stoughton, 1969)
Peter Cahalan, *Belgian Refugee Relief in England during the Great War* (New York and London, Garland, 1982)
Eric Cahm, *The Dreyfus Affair in French Society and Politics* (London, Longman, 1996)
Hilda Cashmore 1876–1943 (Gloucester, printed for private circulation by John Bellows, 1944)
Martin Ceadel, *Pacifism in Britain, 1914–1945: the Defining of a Faith* (Oxford, Clarendon Press, 1980)
———, *Semi-detached Idealists: the British peace movement and international relations, 1854–1945* (Oxford and New York, Oxford University Press, 2000)
David Cesarani, *The 'Jewish Chronicle' and Anglo-Jewry* (Cambridge, Cambridge University Press, 1994)
———, ed., *The Making of Anglo-Jewry* (Oxford, Basil Blackwell, 1989)
Andrew Chandler, ed., *The Church and Humanity: the Life and Work of George Bell, 1883–1958* (Farnham, Ashgate, 2012)
Bryan Cheyette and Nadia Valman, eds, *The Image of the Jew in European Liberal Culture 1789–1914* (London, Vallentine Mitchell, 2004)
Essex Cholmondeley, *The Story of Charlotte Mason 1842–1923* (London, Dent, 1960)
Susan Cohen, *Rescue the Perishing: Eleanor Rathbone and the Refugees* (London, Vallentine Mitchell, 2010)
Christine Collette, *For Labour and for Women: the Women's Labour League 1906–1918* (Manchester, Manchester University Press, 1989)
Mary Gavin Clarke, *A Short Life of Ninety Years* (Edinburgh, Astrid and Martin Huggins, 1973)
Christine Collette, *For Labour and for Women: the Women's Labour League, 1906–1918* (Manchester, Manchester University Press, 1989)
Margaret A. Coombs, *Charlotte Mason: Hidden Heritage and Educational Influence* (Cambridge, Lutterworth Press, 2015)

Jane Cox (ed.), *A Singular Marriage: a Labour Love Story in Letters and Diaries; Ramsay and Margaret Macdonald* (London, Harrap, 1988)
Elizabeth Crawford, *The Women's Suffrage Movement: a Reference Guide 1866–1928* (London, UCL Press, 1999)
Lawrence Darton, *An Account of the Work of the Friends Committee for Refugees and Aliens, first known as the Germany Emergency Committee of the Society of Friends,1933–50* (FRCA, duplicated text, 1954)
Mary Davis, *Sylvia Pankhurst: a Life in Radical Politics* (London, Pluto Press, 1999)
Harry Defries, *Conservative Party attitudes to Jews 1900–1950* (London, Frank Cass, 2001)
Todd M. Endelman, *Radical Assimilation in English Jewish History, 1656–1945* (Bloomington, Indiana University Press, 1990)
——, *The Jews of Britain 1656 to2000* (Berkeley and Los Angeles, University of California Press, 2002)
Lillian Faderman, *Surpassing the Love of Men: Romantic Friendship and Love between Women From the Renaissance to the Present* (New York, Morrow, 1981)
Vera K. Fast, *The Children's Exodus: a History of the Kindertransport* (London, I.B. Tauris, 2011)
David Feldman, *Englishmen and Jews: Social Relations and Political Culture, 1840–1914* (New Haven and London, Yale University Press, 1994)
The First 50 Years: a Record of Liberal Judaism in England, 1900–1950 (London, Liberal Jewish Synagogue, 1950)
Ian Christopher Fletcher, Laura E. Nym Mayhall and Philippa Levine, eds, *Women's Suffrage in the British Empire: Citizenship, Nation and Race* (London, Routledge, 2000)
Sheila Fletcher *Maude Royden* (Oxford and Cambridge Mass., Basil Blackwell, 1989)
Ute Frevert, *Women in German History: from Bourgeois Emancipation to Sexual Liberation* (Oxford, Berg Publishers, 1989)
Michael Galchinsky, *The Origin of the Modern Jewish Woman Writer: Romance and Reform in Victorian England* (Detroit, Wayne State University Press, 1996)
Rosalie Gassman-Sherr, *The Story of the Federation of Women Zionists of Great Britain and Ireland, 1919–1968* (London, Federation of Women Zionists, 1968)
Karen Gershon, ed. Phyllis Lassner and Peter Lawson, *A Tempered Wind* (Evanston, Northwestern University Press, 2009)
Monk Gibbon, *Netta* (London, Routledge and Kegan Paul, 1960)
Kathryn Gleadle, *The Early Feminists: Radical Unitarians and the Emergence of the Women's Rights Movements, 1831–1851* (New York, St Martin's Press; London, Macmillan, 1995)
Simon Goodenough, *Jam and Jerusalem* (Glasgow, Collins, 1977)

Lawrence Goldman, *Science, Reform and Politics in Victorian Britain: the Social Science Association, 1857–1886* (New York, Cambridge University Press, 2002)
Amy Zahl Gottlieb, *Men of Vision: Anglo-Jewry's Aid to Victims of the Nazi Regime, 1933–1945* (London, Weidenfeld & Nicolson, 1998)
Julie V. Gottlieb, *Feminine Fascism: Women in Britain's fascist movement 1923–1945* (London, I.B. Tauris, 2000)
Richard Griffiths, *Patriotism Perverted: Captain Ramsey, the Right Club and English Anti-semitism, 1939–40* (London, Constable, 1998)
Matthew Grimley, *Citizenship, Community and the Church of England: Liberal Anglican Theories of the State between the Wars* (Oxford, Clarendon Press, 2004)
Brian Harrison, *Prudent Revolutionaries: Portraits of British Feminists between the Wars* (Oxford, Clarendon Press, 1987)
Naomi Hetherington and Nadia Valman, eds, *Amy Levy: Critical Essays* (Athens, Ohio University Press, 2010)
Sandra Stanley Holton, *Quaker Women: Personal Life, Memory and Radicalism in the Lives of Women Friends, 1780–1930* (London, Routledge, 2007)
———, *Suffrage Days: Stories from the Suffrage Movement* (London, Routledge, 1996)
———, with June Purvis, eds., *Votes for Women* (London, Routledge, 2000)
Val Horsler, *Women's Century: an Illustrated History of the Women's Institute* (London, Third Millenium Publishing, 2015
Paula E. Hyman, *Gender and Assimilation in Modern Jewish History; the Roles and Representation of Women* (Seattle, University of Washington Press, 1995).
[Isaacs] *For the Record: the Memoirs of Eva, Marchioness of Reading* (London, Hutchinson, 1972)
Louise A. Jackson, *Child Sexual Abuse in Victorian England* (London, Routledge, 2000)
Stanley Jackson, *A Short Walk from the Temple* (London, Michael Joseph, 1970)
Louis Jacobs, *Helping with Inquiries* (London, Vallentine Mitchell, 1989)
Patricia Jalland, ed., *Octavia Wilberforce: the Autobiography of a Pioneer Woman Doctor* (London, Cassell, 1989)
Jane Jordan, *Josephine Butler* (London, John Murray. 2001)
Zoe Josephs, *Survivors: Jewish Refugees in Birmingham 1933–1945* (Oldbury, Meridian, 1988)
Anthony Julius, *T.S. Eliot, Anti-Semitism and Literary Form* (Cambridge, Cambridge University Press, 1995)
———, *Trials of the Diaspora: a History of Anti-Semitism in England* (Oxford, Oxford University Press, 2010)
Marion A. Kaplan, *The Jewish Feminist Movement in Germany: the Campaigns of the Jüdische Frauenbund 1904–1938* (Westport and London, Greenwood, 1979)
Yvonne Kapp, *Eleanor Marx* Vol. I (London, Virago, 1979)

Jonathan Karp and Adam Sutcliffe, eds, *Philosemitism in History* (Cambridge, Cambridge University Press, 2011)
John Henry Somerset Kent, *William Temple: Church, State and Society in Britain, 1880–1950* (Cambridge, Cambridge University Press, 1992)
Susan Kingsley Kent, *Sex and Suffrage in Britain 1860–1914* (Princeton, Princeton University Press, 1987)
Melissa R. Klapper, *Jewish girls Coming of Age in America, 1860–1920* (New York, New York University Press, 2005)
———, *Ballots, Babies and Banners of Peace: American Jewish Women's Activism 1890–1940* (New York, New York University Press, 2013)
Norman Kleeblatt, ed., *John Singer Sargent: Portraits of the Wertheimer Family* (New York, Jewish Museum, Exhibition catalogue 1999)
Tony Kushner and Kenneth Lunn, (eds.), *The Politics of Marginality: Race, the Radical Right and Minorities in Twentieth Century Britain* (London, Cass, 1990)
Tony Kushner and Nadia Valman (eds), *Remembering Cable Street: Fascism and Anti-Fascism in British Society* (London, Vallentine Mitchell, 2000)
Linda Kuzmack *Woman's Cause: The Jewish Woman's Movement in England and the United States, 1881–1933* (Columbus, Ohio State University Press, 1986)
Phyllis Lassner and Lara Trubowitz, eds, *Antisemitism and Philosemitism in the Twentieth and Twenty-first Centuries* (Newark, University of Delaware Press, 2008)
Jennie Lee, *This Great Journey* (London, Macgibbon & Kee, 1963)
———, *My Life with Nye* (London, J. Cape, 1980)
Henrietta Leslie, *More Ha'pence than kicks, being some things remembered* (London, Macdonald, 1943)
Naomi B. Levine, *Politics, Religion and Love: the story of H.H. Asquith, Venetia Stanley, and Edwin Montagu* (New York, New York University Press, 1991)
Donald M. Lewis, *The Origins of Christian Zionism: Lord Shaftesbury and Evangelical Support for a Jewish Homeland* (Cambridge, Cambridge University Press, 2010)
[Liberal Judaism] *The First 50 Years: A Record of Liberal Judaism In England, 1900–1950* (London: The Younger Members Organization and the Alumni Society of the Liberal Jewish Synagogue, 1950)
Jill Liddington and Jill Norris, *One Hand Tied Behind Us: the Rise of the Women's Suffrage Movement* (London, Virago, 1978)
Rainer Liedtke, *Jewish Welfare in Hamburg and Manchester c. 1850–1914* (Oxford, Clarendon Press, 1998)
Louise London, *Whitehall and the Jews, 1933–1948: British Immigration Policy, Jewish Refugees, and the Holocaust* (New York, Cambridge University Press, 1999).
Mary McCune, *"The Whole Wide World, Without Limits": International Relief, Gender Politics, and American Jewish Women, 1893–1930* (Detroit, Wayne State University Press, 2005)

Brenda Maddox, *Rosalind Franklin, the Dark Lady of DNA* (New York, HarperCollins, 2002)
Lara V. Marks, *Model Mothers: Jewish Mothers and Maternity Provision in East London 1870–1939* (Oxford, Clarendon Press, 1994)
——, *Metropolitan Maternity: Maternal and Infant Welfare Services in Early Twentieth Century London* (Amsterdam and Atlanta, Rodopi, 1996)
David Marquand, *James Ramsay MacDonald* (London, Cape, 1977)
Jan Marsh, *Christina Rossetti: a Writer's Life* (London, Viking, 1995)
Helen Mathers, *Patron Saint of Prostitutes: Josephine Butler and a Victorian Scandal* (Stroud, The History Press, 2014)
Walter Robert Matthews, *Memories and meanings* (London, Hodder & Stoughton, 1969)
Pauline C. Metcalf, *Syrie Maugham: Staging Glamorous Interiors* (New York, Acanthus Press, 2010)
Clare Midgley, *Women against Slavery: the British Campaigns 1780–1870* (London, Routledge, 1992)
Lilian H. Montagu, *The Faith of a Jewish Woman* (London, Allen & Unwin, 1943)
——, *My Club and I* (London, Neville Spearman Ltd & Herbert Joseph Ltd, 1954)
Sue Morgan and Jacqueline de Vries, eds, *Women, Gender and Religious Cultures in Britain, 1800–1940* (London, Routledge, 2010)
Sioban Nelson, *Say Little, Do Much: Nursing, Nuns and Hospitals in the Nineteenth Century* (Philadelphia, University of Pennsylvia Press, 2001)
Carol Ockman, *Ingres's Eroticized Bodies: Retracing the Serpentine Line* (London, New Haven, Yale University Press, 1995)
Sybil Oldfield, *Women Humanitarians: a Biographical Dictionary of British Women Active between 1900 and 1950* (London, Continuum, 2001)
John Richard Orens, *Stewart Headlam's Radical Anglicanism: the Mass, the Masses and the Music Hall* (Urbana, University of Illinois Press, 2003)
Oxford Dictionary of National Biography
James Parkes, *Voyage of Discoveries* (London, Gollancz, 1969)
Susan Pedersen, *Eleanor Rathbone and the Politics of Conscience* (London, New Haven, Yale University Press, 2004)
F. K. Prochaska *Women and Philanthropy in 19th Century England* (Oxford, Clarendon Press, 1980)
Peter G. J. Pulzer, *The Rise of Political Anti-Semitism in Germany and Austria* (New York, John Wiley, 1964)
Winifred Raphael, *Gertrude Emily Spielman [sic] 1864–1949* (Sevenoaks, Caxton and Holmesdale Press, 1950)
Lawrence Rigal and Rosita Rosenberg, *Liberal Judaism: the First Hundred Years* (London, Union of Progressive and Liberal Synagogues, 2004)
Meri-Jane Rochelson, *A Jew in the Public Arena: the Career of Israel Zangwill* (Detroit, Wayne State University Press, 2008)

Sheila Rowbotham, *Hidden from History: 300 Years of Women's Oppression and the Fight Against It* (London, Pluto Press, 1973).
W. D. Rubinstein, *A History of the Jews in the English-Speaking World: Great Britain* (Basingstoke, Macmillan, 1996)
W. D. Rubinstein and H. D. Rubinstein, *Philosemitism: Admiration and Support for Jews in the English-speaking World 1840–1939* (Basingstoke, Macmillan, 1999)
Pamela Shatzkes, *Holocaust and Rescue: Impotent or Indifferent? Anglo-Jewry 1938–1945* (London, Vallentine Mitchell, 2002)
Israel Joshua Singer, *Of a World That Is No More* (London, Faber, 1970)
Israel Moses Sieff, *Memoirs* (London, Weidenfeld & Nicolson, 1970)
Mrinalini Sinha, *Colonial Masculinity: the Effeminate Bengali and the Manly Englishman in the Late Nineteenth Century* (Manchester, Manchester University Press, 1995)
Harold L. Smith, *The British Women's Suffrage Campaign 1866–1928*, 2nd edn revised (Harlow, Longman, 2010)
Bertha Sokoloff, *Edith and Stepney: the Life of Edith Ramsay* (London, Stepney Books, 1987)
Katherine Storr, *Excluded from the Record: Women, Refugees and Relief 1914–1929* (Bern, Oxford, Peter Lang, 2010)
Anne Summers, *Angels and Citizens: British Women as Military Nurses 1854–1914* (Newbury, Threshold, 2nd ed., 2000)
——, *Female Lives, Moral States: Women, Religion and Political Culture in Britain, 1800–1930* (Newbury, Threshold, 2000)
Gill Sutherland, *Faith, Duty and the Power of Mind: the Cloughs and their Circle, 1820-1960* (Cambridge, Cambridge University Press, 2006)
John Sutherland, *Mrs. Humphry Ward: Eminent Victorian, Pre-eminent Edwardian* (Oxford, Clarendon Press, 1990)
Laura Tabili, *Global Migrants, Local Culture: Natives and Newcomers in Provincial England, 1841–1939* (Basingstoke, Palgrave Macmillan, 2011)
Susan Tananbaum, *Jewish Immigrants in London 1880–1939* (London, Pickering and Chatto, 2014)
Derek Taylor, *Solomon Schonfeld: a Purpose in Life* (London, Vallentine Mitchell, 2009)
Mabel Tylecote, *The Education of Women at Manchester University 1883 to 1933* (Manchester, Manchester University Press, 1941)
Ellen M. Umansky, *Lily Montagu and the Advancement of Liberal Judaism* (New York, E. Mellen Press, 1983).
Nadia Valman, *The Jewess in Nineteenth-Century British Literary Culture* (Cambridge, Cambridge University Press, 2007)
Martha Vicinus, ed., *Lesbian Subjects: a feminist studies reader* (Bloomington, Indiana Univerity Press, 1996)
——, *Intimate Friends: Women Who Loved Women, 1778–1928* (Chicago, University of Chicago Press, 2004).

Bernard Wasserstein, *The Secret Lives of Trebitsch Lincoln* (Harmondsworth, Penguin, 1988)
——, *Herbert Samuel: a Political Life* (Oxford, Clarendon Press, 1992)
Chaim Weizmann, *Trial and Error* (London, Hamish Hamilton, 1949)
Alan Wilkinson, *The Church of England and the First World War* (London, Society for the Propagation of Christian Knowledge, 1978)
Bill Williams, *The Making of Manchester Jewry, 1740–1875* (Manchester, Manchester University Press, 1976)
——, *Jewish Manchester: an illustrated History* (Derby, Breedon Books, 2008)
——, *"Jews and other Foreigners": Manchester and the Rescue of the Victims of European Fascism, 1933–1940* (Manchester, Manchester University Press, 2011)
Sophia A. Van Wingerden, *The Women's Suffrage Movement in Britain 1866–1928* (Basingstoke, Macmillan, 1999)

Secondary Sources – articles published after 1940

Lawrence Barmann, 'Confronting Secularisation: Origins of the London Society for the Study of Religion', *Church History* 62,1 (1993)
Laura Beers, '"Women for Westminster", Feminism, and the Limits of Non-partisan Associational Culture', in Julie Gottlieb and Richard Toye, eds., *The Aftermath of Suffrage: Women, Gender and Politics in Britain, 1918–1945* (Basingstoke and New York, Palgrave, 2013)
Michael Bentley, ed., *Public and Private Doctrine: Essays in British History Presented to Maurice Cowling* (Cambridge, Cambridge University Press, 1993)
Cecil Bloom, 'The British Labour Party and Palestine, 1917-1948', *Jewish Historical Studies* 36 (1999-2001)
Françoise Blum, 'Itinéraires féministes à la lumière de l'Affaire', in Michel Leymarie, ed., *La Posterité de L'affaire Dreyfus* (Villeneuve-d'Ascq, presses universitaires du septentrion, 1998)
Tom Buchanan, 'The Role of the British Labour Movement in the Origins and Work of the Basque Children's Committee, 1937-9', *European History Quarterly* 18.2 (1988)
Rickie Burman, '"She looketh well to the Ways of her Household"' in Gail Malmgreen, ed., *Religion in the Lives of English Women, 1760–1930* (Beckenham, Croom Helm, 1986)
——, 'Jewish Women and the Household Economy in Manchester, c. 1890–1920' in David Cesarani, ed., *The Making of Modern Anglo-Jewry* (Oxford, Blackwell, 1990)
——, 'Middle-class Anglo-Jewish Lady Philanthropists and East European Jewish Women', in Joan Grant, ed., *Women, Migration and Empire* (Stoke-on-Trent, Trentham, 1996)

——, 'Women in Jewish Religious Life: Manchester 1880–1930' in James Obelkevich, Lyndal Roper and Raphael Samuel, eds, *Disciplines of Faith: Studies in Religion, Politics and Patriarchy* (London, Routledge and Kegan Paul, 1987)

Andrew Chandler, 'A Question of Fundamental Principles. The Church of England and the Jews of Germany 1933–1937', *Leo Baeck Institute Yearbook* 38 (New York, Leo Baeck Institute, 1993)

——, 'The Church of England and the Jews of Germany and Austria in 1938', *Leo Baeck Institute Yearbook* 40 (New York, Leo Baeck Institute, 1995)

——, 'George Bell and the Internment Crisis of 1940' in Andrew Chandler, ed., *The Church and Humanity: the Life and Work of George Bell, 1883–1958* (Farnham, Ashgate, 2012)

Christopher Clark, 'The Jews and the German State in the Wilhelmine Era' in Michael Brenner, Rainer Liedtke and David Rechter, eds, *Two Nations: British and German Jews in Comparative Perspective* (Tübingen, M. Siebeck, 1999)

Martyn Cornick, 'The Dreyfus Affair - Another Year, Another Centenary. British opinion and the Rennes Verdict, September 1899', *Modern and Contemporary France* 7:4 (1999)

Martin Durham, 'Women and Fascism. Women and the British Union of Fascists, 1932–1940', in Tony Kushner and Kenneth Lunn, eds, *the Politics of Marginality: Race, the Radical Right and Minorities in Twentieth Century Britain* (London, Cass, 1990)

Arthur Exell, 'Morris Motors in the 1930s: Part II', *History Workshop Journal* 7 (1979)

Mary Ford, 'The Arrival of Jewish Refugee Children in England 1938–9', *Immigrants and Minorities* 2 (July 1983)

Jessica Gerard 'Ladies Bountiful: Women of the Landed Classes and Rural Philanthropy', *Victorian Studies* 30.2 (1987)

Veronica Gillespie, 'Working with the *"Kindertransports"*' in Sybil Oldfield, ed. *This Working-day World: Women's Lives and Culture(s) in Britain 1914–1945* (London, Taylor & Francis, 1994)

Alex Goody, 'Passing in the City: the Liminal Spaces of Levy's late work' in Naomi Hetherington and Nadia Valman, eds, *Amy Levy: critical essays* (Athens, Ohio University Press, 2010)

Julie V. Gottlieb, 'Women and Fascism in the East End' in Tony Kushner and Nadia Valman, eds, *Remembering Cable Street: Fascism and Anti-Fascism in British Society* (London, Vallentine Mitchell, 2000)

——, 'Varieties of Feminist Responses to Fascism in Inter-war Britain' in Nigel Copsey and Andrzej Olechnowicz, eds, *Varieties of Anti-fascism: Britain in the Inter-war Period* (Basingstoke, Palgrave Macmillan, 2010)

Abigail Green, 'Rethinking Sir Moses Montefiore: Religion, Nationhood, and International Philanthropy in the Nineteenth Century', *American Historical Review* 110.3(2005)

Ruth Harris, 'Letters to Lucie: Spirituality, Friendship and Politics during the Dreyfus Affair' in Ruth Harris and Lyndal Roper, eds, *The Art of Survival: Gender and History in Europe, 1450–2000* (Oxford, Oxford University Press, 2006)

Vanessa Heggie, 'Jewish Medical Charity in Manchester: Reforming Alien Bodies', *Bulletin of the John Rylands University Library of Manchester* 87.1 (2005)

Claire Hirshfield, 'The Anglo-Boer War and the Issue of Jewish Culpability', *Contemporary Review* 15.4 (1980)

Paula E. Hyman, 'Does Gender Matter? Locating Women in European Jewish History' in Jeremy Cohen and Moshe Rosman, eds, *Rethinking European Jewish History* (Portman, Littman Library, 2009)

Helen Jones, 'National, Community and Personal Priorities: British Women's Responses to Refugees From the Nazis, from the Mid-1930s to Early 1940s', *Women's History Review* 21.1 (2012)

Tony Kushner, 'Sex And Semitism: Jewish Women in Britain in War and Peace' in Panikos Panayi, ed., *Minorities in Wartime: National and Racial Groupings in Europe, North America and Australia, during the Two World Wars* (Oxford, Berg, 1993)

——, 'Jew and Non-Jew in the East End of London: Towards an Anthropology of "Everyday" Relations' in Geoffrey Alderman and Colin Holmes eds, *Outsiders and Outcasts: Essays in Honour of William J. Fishman* (London, Duckworth, 1993)

——, 'Politics and Race, Gender and Class: Refugees, Fascists and Domestic Service in Britain, 1933–1940', in Tony Kushner and Kenneth Lunn, eds, *The Politics of Marginality: Race, the Radical Right and Minorities in Twentieth Century Britain* (London, Cass, 1990)

——, 'Beyond the Pale? British Reactions to Nazi Anti-Semitism, 1933–1939', in *The Politics of Marginality: Race, the Radical Right and Minorities in Twentieth Century Britain* (London, Cass, 1990)

——, 'An Alien Occupation— Jewish Refugees and Domestic Service in Britain, 1933–1948 'in Werner Eugen Mosse, ed., *Second Chance: Two Centuries of German-speaking Jews in the United Kingdom* (Tübingen, J.C.B. Mohr, 1991)

——, 'Local Heroes: Belgian Refugees in Britain during the First World War', *Immigrants and Minorities* 18.1 (1999)

Luisa Levi D'Ancona, '"Notabili e Dame": nella Filantropia Ebraica Ottocentescas: casi di studio in Francia, Italia e Inghilterra', *Quaderni Storici* n.s. 114 (2003).

——. 'Jewish Women in Non-Jewish Philanthropy in Italy (1870–1938', *Nashim* 20 (2010)

Elkan Levy, 'The New West End Synagogue 1879–2004', www.newwestend.org.uk/docs/EDLlecture.pdf

Thomas P. Linehan, 'Fascist Perceptions of Cable Street' in Tony Kushner and Nadia Valman, eds, *Remembering Cable Street: Fascism and Anti-Fascism in British Society* (London, Vallentine Mitchell, 2000)

Louise London, 'Jewish Refugees, Anglo-Jewry and British Government Policy 1930–40' in David Cesarani, ed., *The Making of Modern Anglo-Jewry* (Oxford, Blackwell, 1990)

Ellen Frank Mappen, Introduction to Clementina Black, *Married Women's Work* [1915] (republished London, Virago, 1983)

———, 'Strategists for Change: Social Feminist Approaches to the Problems of Women's Work' in Angela V. John, ed., *Unequal Opportunities: Women's Employment in England 1800–1918* (Oxford, Blackwell, 1986)

———, Introduction to Clementina Black, *Married Women's Work* [1915] (republished London, Virago, 1983)

Clare Midgley, 'Ethnicity, "Race" and Empire' in June Purvis, ed., *Women's History: Britain, 1850–1945: an Introduction* (London, UCL Press, 1995)

———, 'The Ambiguities of Aid and Agency: Representing Refugee Children in England, 1937–8', *Cultural and Social History* 6.1 (2000)

Janaki Nair '"Imperial Reason": National Honour and New Patriarchal Compacts in Early Twentieth-century India', *History Workshop Journal* 66 (2008)

Mica Nava, 'Sometimes Antagonistic, Sometimes Ardently Sympathetic: Contradictory Responses to Migrants in Postwar Britain', *Ethnicities* (2013)

Sybil Oldfield, '"It is usually She": the Role of British Women in the Rescue and Care of the Kindertransport Kinder', *Shofar: an Interdisciplinary Journal Of Jewish Studies*, xxiii (2004)

Mark Rowland, 'COPEC' at http://www.davidalton.com/rowland2.html

William Wynn Simpson, 'Jewish-Christian relations since the Inception of the Council of Christians and Jews', *Jewish Historical Studies* xxviii (1981–2)

Jean Spence, 'Working for Jewish Girls: Lily Montagu, Girls' Clubs and Industrial Reform 1890–1914', *Women's History Review* 13.3 (2004)

Stephanie Spencer, '"Knowledge as the Necessary Food of the Mind": Charlotte Mason's Philosophy of Education' in Jean Spence, Sarah Aiston, Maureen M. Meikle, eds, *Women, Education, and Agency, 1600–2000* (London, Routledge, 2010)

Ronald Stent, 'Jewish Refugee Organisations' in Werner Eugen Mosse, ed., *Second Chance: Two Centuries of German-speaking Jews in the United Kingdom* (Tübingen, J.C.B. Mohr, 1991)

Anne Summers, 'A Home from Home—Women's Philanthropic Work in the Nineteenth Century' in Sandra Burman, ed., *Fit Work for Women* (London, Croom Helm, 1979)

———, 'False Start or Brave Beginning? The Society of Jews and Christians, 1924–1944', *Journal of Ecclesiastical History* 65.4 (2014)

Martin Summers, 'Diasporic Brotherhood: Freemasonry and the Transnational Production of Black Middle-Class Masculinity', *Gender and History* 15.3 (2003)

Susan L. Tananbaum, 'Philanthropy and Identity: Gender and Ethnicity in London', *Journal of Social History* 30 (1997)

Avram Taylor, '"Are you a Billy, or a Dan, or an old tin can?" Street Violence and Relations between Catholics, Jews and Protestants in the Gorbals during the Inter-war Years', *Urban History* 41.1 (2014)

Nadia Valman, 'Jewish Girls and the Battle of Cable Street' in Tony Kushner and Nadia Valman eds, *Remembering Cable Street: Fascism and Anti-Fascism in British Society* (London, Vallentine Mitchell, 2000)

Jacqueline de Vries 'Challenging Traditions: Denominational Feminism in Britain, 1910–1920' in Billie Melman, ed., *Borderlines: Genders and Identities in War and Peace 1870–1930* (London, Routledge, 1998)

——, 'More than Paradoxes to Offer: Feminism, History and Religious Cultures' in Susan Morgan and Jacqueline de Vries, eds, *Women, Gender and Religious Cultures* (London, Routledge, 2010)

Paul Weindling, 'The Contribution of Central European Jews to Medical Science and Practice in Britain, the 1930s–1950s' in Werner Eugen Mosse, ed., *Second Chance: Two Centuries of German-speaking Jews in the United Kingdom* (Tübingen, J.C.B. Mohr, 1991)

——, 'From Refugee Assistance to Freedom of Learning: the Strategic Vision of A.V. Hill, 1933–1964' in Shula Marks, Paul Weindling and Laura Wintour, eds, *In Defence of Learning: the Plight, Persecution and Placement of Academic Refugees, 1933–1980s* (Oxford, Oxford University Press, 2011)

Julie Wheelwright, '"Colonel" Barker: a Case Study in the Contradictions of Fascism' in Tony Kushner and Kenneth Lunn, eds, *The Politics of Marginality: Race, the Radical Right and Minorities in Twentieth Century Britain* (London, Cass, 1990)

Bill Williams, 'The Anti-Semitism of Tolerance: Middle-Class Manchester and the Jews 1870–1900' in Alan J. Kidd and K.W. Roberts, eds, *City, Class and Culture: Studies of Social Policy and Cultural Production in Victorian Manchester* (Manchester, Manchester University Press, 1985).

Philip Williamson, 'The Doctrinal Politics of Stanley Baldwin' in Michael Bentley, ed., *Public and Private Doctrine: Essays in British History Presented to Maurice Cowling* (Cambridge, Cambridge University Press, 1993)

——, 'Christian Conservatives and Totalitarian Challenge 1933–40', *English Historical Review* 115.462 (2000)

——, 'National Days of Prayer: the Churches, the State and Public Worship in Britain 1899–1957', *English Historical Review*, 128.531 (2013)

David Wills, 'An Appreciation of Marjorie E. Franklin', *Studies in Environment Therapy* 1 (1968)

Stephen Yeo, 'A New Life: the Religion of Socialism in Britain 1883–1896', *History Workshop Journal* 4 (1977)

Secondary Sources – Other Unpublished Theses

Ruth Abrams, *Jewish Women and the International Woman Suffrage Alliance 1899–1926* (Ph.D., Brandeis University 1996)

Dan Lyndon, '"It is the Joy of the Righteous to do Justice": Jews and the British Suffrage Campaign' (MA, Westminster University 1997)

Websites

http://dreyfus.mahj.org/consultation/index.php
http://www.quakersintheworld.org/quakers-in-action/182; http://www.psychoanalytikerinnen.de/greatbritain_biographies.html#Franklin
http://www.scotlandspeople.gov.uk/

Personal Information

Esther Croxall Higgins, Carmen Mangion, David Jacobs

Index

A
Aberdeen, Lady. *See* Hamilton-Gordon
Adler, Chief Rabbi Dr. Hermann, 25, 41, 45n13
Adler, Henrietta (Nettie), 41, 63, 64, 67, 70, 80n23, 81n43, 145, 146
Adler, (Mrs Hermann) Rachel, 25
Alderman, Geoffrey, 139n1, 196n50
Alien Immigration, Royal Commission on, 41
Aliens Act, 1905, 2, 41
Allenby, General, 43, 159
Allen, Mary S., 137, 140n5
Altschul, Professor Annie, 195n43
Anglo-Boer War, 10, 41, 44, 76, 105
Anti-semitism, perceptions of, 5–7, 9–11, 76, 104, 105, 136–38, 201, 202
Ashby, Margery Corbett, 165, 166, 168–70, 174n57, 174n65
Ashwell, Lena, 50
Atholl, Katherine, Duchess of, 177
Auerbach, Helena, 9, 18n33, 33, 43, 47n48, 64, 66, 76
Auxiliary Movement, 147

Ayrton *formerly* Marks, Hertha, 10, 17n28

B
Balfour Declaration 1917, 143, 156, 165
Balfour, Lady Frances, 37, 45n15
Balfour, Lord Arthur James, 156
Balgarnie, Florence, 50
Baptist Union, 147
Barnett, Canon Samuel, 14, 19n52, 25, 31n4
Barnett, Henrietta, 25
Battersea, Lady. *See* Flower
Baylee, Rev. Joseph, 130n5
BCL. *See* British Commonwealth League (BCL)
Beale, Dorothea, 116
Beckett, John, 148, 152n38
Bedales School, 122
Bedford, Adeline Duchess of, 46n30
Behrens (Mrs. Edward), Abigail, 56, 60
Behrens, Edward, 60

Behrens, Ethel, 141, 150n2, 181
Bell, Adrian, 178
Bell, George, Bishop of Chichester, 180, 185
Bendit, Francis, 185
Bendit, Gladys. *See* Skelton
Bentwich, Helen, 78n4, 184–85, 195n47
Bentwich, Norman, 184, 185
Bentwich, Rosalind, 185
Bernstein, *afterw.* Summers, Rachel, 205–08
Bevan, Aneurin (Nye), 161, 163
Billig, Dr. Hannah, 138
Birnstingl, K. S., 75
Bishop Otter Memorial College, 115, 130n4, 130n6
Black, Clementina, 91, 95–9, 109n54
Blond,. *See also* Marks afterw. Laski, Elaine
B'nei Brith, 164
Bodichon, Barbara, 10
Bondfield, Margaret, 9, 17n24, 91
Booth, Charles, 38
Booth, Mrs. Alfred, 38
Bosanquet, Helen, 41
British Commonwealth League (BCL), 164–6
British Federation of University Women (BFUW), 182, 194n35
British Peace Party, 148
British Red Cross, 34, 143, 168, 173n53
British Society for the Propagation of the Gospel among the Jews, 148
British Union of Fascists (BUF), 137, 138, 165
Brittain, Vera, 9
Brixton Synagogue Hebrew and Religion Class, 206
Brooke, Margaret, Maharanee of Sarawak, 50
Browning, Louisa, 10

Browning, Robert, 10, 17n29, 206, 208
Bryant, Dr Sophie, 50
Bund Deutscher Frauenvereine, 182
Bunting, Percy, 50
Burdett-Coutts, Baroness Angela, 50–2
Burkill, Greta, 186
Burkitt, Francis Crawford, 18n55
Burman, Rickie, 82n66
Burrell, Lady Anne, 9, 10, 17n27
Burstall, Joan, 158
Buss, Frances, 116
Butler, Iris, 202
Butler, Josephine, 1, 11, 14n1, 14n2, 24, 28, 50, 53, 61n11
Butler, Rev. George, 1
Buxton, Dorothy, 182
Byvoet, Miss, 102, 110n71

C
Cable Street, 15n10, 137
Cadbury, Dame Elizabeth, 105, 111n83, 145
Cadbury family, 161, 178
Carpenter, Mary, 24
'Cat and Mouse Act,' 1913, 71
Catholic Guild of Israel, 146
Catholicism, Protestant attitudes to, 10, 13, 23, 37, 42, 53, 98, 115
Catholic Women's Suffrage Society, 66
Catlin, George, 9
Central Association for the Employment of Women, 104
Central British Fund for German Jewry, 163–4, 180
Central Conference Council, 37
Cesarani, David, 6
Chalmers, Lady Iris, 160
Chamberlain, Joseph, 59
Chant, Laura Ormiston, 50, 51
Charity Organisation Society, 41, 77n1

Chesterton, Cecil, 176, 190
Chief Rabbi. *See also* Adler, Dr Hermann; Hertz, Dr Joseph
Christian Social Union, 143
Christ's Hospital, Hertford, 126
Church and Stage Guild, 207
Church League for Women's Suffrage, 66, 68, 70, 71, 82n58, 144
Church Mission to the Jews, 147, 149
Clarke, Mary G., 158
Clifford, Mary, 38, 39, 43, 46n29
Clough, Anne Jemima, 116, 123, 130n7
Clubs' Industrial Association, 92, 94, 99
Cohen (Mrs. Nathaniel L.) Julia Matilda, 29, 30, 32n13, 40, 42, 107n27
Cohen, Lucy, 33
Cohen, Nellie, 64
Cohen, Percy, 80n25
Cohen (Mrs. Nathaniel) Rebecca, 36, 37, 45n17
Cohen, Rose, 64
Coke, Katherine, 171n12
Coke, Reginald, 171n12
Collet, Clara, 145
Communist Party, 122, 132n32, 138, 177, 192n11
Conference on Politics, Economics and Citizenship (COPEC), 143, 144, 151n9
Conservative and Unionist Woman Franchise Association, 64
conversion, 6, 11, 12, 26, 29, 42, 44, 53, 146, 147, 149, 187. *See also* Missions to Jews, Philosemitism
Conway, Katherine St. John, 47n45
Co-operative Wholesale Society, 166
COPEC. *See* Conference on Politics, Economics and Citizenship (COPEC)
Corbett-Ashby,. *See* Ashby

Corelli, Marie, 50
Costley-White, Rev. Dr. Harold, 128
Council for the Amelioration of the Legal Position of the Jewess, 73, 82n64, 157
Council of Christians and Jews (CCJ), 149, 153n41, 196n59, 203
Countrywomen of the World, 164
Courtauld family, 161
Creighton, Louise, 38
Criminal Law Amendment Act, 1885, 45n13
Crowdy, Rachel, 177, 193n12

D
Darwin, Francis, 50
Davenport-Hill, Florence, 50
Davenport-Hill, Rosamond, 50
Davidson, Randall, Archbishop of Canterbury, 143
D'Avigdor, Sylvie, 93, 107n24
Davis, Emily, 33
Davison Infant School, Worthing, 115
Day, Father Arthur, S.J., 146, 147
Deedes, Sir Wyndham Henry, 185
Delawarr, Countess Muriel, 50
Denman, Lady Gertrude, 8–10
Despard, Charlotte, 105, 111n83
District visiting, 27, 55
domestic service, 139n4, 183, 187, 190
Donnell, Laura, 68–70
Doreck, Beata, 106n3
Doreck College, Bayswater, 88, 119
Douie, Vera, 169
Dreyfus, Captain Alfred, 1, 6, 11, 49–54, 57–9, 61n11, 156
Dreyfus, Charles, 156
Dreyfus, Hedwig, 57
Dreyfus, Lucie, 1, 6, 10, 11, 49–54, 57–60
Drummond, Flora, 76, 136

E

East London Federation of Suffragettes, 64, 68, 70
Eccles, Charlotte O'Connor, 50, 51
Eder, Dr. David, 148, 159
Eder, Edith, 159
Education Act, 1870, 115
Edward, Prince of Wales, 160
Elgar, Edward, 78n10
Elmy, Elizabeth Wolstoneholme, 74, 83n69
Emanuel, Mrs, 35
Equal Citizenship (Blanket) Bill, 169
Equal Compensation for War injuries, movement, 169
Erleigh, Viscountess,. *See* Isaacs
Evans, Dorothy, 169, 170
Exell, Arthur and Mabel, 178

F

Fabian Society, 38, 206
Farr, Florence, 185
Fast, Vera, 185
Fawcett, Millicent, 10, 18n33, 40, 43, 76
Federation of Synagogues, 24, 30, 73, 95
Federation of Women Zionists (FWZ), 156–7, 159, 163–7, 201
Fellner, Ruth, 181
'Feminisation of religion', 73
Ferenczi, Sandor, 124
Fischl, Joan, 181
Fitzgerald *née* Bischoffsheim, Lady Lily, 160
Fleming *née* Healey, Selina, 116
Flower, Cyril, 6, 29
Flower *née* Rothschild, Constance (Lady Battersea), 6, 29, 30, 34–6, 39–41, 43, 44n8, 46n30, 47n38
Fogerty, Elsie, 50
Franklin, Alice, 70, 81n43
Franklin, Angela Wai Netta, 121
Franklin, Cyril, 122
Franklin, Dr. Marjorie, 122–5
Franklin, Ernest, 113, 129
Franklin, Geoffrey, 121, 122, 132n25
Franklin Helen,. *See* Bentwich
Franklin, Hugh, 64, 68, 74, 75, 78n4
Franklin, Michael, 121, 122
Franklin *née* Montagu, Henrietta (Netta), 8, 9, 18n33, 39, 41, 64–6, 77, 91, 93, 95, 100–3, 106n3, 111n84, 113–30, 141, 145, 149, 182, 184
Franklin, Olive, 122, 132n28, 132n32
Franklin, Rosalind, 202
Franklin, Ruth, 66
Franklin, Sydney, 122
Fraser, James, Bishop of Manchester, 46n37, 56
Free Church League for Woman Suffrage, 66
Free Church Suffrage Times, 71
Friends' Germany Emergency Committee (GEC), 163, 165, 180–82, 185, 194n29
Friends' League for Women's Suffrage, 66
Friends' Penal Reform Committee, 124
Friends, Society of, 148, 152n38, 180, 182. *See also* Quakers
Friends' War Victims Relief Committee, 121
Froebel, Friedrich, 106n3, 116, 131n8
Fry, Elizabeth, 24, 28
Fry, Ruth, 149
Fullerton, Lady Georgiana, 34, 44n6
FWZ. *See* Federation of Women Zionists (FWZ)

G

Gamble, Sarah Anne, 53, 55, 57
Garbett, Cyril, Bishop of Southwark, 142

INDEX   233

Gestetner Company, 181
Gibson, Frances, 128
Girton College, 10, 33, 121, 132n32, 185, 196n48
Gladstone, family, 50
Gladstone, Margaret Ethel. *See* MacDonald
Gladstone, Professor John Hall, 88, 105n2
Gladstone, William Ewart, 88, 110n62
Gliksten, Millie, 64
Glover, Edward, 124
Glover, Mrs. Arnold, 144
Goldsmid, Anna Maria, 29
Goldsmid, Lady Louisa, 33
Goodfellow, Miss Lorel, 145
Graves, Mrs [Beatrice Mary], 105, 111n84
Gray, Revd. A. Herbert, 148, 187
Greene, Ben, 152n38
Green, Norah, 104
Green, Rev. G. G., 71, 74
Grice, Miss A. M., 207
Groveham, Lizzie, 115, 131n22

H
Halifax, Lady Dorothy, 202
Hamburger, Fräulein, 125
Hamilton-Gordon, Ishbel Maria, Marchioness of Aberdeen and Temair, 145
Hamilton Miss, of the MSSA, 56
Hands, Lizzie, 82n64, 157, 164, 166
Hardie, Keir, 50, 59
Hardie, Mrs. James, 56
Hardisty, Dorothy, 186
Harrison, Professor Sir Brian, 7
Harrison, Tom, 168
Hart, Henry D'Arcy, 88, 89, 106n5
Hart, Philip D'Arcy, 106n5
Harvey, Oliver, 58
Headlam, Revd. Stewart, 207, 208n4
Henriques, (Mrs. E. M.) Emily, 56

Herbert, Lucy, 102, 110n75
Herbert, Mrs, 34
Hertz, Chief Rabbi Dr Joseph, 141, 142, 186-7
Herzl, Theodor, 156
Hicks, Edward Lee, Bishop of Lincoln, 71
Hill, Octavia, 25, 41
Hirsch, Baron Maurice, 160
Hitler, Adolf, 6, 136, 137, 148, 162-4, 168
Hoare, Sir Samuel, 196n50
Hochmann (also Hochman and Hockman), Rev. Joseph, 65, 71, 74, 77, 78n10
Hochmann, Vera, 78n10
Holtby, Winifred, 9
Home and Colonial Society, 115, 116
Home Education, 116, 117
Horton, Gertrude, 46n34
Household, Horace West, 127, 128
House of Education, Ambleside, 116, 125, 126, 128, 129
Hubback, Eva, 10
Hügel, Baron Friedrich von, 72
Hughes, Mary, 70
Hyam, Hannah, 64, 66, 67, 70, 71, 146

I
ICW. *See* International Council of Women (ICW)
Independent Labour Party (ILP), 59, 91-3
Independent Labour Party News, 59
interfaith activities, 72, 142, 149
International Council of Women (ICW), 121, 182, 183
International Women's News, 168-70
International Women's Suffrage Alliance, 169
Isaacs, Annie, 60
Isaacs Estelle (Stella), 60, 62n28

Isaacs, Lady Alice, Marchioness of Reading, 202
Isaacs, Lady Eva, Marchioness of Reading, 39, 164, 186
Isaacs, Rufus, Marquess of Reading, 76, 202

J
Jameson, Leander Starr, 59
Janes, Emily, 104
Jeans, Norah, 170
Jeune, Lady Mary, 35
Jewish Association for the Protection of Girls and Women (JAPGW), 34–7, 40, 41, 45n13, 187, 188, 197n63
Jewish Board of Deputies, 166, 180
Jewish Board of Guardians, 27, 28, 63, 91
Jewish Chronicle (JC), 25, 32n13, 65, 67–9, 74–6, 80n24, 80n25, 80n28, 81n43, 91, 99, 146, 157
Jewish Ladies' Loan and Benevolent Society, 34
Jewish Ladies' Visiting Association (JLVA), 46n37, 56, 57, 60
Jewish League for Woman Suffrage (JLWS), 13, 63–9, 71–6, 79n16, 80n24 80n28, 103, 113, 141, 157, 200
Jewish Literary Societies, 64, 65, 82n64, 157
Jewish Peace Society (JPS), 82n64
Jewish Quarterly Review, 65, 79n13
Jewish Refugees Committee, 163
Jewish Religious Union, 24, 65, 79n14, 94, 95, 113, 142
Jewish Review, 64–5
Jewish Study Society, 65
Jews' Free School, 34
Jews' Relief Act, 2, 1858

Jews' Temporary Shelter (JTS), 188–90
Jones, Clifford, 134n63
Jones, Helen, 31n8, 191
Joseph, Lizzie (Mrs. Nathan) , 37, 46n26
Julius, Anthony, 139n2, 202

K
Kaye, Dr. Elaine, 208
Kelly, Kathleen, 189–90
Kindertransport, 152n38, 184–86, 195n47
King Alfred School, 122
King's College Hospital, 42
Kipling, Rudyard, 146
Kitching, Elsie, 128, 129, 131n22
Klapper, Melissa R., 13
Kristallnacht, 152n38
Kuzmack, Linda, 77, 79n16, 80n28, 80n37

L
Labour Party, 5, 98, 110n66, 160, 162, 166, 172n26, 177, 192n11, 195n47
Lacy, Helen Elizabeth, 206–7
Langtry, Lily, 50
Lawrence, Emmeline Pethick, 18n32, 75–6
Lawrence, Susan, MP, 166
Lazarnick, Dora, 69
League of Nations, 136, 138, 142, 156, 185, 193n12
League of Nations Union, 142, 165
Lee, Jennie, 161–3, 168–70, 172n24
Leno, Dan, 50
Leslie, Henrietta, 75
Lesser Half, The, 169

Levertoff, Revd. Paul, 147, 152n26
Levy, Amy, 83n67, 110n68
Liberal Judaism, 74, 79n13, 94, 99, 141–4, 146, 149–50. *See also* Montagu, Lilian
Liberal Party, 5, 68, 88, 89, 91, 92, 109n62
Lincoln, Tribich, 69, 80n36
Livingstone, Rev. Isaac, 144
London and National Society for Women's Service, 169
London Hospital, 42, 160
London, Louise, 6
London Shakespeare League, 206, 207
London Society for the Study of Religion, 72, 81n55
London Society for Women's Suffrage, 66, 68, 70, 111n84
Lonsdale, Margaret, 50
Loubet, President Emile, 49
Lowe, Clara, 12
Lutyens, Lady Emily, 160
Lutyens, Robert, 171n11
Lyndon, Dan, 79n16

M
Macadam, Elizabeth, 9
MacDonald, David, 95, 96, 108n35
MacDonald, James Ramsay, 87, 90, 92, 93, 100–3, 105, 144
MacDonald, Margaret Ethel, 11, 87–105, 106n9, 106n12, 107n19
Mackereth, F. G., 98
MacMillan, Margaret, 9
MacMillan, Rachel, 9
Macpherson, Annie, 11–12
Maddox, Brenda, 202
Manchester and Salford Sanitary Association (MSSA), 46n37, 55–7, 61n15

Manchester Guardian, 53, 59, 146, 156, 159, 161
Manchester High School for Girls, 158
Manchester Relief Fund for Russian Jews, 56
Manchester University, Women's Department, 158
Mannin, Ethel, 148
Manning, Cardinal, 37
Manning, Leah, M.P., 177
Mann, Tom, 93
Marks *afterw.* Laski *afterw.* Blond, Elaine, 60, 156, 158, 159, 164, 170, 171n5, 186, 187
Marks and Spencer, 156, 161
Marks, Hannah, 157–8
Marks, Lara, 110n67
Marks, Michael, 157–8, 160, 161
Marks, Miriam, 159
Marks, Rebecca,. *See* Sieff
Marks, Simon, 156, 161
Marofsky (also Marovsky), Fanny, 126, 128, 130, 134n63
Marshall, Miss, 147
Marsh, Catherine, 50
Marsh, Jan, 11, 18n37
Marx, Eleanor, 17n28
Mason, Charlotte Maria Shaw, 8, 9, 11, 18n33, 77, 113–27, 130, 131n8, 131n22
Mass Observation, 168
Mattuck, Rabbi Israel, 74, 75, 144, 147, 181, 196n58
Maugham, Syrie, 160, 171n11
McArthur, Irene, 144–6
McCormick, Very Rev. Joseph Gough, 144, 151n10
McKenna, Reginald, 176
McShane, Yolande, 137, 140n5
Melchett, Lady Violet, 160
Meredith, George, 50

Metropolitan Association for Befriending Young Servants, 41, 45n15
Meyer, Adolf, 124
Middleton, Mary, 100, 101
Miller, Jean, 147
Ministry of Information, 168
Missions to Jews, 11, 24, 147, 148
Model, Alice, 157
Mond, Sir Alfred, 74, 160
Montagu *afterw.* D'Arcy Hart, Ethel, 88, 106n5
Montagu, Edwin, 100, 109n58
Montagu, Lilian H. (Lily)
   autobiographical and religious writing, 65, 77, 79n13, 103–5, 149
   fictional writing, 93, 94
   friendship with MacDonald family, 88–90, 92, 93, 101–5
   interfaith activism, 12, 141–53
   progressive Judaism, 12, 13n79, 65, 94, 95, 125, 145
   social and political causes, 64, 92, 94, 105
   youth work, 89, 91, 92, 94, 99, 111n83
Montagu, Marian, 9, 65, 94, 95, 99, 100, 104, 108n48
Montagu, Samuel, *afterw.* Baron Montagu of Swaythling, 30, 32n18, 65, 88, 89, 99, 109n62, 113, 122
Montefiore, Claude Joseph Goldsmid, 65, 72, 79n13, 92, 94
More, Hannah, 28
Moses, Miriam, 70, 71, 81n43, 145
Mosley, Sir Oswald, 137–8
Mountbatten, Lady Edwina, 171n11, 175n53
Mountbatten, Lady Irene, Marchioness of Carisbrooke, 160
Mundella, Anthony John, 29

N
National Association for the Promotion of Social Science, 55, 64
National Council of Girls' Clubs, 168
National Council of Women (NCW), 7, 36, 39, 104, 113, 127, 145, 164, 168, 175, 182–4
National Peace Council, 141, 142, 164
National Union of Societies for Equal Citizenship, 168
National Union of Women's Suffrage Societies (NUWSS), 33, 43, 64, 66, 72, 175
National Union of Women Workers (NUWW), 36–41, 43, 63, 92, 94, 95, 99, 101. *See also* National Council of Women (NCW)
National Vigilance Association, 35, 45n13, 45n15, 175, 188
Nazism, 138, 139, 148, 149, 162, 167, 177, 178, 180, 182, 184, 191
Nazi-Soviet Pact, 167
News from Nowhere, 166
New Statesman, 206
New West End Synagogue, 65, 68, 73, 78n10, 81n55, 91
Nonconformity, 23, 38, 67, 71–2
Norwood Orphanage, 34
Nuremberg Laws, 1935, 180, 185

O
Oaths Act, 1866, 2
Oldfield, Sybil, 152n38, 186
Old Vic Theatre, 206
Oppenheim, Mrs, 35
Overstone School, 129

P

Pacifism, 111n83, 130, 138, 141
Pailthorpe, Grace, 124
Palestine, 10, 47n48, 136, 142, 152n35, 156, 157, 160, 163–7, 169, 171n16, 172n26, 179, 181, 184–5, 187, 192
Pankhurst, Adela, 9, 171n5
Pankhurst, Christabel, 9, 68, 171n5
Pankhurst, Emmeline, 68, 75
Pankhurst, family, 8, 60, 64, 69
Pankhurst, Sylvia, 9, 18n31, 64, 68–9, 76, 78n5, 171n5
Pappenheim, Bertha, 65
Papworth, Lucy Wyatt, 96–9, 102, 108n35
Parents' National Education Union (PNEU), 33, 102, 113, 114, 116–18, 120–2, 124–7, 129, 130, 130n1, 145
Parents' Review, 114, 118, 123, 128
Parish, Ellen, 125–8
Parkes, Revd James, 147–50
Peace Army, 152n35
Peace News, 148
Peace Pledge Union, 152n38, 177
Pennethorne, Amy, 129
Pestalozzi, Johann Heinrich, 116, 131n8
Petrie, Dr. Telford, 128
Philosemitism, 11, 16n12, 18n36, 150, 203. *See also* Conversion
Picton-Turbervill, Edith, MP, 8, 16n21
Political and Economic Planning (PEP), 161
Portman Clinic, 124
Primrose, Archibald, Lord Rosebery, 6, 50

Q

'Q camps', 124
Quakers, 23, 70, 180, 182
Queen Charlotte's Hospital, 160
Quilliam Foundation, 203

R

Ramsay, Edith, 138, 140n9
Rathbone, Eleanor, MP, 9, 177, 182
Refugee agencies
 for Basque children, 177–9
 for Belgians, 175–6
 for Germans and Austrians, 6, 7, 139, 162–4, 178–92, 193n24
Refugees
 Basque, 177–9
 Belgian, 175, 176, 178, 179, 192n1, 192n2
 German and Austrian, 6, 7, 11, 136, 162, 163, 167, 178–92, 193n24
Renshaw, Mrs, of the MSSA, 56
Rhodes, Cecil, 59
Rickards, Esther, 68
Rickards, Phoebe, 68, 80n30
Roberts, Charlotte, 52
Robins, Elizabeth, 131n22
Rothschild *afterw*. Yorke, Annie, 6, 41
Rothschild, Anthony, 164
Rothschild, Charlotte, 29, 34, 44n6
Rothschild, Constance,. *See* Flower
Rothschild, Hannah, 6, 50
Rothschild, Juliana (Baroness Mayer), 33
Rothschild, Louise, 40
Rothschild, Yvonne, 164
Rowntree family, 161
Royden, Maude, 145, 148, 152n35, 153n39

Russell, Countess Mabel, 50
Russell, Miss, suffragist, 68

S
Sacher, Harry, 156, 159
Salaman, Annette (Annie), 29
Salaman, Nina Davis, 76, 157
Salomon, Rabbi Dr. Berendt, 144
Salomons, Mrs E., 56
Same-sex relationships, 8–9, 120
Samuel, Ida, 70, 71, 81n43, 138, 145
Samuel, Louise, 64, 67
Samuel, Viscount Herbert, 76, 137, 176, 184, 185
Save the Children Fund, 182, 185
Saviour of the World, The, 119, 125, 126
Schiff, Otto, 176
Schmideberg, Melitta, 124
Schneiderman, J. H., 69
Schonfeld, Rabbi Solomon, 186
Scott, Charles Prestwich, 156
Scottish Churches' League for Women's Suffrage, 66, 72
Scott, Lady Selina, 50
Shaftesbury, Lord, 33
Sidebotham, Herbert, 159
Sieff, Israel, 156, 159, 161, 162
Sieff née Marks, Rebecca, 156–70, 185–87, 201
Simmons, Anna, 40, 55–7, 61n21
Simmons, Rev. Laurence, 40
Simon née Salaman, Lady Rachel, 29
Simon, Sir John, 29
Simons, Mrs. Salis, 56
Simpson, Rev. William Wynn, 149
Simpson, Rose, 167, 173n48
Six Point Group, 169
Skelton *née* Williams, *afterw.* Bendit, Gladys, 185, 196n48
Small, Mrs, 58

Smith, Arthur Lionel, Master of Balliol, 142
Smith, Constance, 144, 145
Smyth, Canon John Paterson, 125, 133n44
Snowden, Viscountess Ethel, 160
Society of Jews and Christians, 104, 140n9, 144–50, 153n40, 155, 203
Soldiers' and Sailors' Families Association, 41
Somerset, Lady Henry, 46n30, 50
Spanish Civil War, 177, 178, 192n11
Spielmann (also Spielman), Gertrude, 40, 63–5, 74
Stanley, Venetia, 100
Steer, Mary H., 24, 25, 52, 70
St. George's Hospital, 42
Stopes, Charlotte Carmichael, 72
Strachey, Philippa, 66
Streeter, Miss, 98
Student Christian Movement, 147
Summerskill, Dr. Edith, 169
Surrey Lane Central School for Girls, 205
Swanwick, Helena, 50

T
Tabili, Laura, 137–8
TAS. *See* Travellers' Aid Society (TAS)
Tawney, Richard Henry, 151n16
Temperance movement, 38, 51, 55, 57, 67, 93
Temple, Frederick, Bishop of London, 116, 125
Temple, William, Archbishop of Canterbury, 147, 149, 196n59
Terry, Ellen, 50
Thomson, Helen B., 55
Threefold Cord, The, 37

Townswomen's Guild, 46n34, 70, 114, 168
Travellers' Aid Society (TAS), 35–7, 40, 45n15, 187, 188

U
United Suffragists, 64
United Synagogue of Great Britain and the Empire, 13, 23, 30, 73, 95, 143
Unwin, Jane Cobden, 50

V
Vaudrey, Eleanor, 55, 57
Victoria League, 41

W
Waley, Jacob, 32n13
Ward *afterw.* Montefiore, Florence, 94
Ward, Maud, 9
Ward *née* Arnold, Mrs. Humphry, 123
Waring, Lady Clementine, 160
Waugh, Rev. Benjamin, 70
Waugh, Rosa, 70
WCG. *See* Women's Co-operative Guild (WCG)
Webb, Beatrice, 17n28, 38, 39, 42, 46n32
Webb, Dr. Helen, 120, 121, 132b6
Wedgwood, Josiah, 166
Weizmann, Dr. Chaim, 156, 159, 160, 171n2
Weizmann, Vera, 159, 160
Welldon, James, Dean of Durham, 142
Wellesley *née* Fitzgerald, Nesta, 160
West Central Jewish Girls' Club, 67, 80n24, 91, 94
White, Arnold, 50
White Slave Trade, 67, 68
WIC. *See* Women's Industrial Council (WIC)
Wicksteed, Joseph, 72
Wilberforce, Octavia, 131n22
Wilkinson, Ellen, MP, 177
Williams, F.C.A., 130n4, 130n6
Wise, Dorothy, 70, 144
Woman's Life, 51
Woman's Signal, The, 38, 46n30, 52
Women for Westminster, 169–70, 174n59
Women's Anglo-Soviet Committee, 167, 173n53
Women's Appeal Committee for German-Jewish women and children, 163, 164
Women's Christian Temperance Association, 55
Women's Citizens' Associations, 7, 165, 182
Women's Co-operative Guild, 165–8, 177
Women's Equality Party, 170
Women's Freedom League, 168
Women's Guild of Empire, 137
Women's Industrial Council (WIC), 91, 92, 95–9, 104, 105, 108n34, 113, 144
Women's Industrial News, 98–9
Women's Institute, 9, 33, 46n34, 114
Women's International League for Peace and Freedom, 164
Women's International Zionist Organisation (WIZO), 157, 159, 164, 165, 167, 171n16
Women's Labour League, 94–5, 100, 101, 103, 110n66
Women's Publicity Planning Association (WPPA), 168–9, 174n59

Women's Social and Political Union (WSPU), 60, 64, 75
Women Transport Workers' Union, 165
Wooldridge, Martha Lugg, 207
Woolf, Flora Sidney, 80n28
Woolf, Leonard, 80n28
Working girls' clubs, 41, 67, 99, 144, 145, 168
Wright, Miss, of the MSSA, 56
WSPU. *See* Women's Social and Political Union (WSPU)

Y
Yorke, Hon. Eliot, 6
Young Men's Christian Association, 88
Young Women's Christian Association (YWCA), 35, 37, 45n15, 146

Z
Zangwill, Edith Ayrton, 141, 157
Zangwill, Israel, 64, 74–6, 78n10
Zionism, 16n14, 18n36, 155–74, 187
Zionist Commission, 159

Printed by Printforce, the Netherlands